THE JEWISH WOMAN IN CONTEMP(

To Jane

Warm greetings

Adrienne Baker

THE JEWISH WOMAN IN CONTEMPORARY SOCIETY

Transitions and Traditions

Adrienne Baker
Course Director and Tutor, Diploma in Counselling, Regent's College, London and Lecturer in Women's Studies, Birkbeck College, London

Preface by Susie Orbach

Jo Campling
Consultant Editor

150th YEAR

MACMILLAN

First published 1993 by
THE MACMILLAN PRESS LTD
Houndmills, Basingstoke, Hampshire RG21 2XS
and London
Companies and representatives
throughout the world

ISBN 0–333 53760–2 hardcover
ISBN 0–333 53761–0 paperback

A catalogue record for this book is available
from the British Library

Printed in Hong Kong

To Harvey

Contents

vii

Preface
Susie Orbach

As a second generation secular Jew, part of the 9 per cent of British and American Jewry who have no religious affiliation and practise none of the fundamental pietistic precepts associated with Judaism, I found Adrienne Baker's book covering the wider spectrum of Jewish communal activity an eye opener on the one hand and a cause for self-reflection on the other.

The secular Jewish world assumes that to be a Jew a sufficient starting-point is the statement of ethnic affiliation. For the generation raised in the wake of the Holocaust, there is an imperative to claim that ethnicity and that history; to not deny that aspect of one's personal and family heritage. One has been raised to be ever so slightly 'set apart' from the general culture. One learns to be alert to racism and anti-semitism; to be cautious and vigilant; to watch out for the consequences of being a Jew without really being able to put much substance to what being a Jew means. And yet the need to identify as such, the wish to place oneself as an American *Jew* or a British *Jew* is significant and transcends religiosity and observance.

What intrigued me in reading this book was the heterogeneous nature of the community which the secular Jew is both connected to and excluded from. I was delighted to learn more about the 300,000 people in the UK and the six million people in the United States with whom I, by the statement that I am a Jew, identify.

In her survey of current trends among the many religious Jewish communities, Adrienne Baker shows how each branch of Judaism has given itself a defined purpose reflecting a specific ideology. We learn about gender politics within the more progressive or liberal tendencies and the meaning of femininity in the conservative and ultra-right Jewish communities.

I was shamed by some of what I learnt about the repression and oppression within certain communities. At the same time I was impressed by the struggles of religious contemporaries who are creating forms of community, including study and worship which reflect the position of post-diaspora Jews. I was impressed too by the headway that gender-conscious Jews have made in rethinking issues of sexuality, including lesbianism, and in redefining sex roles: including the most welcome ordination of women rabbis. I was stunned to discover that the adage that a child is only a Jew through matrilineal descent is a law which has now been challenged by Progressive Jews.

But the question I was left with after reading this book, a book which tells us that one-third of Jews are marrying out, was this. What is the significance of naming oneself a Jew? While for many many Jews this has a religious answer, what does this mean for a secular Jew? What is the significance and meaning of giving that identity to the next generation? For society as a whole, this is still a political question. Jews are not seen as the sum of their religious observances, or their people's history: they are seen as a political or sociological category. As long as that remains the case, then we need to retain that identity, but there is also a need for us to understand who Jews are rather than be allowed to project on to them what we need them to be. This book is a useful introduction to contemporary Jewish culture through the perspective of women's experience. In letting us into those communities we begin to understand more about who we are, whether within the spectrum of Jews or within contemporary femininity.

Susie Orbach 1992

Acknowledgements

Most of all, it is the women who have talked to me about the special meaning to them of being Jewish whom I want to acknowledge. They have talked and I have listened and then together we have discussed these things, in study groups and informal gatherings and in interviews – and, as well as sharing their thoughts, they have often given me their hospitality, too, and much wonderful Jewish cooking!

My thanks go to my editor, Jo Campling, for her interest and encouragement and to Kate Loewenthal, who was my PhD mentor and whose enthusiasm for learning more about ourselves as Jewish women is with me still. Then, too, I must thank Ezra Kahn, the librarian of Jews' College library, for his patience and his suggestions.

The excerpt from 'At the new moon: Rosh Hodesh' on p. 81 by Marge Piercy (copyright © 1987, 1992 by Marge Piercy and Middlemarsh, Inc.) is used by permission of the author and A.M. Heath and Company, Ltd. The poem was first published in *Tikkun* and is included in *Mars and her Children* published by Alfred A. Knopf, Inc.

I want also to express my appreciation to Vicky Brohan for all her wonderful help and friendship and to my many friends whose ideas and support have been so important to me.

I am grateful for the ideas and criticisms and stimulus of my daughters, Caroline and Marion, and my son, Larry.

Finally and especially, I value the endless encouragement and love of my husband, Harvey. They have been there for me all the way along.

A Woman Of Worth

A Woman of Worth, who can find? For her price is beyond rubies. The heart of her husband trusteth in her and he shall have no lack of gain. She doeth him good and not evil all the days of her life. She seeketh wool and flax, and worketh willingly with her hands... She bringeth food from afar. She riseth also while it is yet night, and setteth forth provision for her household... She considereth a field and buyeth it: with the fruit of her hands she planteth a vineyard. She girdeth her loins with strength and maketh strong her arms. She perceiveth that her earnings are good: her lamp goeth not out by night. She putteth her hands to the distaff and her hands hold the spindle. She stretcheth out her hand to the poor; yea, she putteth forth her hands to the needy.... Her husband is known in the gates, when he sitteth among the elders of the land.... Strength and majesty are her clothing;... She openeth her mouth with wisdom and the law of lovingkindness is on her tongue. She looketh well to the ways of her household and eateth not the bread of idleness. Her children rise up and call her happy; her husband also and he praiseth her, saying: 'Many daughters have done worthily, but thou excellest them all. Favour is false and beauty is vain; but a woman that feareth the Lord, she shall be praised. Give her of the fruit of her hands; and let her works praise her in the gates.'

Proverbs xxxi, 10–31

This ancient text is sung in Hebrew to the wife each Friday evening at the commencement of the Shabbat.

Introduction

Religion is not a part of me; it is me. Religion comes into everything.
The world out there is the world in here.

(Orthodox woman; teacher; mother).

I feel very Jewish. I am aware of being Jewish all the time. That is from
my having gone through the Holocaust. I don't believe in God but I feel
Jewish and I want my children to feel Jewish.

(Secular Jewish woman; educational psychologist; mother).

A non-Jewish woman may ask her friend, 'What does it mean to you,
being Jewish?'. It is a question with many answers. For the Orthodox
woman there is no difficulty in replying; it means living a religious way of
life in which serving God totally defines her self-perception, her roles, her
marital relationship, the way she brings up her children, as well as every
aspect of her day-to-day routine, down to the minutest detail of how she
prepares her family's food.

At the other end of the continuum, the 'secular' Jewish woman will
define being Jewish in terms of belonging, although not necessarily to a
specific Jewish community. Her sense of cultural identity is composed of
memories and of unconsciously internalized expectations. There also
lingers an awareness of shared experiences and ways of understanding.

It is important to understand both perspectives, for within the expectations of even the totally non-religious woman are values deriving from
religion. Nor, of course, are women grouped only at the extremes; the
majority of Jewish women in contemporary society occupy a place along
the religious/non-religious continuum. Many observe some of the rituals
and some of the requirements of religious law (*halacha*). At the same
time, nearly all have a social awareness of their Jewish ethnic identity.
Moreover, they draw on both a written and an oral tradition, passed on
through the family from generation to generation, which conveys values
and a way of life. For the woman, this way of life has always given central
place to the roles of wife and mother.

So, what *does* it mean, being Jewish? The answers come from many
perspectives, for the Jewish identity is a complex interweaving of religious
and ethnic elements. At its core, too, is a shared history, a collective
memory of periods in which Jews suffered prejudice and persecution and
of periods of wandering and resettlement in new lands. It is a history of
migration in which two factors have given stability: religion and the

1

family. And in more recent times, the Holocaust and the establishment of the State of Israel have added extra dimensions to the sense of responsibility which being a Jew has always involved.

Erikson (1960) defined identity as 'the reflection in the individual of an essential aspect of a group's inner coherence'. We may rightly ask what the relevance of this can be to the Jewish woman today – to the woman who fully participates in the wider, secular society or the woman who may no longer observe anything to do with an ancient religion and who may celebrate her freedom from a seemingly-patriarchal culture.

Because our lives never take place in a vaccuum we are, without realising it, powerfully influenced. As women, we are influenced, firstly, by our own mother's culturally-defined self-image, which we internalize (Eichenbaum and Orbach, 1983). And, secondly, we are shaped by the culture in which we mature, a culture which is initially filtered through our family of origin. The Jewish culture presents many contradictions; it is, of course, male-defined – its religious laws, its allocation of roles and status, its language and symbols and its myths. At the same time – and this is so in reality, as well as in the platitudes of apologists – women in Judaism have always had a pivotal role: not only as the idealized wife-mother, central to all religions, but as the one who holds things together, whether this is during times of upheaval, with the threat of anti-Semitism, or during times of comparative calm, with the paradoxical threat of assimilation.

As a result, women in this culture, even though they have always been – and still are – greatly disadvantaged in religious law, have never been passive and oppressed (Myerhoff, 1978; Webber, 1983; Neuberger, 1983; Burman, 1986; 1990). They have always transcended restrictive roles and established their own areas of dignity and purpose. They have been influenced by and have also always covertly influenced their particular world, but it has been done whilst maintaining traditional attitudes which place the family in the centre of that world. And maybe that is why feminism – both as a different way of understanding long-established systems and as a movement urging women to think more deeply about their lives – has met with such ambivalence: it has been resisted and it has been embraced.

How feminism has brought about change for women within this culture is an underlying theme of this book. It is a theme discussed in the context of two very different societies, the United States and Britain. So, in answering the question, 'What does it mean to you, being Jewish?' we shall begin by looking at the dynamic relationship between women and their contextual world – how women are influenced by and simultaneously influence the age-old culture of which, one way or another, they are a part.

And, at the same time, we shall explore not only the forces within that culture but also the forces without – and the way in which new ideas, new ways of thinking, are gradually heard, discussed, reflected upon and partly incorporated into our lives.

Central to the experience of being a Jew is that of being the child, or the grandchild, or the great-grandchild of an immigrant. Yet coming to the United States must have been a very different experience from coming to Britain; one was 'a nation of immigrants', the other was a comparatively settled, comparatively homogeneous society. Then, too, the Jews came from many lands, and they were Ashkenazim or they were Sephardim. Chapter One therefore begins by describing the different waves of immigration into both countries. It then moves forward in time and presents the demographic picture: one with contrasts and similarities, with defection from organized religion alongside a return to Orthodoxy and in which massively increasing rates of intermarriage take place at the same time as a revived interest in Jewish roots and knowledge.

The next chapter considers woman's role in Judaism. Within the Jewish identity both religious and ethnic cultural influences are inextricably interwoven. Throughout both these strands, but derived from religion, is an emphasis on the woman's role within the family. The Jewish feminist perspective on which this discussion is based highlights the extent to which traditional expectations still influence Jewish women's self-perception, and why they do so.

Myths and stereotypes surround the role of Jewish woman and understandably so, for since biblical times she has been depicted with ambiguity. These polarized images also, of course, suggest men's ambivalence at the possibility of women's inappropriate strivings.

Chapter Three concerns itself with woman's status in religious law. The *halacha*, in which this is codified, maintains an essentially male worldview. It is a system which religious women have been discouraged from studying and which Orthodox men are reluctant to change. The *halachic* laws, however, affect not only the Orthodox and traditionally observant (and a high proportion of affiliated Jews belong to these two groups), but, particularly in relation to marriage and divorce and to conversion, they may also affect women in Reform and Progressive synagogue groups.

The chapter which follows begins by discussing the spectrum of synagogue observance in the States and in Britain. This is the area, probably more than any other, in which feminism has made its greatest, *objectively-observable* achievements. Not surprisingly, these achievements came about earlier and are much more far-reaching in the States, in terms of women's involvement in synagogue ritual and leadership, than in Britain. For it is very clear that American Jewish women – many of whom were amongst the pioneers of the women's movement – internalized the messages of feminism earlier and deeper than their British counterparts. In fact, even now – and even within Reform Judaism (although less so within Liberal Judaism) – many British Jewish women still feel ambivalent about fundamental changes in women's synagogue participation.

Looking separately at the religious scene in both countries, the greatest similarity, not surprisingly, is in Orthodox Judaism. As we move along the Orthodox/non-Orthodox continuum, Britain's United Synagogue is far to the right of the Conservative movement in the States. Similarly, Reform in Britain is less radical than Reform in the States. The chapter then focuses more specifically: firstly on woman's place, if any, in public ritual and secondly on the area which traditionally is her realm, ritual in the home.

And what of the different realities? From a secular Jewish woman we learn what it feels like fully to identify as a Jew and yet as a Jew without religion. It is often a lonely position to occupy, with perceptions of being alienated from the so-called 'normative' community. The chapter ends with a group of women exploring the individual meaning to them of their Jewishness.

Chapter Five considers Orthodox Judaism. It looks at it from three perspectives: firstly, in terms of what it means to be an ultra-Orthodox woman, with all the seeming restrictions. Then it narrows its focus to consider a sub-culture within a sub-culture – the Chassidim. Even more specifically, we then consider the way of life of the Lubavitch Chassidim and their controversial evangelical role. The third part of this chapter explores the pull of Orthodox Judaism for the *ba'alot t'shuva* ('returnees'), many of whom are educated young women who have lived and worked in the secular world, now making a positive choice to become totally committed. It is a paradox of interest to feminist thinkers who ask whether it represents a retreat to safety, or a reclaiming and celebration of all that is uniquely female.

The next section focuses on family life. In Chapter Six we look at the home as the woman's domain and, within it, the mother's role both as conveyor of tradition and as enabler of others. We ask how it is – by what sort of an apprenticeship – that such a powerful message concerning expectations is conveyed from mother to daughter and we shall also consider the role of myths in preserving the status quo. The chapter ends with a discussion of food, both in terms of the dietary laws which are central to Jewish observance; and in relation to the laws of Shabbat and festivals. We also reflect on food in terms of its symbolic meaning.

The internalized expectation is that a 'nice Jewish girl' will marry and have children. Marriage, the wedding ceremony and the 'Laws of Family Purity' are the subjects of Chapter Seven. So, too, is the biblical injunction to 'Be Fruitful and Multiply', as well as attitudes to childlessness, birth control and abortion. This is followed by a consideration of the laws concerning sexual morality. Finally, we approach the frequently-unacknowledged reality: that not all 'nice Jewish girls' marry – some remain single not out of choice, other choose not to marry. And some Jewish women are lesbian. Assumptions about and only-slowly changing attitudes towards single women and lesbian Jewish women are the issues on which this chapter ends.

Chapter Eight occupies itself with two areas of intense anxiety: conversion and inter-faith marriage. It also looks behind the idealized picture of Jewish family life: at domestic violence, family breakdown and single parent families. In all of these, the woman as everlasting carer remains the one carrying the responsibility, and this is a role for which she receives even less support when the family members for whom she cares are elderly or have a handicap.

Within this culture which symbolizes continuity and stability, women – even Orthodox women – have not been immune to the messages of feminism. The final section of this book explores areas in which change is taking place. Education, voluntary work, women earning, women with careers are all discussed in Chapter Nine. It looks at evolving attitudes to women's education within a culture which had traditionally not expected women to have careers or seek positions of leadership. It considers voluntary work to which, so often in the past, a woman's 'desire for purposeful activity was channelled' (Kraemer, 1989). Finally, this chapter discusses work; it shows, despite all that has changed, how much stays the same, primarily the ambivalence inherent in being a working mother. And, inevitably, women's extra-familial work roles have important implications for marriage, child care and communal support.

Finally – but it is not finally, for it has been a theme throughout – Chapter Ten attempts an overview of the impact of feminism on Jewish women in the States and Britain. It looks again at the contradictions, at the way in which women have achieved self-respect but have also been ambivalent about change in this androcentric culture. It considers the areas in which evolution is slowly coming about – most profoundly within women's psyches – and the not-unexpected male resistance to such change. It documents the turbulence, not only within the feminist movement but within Jewish women in the movement, surrounding Israel and anti-Semitism. The chapter ends with a recognition of the extent to which women are doing what we always have done – redefining our expectations whilst preserving our traditional roles, particularly within the family. But it also recognises that new role models are emerging and challenging our old, internalized assumptions. And they are permitting us to re-evaluate our roles and our rights.

Basic to all feminist writing is a belief in the validity of women's perception of reality. For Jewish women, the anthropologists' notion of there being an alternative 'counterpart system' – a reality different from that of men, with different symbols of esteem and satisfaction – is immensely relevant. It does not overlook the imbalance, the inequalities, but it offers insights into why women have continued for so long to fulfil their time-honoured expectations, ostensibly seeking so little change. For to be Jewish is a very complex matter; it means drawing on vibrant threads, of religion, of history, of culture. This book explores their interconnection, and it is in this area of interconnection that we find the richest source for understanding the reality of Jewish women's lives.

Part I
The Cultural Background

1 Setting the Scene

The wonder of it all lies in the capacity of Jews to maintain a sense of common identity and kinship when all the circumstances of their history seemed to favour fragmentation. All that they had in common was their devotion to an ancient faith and the experience of suffering to which their very Jewishness appeared to commit them for all time.

(Abba Eban, 1986).

The experience of being an immigrant is one which continues to have reverberations for the children, grandchildren and even great-grandchildren of the immigrants. The way in which that experience is lived by the generations who follow depends, of course, on many factors, particularly the economic and social status of the immigrant generation and the severity of the situation from which they are fleeing.

How easily the second and third generations adapt to their host culture and even become a part of it is also a complex matter; it depends on the continued importance of that which sets them apart – for the Jews, particularly religion – and, against that, the sense of acceptance or of rejection which they feel in the society to which they have come.

The Jews have had the experience of exile for over 2,500 years. In fact the word 'Diaspora', describing the lands in which Jews outside Israel live, actually means dispersion. Therefore, to understand a little of what it is like to be a Jew in America or Britain today means exploring the history of their coming to these countries – and this is where we begin.

JEWISH IMMIGRATION INTO BRITAIN

The Jews are one of the longest-established ethnic groups in Britain today. There were Jewish communities in England in the early Middle Ages but anti-Semitism was rife and eventually all the Jews were expelled in 1290.

It was not until 1656, under Cromwell's republic, that Jews were re-admitted. Over the next hundred years, it was primarily Sephardim who came to England and settled. They were descendants of Jews who had previously been expelled from Spain and Portugal. These Sephardi settlers were cultured and commercially successful and they became the early Anglo-Jewish establishment. There was also a small Ashkenazi immigration of wealthy German Jews and one of Italian Sephardim early in the eighteenth century. It was not until 1826, though, that all restrictions against Jewish immigration to Britain were lifted. During the mid-nineteenth century Jews came from Iraq and Persia to settle in London; the menfolk were mostly prosperous merchants.

The members of this early Anglo-Jewish community were aware of a need to be as little different as possible from the English; their Jewishness must not in any way make them seem like foreigners. There was therefore increasing tension between these long-established Jewish settlers and the much more unworldly Jews who came in increasing numbers during the late nineteenth century.

It was, in fact, the large-scale immigration between 1881 and 1905 of Ashkenazim from Eastern Europe which dramatically changed the character of British Jewry. During this period, hundreds of thousands of Jews poured into Britain, fleeing increasing economic restrictions, persecution and pogroms in Russia, Poland, Lithuania, Galicia and Roumania. They spoke in Yiddish and they brought with them the Orthodoxy and the customs of their *shtetls* (small Jewish towns). The majority were impoverished and unsophisticated; some were religiously learned; the non-religious amongst them were intellectual and socialist. And it was on this vast and disparate group of newcomers that their established brethren tried to impose an English way of life, at the same time as helping them to settle.

Not surprisingly, there were growing anti-foreign feelings in Britain – feelings reflected in the 1905 Aliens Act, aimed at stemming Jewish immigration. As a result of this legislation, although anti-Semitism in Eastern Europe continued, only a trickle of refugees managed to enter Britain after 1905.

The next large wave of immigration followed Hitler's rise to power in 1933. During these early years of terror, approximately 75,000 Jews, primarily from Nazi Germany and Austria, were able to gain refuge in Britain. Restricted entry remained a major obstacle but, particularly in response to the brutalities of Kristallnacht in 1938 – brutalities which were orchestrated by the Nazi government – the British offered hospitality to the 10,000 children brought by the Children's Transport Programme from Germany, Austria and Czechoslovakia. At the same time, permits were granted to (mainly female) refugees from these countries who were willing to go into domestic service in Britain. But the Jews who came were only a fraction of those who could not gain entry and died. Even post-war, only a very few Holocaust survivors were allowed into Britain.

It was not until the 1950s that immigration became easier. Then, once more, Jews sought refuge in Britain when circumstances in their countries of origin provoked anti-Semitism there. This was so for Jews from the Arab countries who came in three different waves: firstly, as a result of Arab fury at the establishment of Israel in 1948, and then during the Arab-

Israel wars of 1956 and 1967.

A different influx was of Hungarian Jews, when their continued existence there was threatened as a result of the 1956 revolution. Also in 1956,
following the Suez invasion, there was an exodus of Jews dispossessed
and expelled from Egypt, and those with British passports came to Britain.

Whilst a sizeable Persian Jewish community had been established in
London since the 1920s, Sephardi Jews also came during the fifties from
India, Morocco and Aden and many of the Israelis who have settled in
Britain since the 1960s actually originated in Arab countries such as the
Yemen and Iraq.

In contrast to much of the earlier immigration, which was in response to
oppression or persecution of the Jews in their country of origin, the large
South African Jewish influx of the fifties and sixties resulted from their
opposition to the oppression of other peoples, as expressed in apartheid.

The different waves of early immigrants tended to settle in the cities
near to their ports of arrival. The more northerly ports were used by those
from the northern regions of Eastern Europe so that Manchester, Leeds
and Glasgow particularly drew Lithuanian Jews, whilst London drew a
larger proportion from Poland and Central Europe. London again became
the magnet for later groups of immigrants.

The different groups came from widely different socio-economic backgrounds and levels of education. The Central European Jews, for example,
were generally well-educated with relatively high social and economic
status, as were the early Sephardi settlers. In contrast, the Eastern
European and the Oriental immigrants were mainly poor and unworldly.

Coming from a different culture affects not only self-perception but also
expectations. Burman (1990) illustrates this in relation to work: women of
the established Anglo-Jewish community, like their Gentile middle-class
peers,

> drew a sharp distinction between the spheres of home and work, which
> corresponded neatly with a demarcation of sexual spheres. The
> immigrants from Eastern Europe drew upon a different tradition: whilst
> they also perceived the woman's domestic role as of primary
> importance, this did not necessarily entail exclusion from the economic
> sphere. (p. 62)

It was a contrast in attitudes which continued to exert an influence on at
least two generations to follow. But in Britain – as in the States – there
were other outside and internal influences, too, so that being an immigrant,
or the child of an immigrant, was just one facet of the complex and rich
experience of being a Jewish woman.

THE AMERICAN INCOMING

The Jewish population of the United States is estimated at nearly 6 million (*A. J. Y. B.*, 1991). It is by far the largest Jewish community in the world; many more Jews live in the USA than in Israel, which has approximately 4.5 million.

Although large-scale Jewish immigration to the United States did not begin until the 1880s, it is interesting to consider the origins of the earlier Jewish immigrants and the way in which their influence was eventually overtaken by the later influx. The first Jewish settlement in North America was established in New Amsterdam (later New York) in 1654 by a small group of Dutch refugees fleeing the Brazilian Inquisition. They were followed in 1677 by Jews from Surinam and Curacoa who began a community at Newport, Rhode Island. The first synagogue was opened in New York in 1730. Other small and scattered communities were established during the eighteenth century, particularly after the American Declaration of independence in 1776 and the subsequent granting of freedom of religious expression. By the mid-nineteenth century there were 100,000 Jews, some of whom were Sephardim, descendants of the original Spanish and Portuguese settlers of the Colonial period, whilst others were Central European Ashkenazim.

The first major inpouring of 150,000 German and Polish Jews took place between 1860–70. But it was the great exodus from Eastern Europe between 1882 and 1914 which totally changed the composition of the American Jewish community. During this period, over two million Jewish immigrants came to the United States. They were fleeing discrimination, persecution and pogroms and their salvation was America's policy of unrestricted immigration. They came from Russia, Poland, Lithuania, Galicia, Romania, Hungary and Austria and, although the major influx was curtailed by the First World War, they continued to come until 1920.

However, the war ended this ultra-liberal phase and, subsequently, the association of radical Russian Jews with the Bolsheviks led to the imposition of immigrant quotas. Legislation in 1921 and 1924 effectively ended mass Jewish immigration to the USA. During the Nazi era (1933–41), Jewish organizations had to fight hard to enable approximately 250,000 German and Austrian Jews to enter the USA. They represented only a fraction of the refugees fleeing terror.

By the 1960s, the character of the American Jewish community had been strongly defined by two interrelated facts. The first was the speed of its increase – in 1880, there were under a quarter of a million American

Jews; by the mid 1960s there were six million – 3 per cent of the total population: they were no longer an insignificant minority. The second fact was the primarily Eastern European origin of this population growth – with the complex challenge which impoverished immigrants give to the second and third generation.

The immigration quotas of the 1920s were eventually set aside in 1965 and very soon large number of Israelis came – 300,000 had come by 1980, although not ostensibly to settle. Then, during the 1970s, Jews began to arrive from the Soviet Union and from Iran. The Israeli influx is unique for it is the only one in which Jews were not escaping injustice in their country of origin. The paradox is that it has occurred at a time of massive immigration into Israel of Jews from the four corners of the world. There is much ambivalence towards Israelis settling abroad (Shokeid, 1988); it comes from Americans who see them as leaving the land which every Jew regards as a haven and from Israelis in Israel who label them *yordim*, 'those who go down'. They symbolise the conflict between idealism and ambition.

Considering the history of immigration to the States, it is primarily of a people seeking refuge. Other than the recent Israeli settlers, the immigrants had fled from their countries of origin because they were persecuted. Upon arrival in the USA, although they missed aspects of their traditions in the 'old country', they did not yearn to return; nor did they express their loss by trying to reproduce in America their native society.

Goldstein and Goldscheider (1985) document the generational changes, starting with those who came at the turn of the century. The first generation were poor, had little formal education and were unskilled occupationally. Their goal was to survive economically. Imbued with the values of Eastern European ghetto life, they found comfort by continuing to live in tightly-knit communities and in these self-imposed American ghettos, religion played a vital part. Nevertheless, although impoverished, they came with internalized middle-class values – ambition, respect for education and a willingness to defer immediate gratification.

The second generation above all sought economic success and higher social status and, in contrast to their parents, they were receptive to Americanization. They also wanted to lift themselves out of their parents' world – out of the foreignness and the stifling ghetto environment – and they saw they could achieve this through hard work and particularly through education. In America – a nation of immigrants – this second generation was no more alien than other immigrant groups. But it was a generation in flux: its members were becoming Americans, yet the very Jewishness which they were rejecting gave them their identity and sense of belonging. It was a dilemma: being Jewish was both a religious and an ethnic identity (Herman, 1977), yet the religious aspect – particularly their parents' Orthodoxy – no longer seemed relevant. And so many of them began to look for a new, more American type of religious expression.

The first generation was preoccupied with surviving and the second with succeeding. The desires of the third generation were to do with integration, with becoming in every way a part of the American culture. Ironically, it is the legacy of this quest which is seen to underlie the problems of intermarriage and assimilation.

ON BEING AN IMMIGRANT

Although in both Britain and America the major waves of immigration have been of Ashkenazim from Central and Eastern Europe, yet they, and, even more so, the smaller groups of Sephardim, come from many different countries. As a result, Jews in contemporary American and British society draw on an immense diversity of cultures, of languages, of customs and of styles of religious practice. Yet one striking feature of the Jews, whatever their origin, is the sense of responsibility they feel for one another. 'They share a common fate, honour the same Torah, even if in the breach, and are more alike genetically and culturally than they are different' (Elazar, 1989, p. 17).

Nevertheless, coming from a foreign culture – or being the child of immigrant parents – affects a woman in many ways. Four quite different women spoke of how their lives have been coloured by their background:

Fifty-two year old Orthodox Persian woman (who had baked elaborately, especially for my visit). Married thirty-six years, with two married sons. Husband, also Persian, a fur merchant.

> I married at sixteen. In Persia we were living with the Moslems, in the same town. For the Moslems to marry a Jewish girl is a very good thing. We had to marry young, otherwise they would come and say 'we want your daughter for our son'. If you said no, there was a lot of trouble. So it was best that the girls married as soon as they matured – and a girl of sixteen in Persia is very mature, she can look after children, she can look after a home, she can cook, she can bake. So they used to marry their daughters very young – fifteen and sixteen; in the olden days, even

twelve. We were in the Pogrom [persecution] and we had all these Moslem people around us.

I was born in a village called Mashat. Then, when I was one, my parents came to Teheran. I came to England when I married in 1952. My husband also is Persian but he came from England to meet me. They had told him about me. I came to London as a young bride. I lived with my in-laws. They came over from Persia in 1927. Our parents taught us discipline, respect. We never dreamed of going [sleeping] with a boy. The girls here are spoiled. They have everything. We never took anything for granted in Persia.

My mother was a very very good wife and a good mother and she put everybody else before herself. She felt she was unimportant and everybody else was important.

I do a lot of charity work; I visit people in hospital and it gives me a lot of satisfaction. I make the most of my day and if I have in that day two or three *mitzvot* [good deeds], I am satisfied.

Non-religious South African woman, academic, feminist writer and lecturer. Married thirty-four years with three adult children, one married. Husband, also South African and a member of the ANC, also an academic and lecturer.

My transitions have been taken up with problems of being an exile, having no money and moving into areas of work for which I was unprepared. Bringing up children who are not of the English culture. We spoke English and yet we were very different... I've come through enormous trauma, immense pain and suffering.... I have a hundred different parts of me. There's me as an academic; me as a member of the ANC [African Nationalist Congress]; me as a wife; me as a mother.

We are aliens in an alien country and, because we are non-religious, have not been part of the Jewish community.

My mother was first-generation South African. Her mother just eked out an existence and had waited in Moscow for twelve years for her husband to save enough money to bring her over. My father's mother also had suffered and struggled. My mother was only one generation from people who had suffered and struggled and yet she fitted into the middle-class South African life without any difficulty. She was a very wasted woman.

German-born Jewish agnostic woman, married with four daughters.

My parents had to emigrate from Germany during the Nazi period. They suffered financially and had a very difficult time but they tried to give my brother and me always a feeling of security.

Sometimes I think we could do without religion in our day and age, yet the cultural aspect of Judaism is something that I value.... Most of our friends are Jewish, from Germany or South Africa. They are non-believers like ourselves. I feel part of this group of people. Though we don't see very much of one another I know I can always count on them in times of crisis or times of joy. A group of friends who, by choice, are Jewish.

American-born Reform woman, husband from Orthodox background, two sons.

I grew up in America but I never thought of myself as being American because my parents were so obviously European and my home environment was never 'all-American'. My twin sister lives in Washington DC and is married to a non-Jew. Her having 'married out' has affected me more than I realised it would.

ASHKENAZIM AND SEPHARDIM

Despite the varied origins of all the different waves of immigration, the Jews belong to one of two major groupings: the Ashkenazim and the Sephardim. The Ashkenazim, originally meaning Jews of German origin, also include most Jews from northern France and from central and eastern Europe. The Sephardim, originally meaning Jews of Spanish and Portuguese origin, also include Jews from the Mediterranean basin and from the Orient (the term *Mizrachi*, meaning Eastern, is used to describe Jews of the Sephardi tradition coming from the Arab and other Middle Eastern countries and from India).

The cultural background of Ashkenazi and Sephardi Jews is very different and yet, surprisingly, only relatively unimportant differences in customs and ritual now divide them, and marriages between the two groups, although not frequent, take place without any great difficulties in bringing together both cultures. It is interesting, however, to look at each group separately.

The major historical difference between these two groups is that, over a very long period, the Sephardim inhabited a Muslim world, while the Ashkenazim lived among Christians. The Jews of Spain, the original Sephardim, were part of the Muslim world before Christian Spain limited Muslim rule to the south. Whereas historically the Ashkenazim were compelled to live in the narrow ghettos of northern Europe, the Sephardim were usually able to participate fully in the general life of their countries of residence before their flight or expulsion. Elazar (1990) points out that, more important than the specific culture of their particular country of exile, are the rituals and symbols which unite Sephardi Jews: 'the Sephardic world is one, from the Atlantic to the Indian oceans, significantly influenced by its location within Islamic civilization'. (p.15)

The Sephardim

They represent fewer than 3 per cent of the Jews of America and Britain, yet their countries of origin are far and wide. They come from Spain and Portugal, from Turkey and Greece, from Morocco, Yemen, Egypt, Aden, Syria, Lebanon, Tripoli, from Iraq and Iran, from India. For many of them, neither America nor Britain is their first country of migration – it is as if, having once been uprooted, they remain mobile. In fact, for many of the more recent Sephardim, Israel has often been their intermediary home.

In America and Britain, the Sephardim were the first Jewish settlers. The earliest group – descendants of Jews previously expelled from Spain and Portugal – came to America during the Colonial period (1654–1776) and settled in England too during that period. In what became the United States, these Sephardim – although never more than a few hundred – established communities and synagogues, combining their Spanish heritage with their Jewish tradition. Like the early Sephardi settlers in Britain, many of whom played a part in Victorian high society, they were aristocratic and had amongst them many wealthy and notable families. But, although they retained their cultural and religious dominance until the 1820s, they were soon outnumbered by Ashkenazim.

Further waves of Sephardim came to America and Britain as a result of upheavals in their countries of origin. At the beginning of the twentieth century, and particularly following the collapse of the Ottoman Empire, they came from the Balkans and from the Levant. These newcomers were very different from the descendants of the earlier Sephardim of Spanish and Portuguese origin and they often chose to found their own separate congregations.

In the aftermath of the Second World War, more Sephardi refugees came from the Balkans. Then, in the 1950s and 1960s, in the wake of decolonization in Africa and Asia, Jews came to America and Britain from Iraq, Persia, Egypt, North Africa and Lebanon. Still later, two further incomings were of Sephardi Jews from Israel, particularly after the 1973

Yom Kippur war, and then of Iranian Jews, leaving in their thousands after the overthrow of the Shah.

Yet with all of these waves of immigration, the Sephardim remain only a small minority of the Jewish communities in America and Britain – less than 3 per cent in either country – and their congregations and synagogues tend to be separate from the mainstream. For, despite being a tiny minority, the Sephardim retain from their different cultures of origin a way of life and a set of traditions which, in their vibrancy and colour, seem to set them apart from the Ashkenazim, with their more austere northern European backgrounds.

Within the different groups of Sephardim, there are inevitably many distinctions: education, wealth and culture of origin are the obvious dividers. The descendants of the early Spanish and Portuguese settlers have the sophistication of long-established and often distinguished families, as do the Jews from Iraq and Iran who built up great wealth in trade with India and the Far East. In contrast, many of the Oriental Jews remain poor and, particularly with the men, there remains a cultural gulf between their understandings and those of their host country.

Yet it is a curious paradox that – despite originating from at least eighteen different countries – Sephardi Jews, unlike the Ashkenazim, accept the same standards of observance; they have never had a Reform movement within their communities for there is a tolerance and a flexibility which has not necessitated it.

Just as the early immigrant generations of Ashkenazim spoke Yiddish, the colloquial speech of the Sephardim, particularly the less sophisticated and the older generation, remains Ladino. It is a 'popular' speech giving a sense of continuity with their culture of origin, and yet it is also a language full of poetry and song. There is even a translation of the Bible in Ladino intended particularly for women (*Me'am Lo'ez*) and aimed at making the biblical commentaries more accessible.

Women in Sephardi tradition

Regardless of the differences in background and culture of origin, there are many similarities in attitudes and expectations of Sephardi women. Firstly, for a woman to choose to remain unmarried is seen, even in sophisticated families, as highly undesirable. Then, having married, whether rich or poor, whether educated or not, the Sephardi woman even today will meet with great opposition if she should want to work. Her rightful role is seen to be presiding over her home, caring for her children, becoming expert at the elaborate foods which remain a feature of Sephardi family life and – particularly with the more affluent – involved with cultural and communal activities.

Even more entrenched attitudes influence Oriental Jews from Islamic countries, for they combine both Jewish and Islamic attitudes towards women. Family life is highly patriarchal and status belongs to the father and then the eldest son. The woman's role is to bear and raise children, with barrenness considered a curse caused by the 'evil eye'; in fact, many of the poorer Oriental men, unable to succeed in financial terms, achieve status in terms of their virility, demonstrated by the number of their children. Yet, however poor, the Oriental husband will not tolerate his wife's working outside the home; to need her earnings would undermine his pride and honour. And not infrequently, marital conflict – and even wife-beating – results from the woman's internalizing the very different – and unacceptable – expectations of her host culture.

The Sephardi communities encompass many contrasts and often, particularly in their attitudes to women, they retain values which seem anachronistic today. Yet, both in the popular imagination and in reality, the Sephardim are seen as more exotic than the Ashkenazim in all aspects of their lives – their rituals, their customs, their foods. In their synagogues they have a liturgy enriched by the poets of the Spanish golden age (Ibn Gabirol and Yehuda Halevi) and their ceremonies convey an aesthetic dimension missing from the Ashkenazi tradition. In their homes, too, and in their *succoth* (simple dwellings for the festival of Tabernacles) they celebrate colour and beauty with Oriental wall rugs, pictures and brass ornaments. Most of all, in their sweet, rich, elaborate and artistic cooking they show the diversity of their cultural heritage. It is a heritage which, in its all-embracing quality, vividly defines the expectations of a woman's life.

The Ashkenazim

'Ashkenaz' is the Hebrew for Germany, just as 'Sepharad' is the Hebrew word for Spain. In the Middle Ages, many of the Jews of north-west Europe migrated to eastern Europe, taking with them both the name and a German-type language, Yiddish, which is still spoken today by elderly Ashkenazim. Paradoxically, in contemporary society Yiddish is being revived by Jews at opposite ends of the spectrum: by modern Jews, seeking to retrieve aspects of their ancient heritage and, in vivid contrast, it has become once more the language of the ultra-Orthodox, seeking to segregate themselves from the secular world.

The vast majority of American and British Jews are Ashkenazim, descendants of those who fled from persecution. They are the children or grandchildren or great-grandchildren of two large waves of immigration. The first major influx followed the murder of Alexander II in Russia in 1881 – an event which unleashed state-instigated pogroms throughout the anti-Semitic countries of Eastern Europe. Refugees came in their thousands to Britain until stopped by the 1905 Aliens Act and over two million Jews poured into the States until prevented by similar legislation in the 1920s. They arrived, impoverished, from Russia and Poland, from Lithuania, Galicia and Roumania.

But it was the survivors of the Holocaust who have even more influenced the character of the generations since. During the Nazi era, and struggling against legal restrictions in America and Britain, they came from Germany, Austria, Hungary and Czechoslovakia – and it is their legacy which still leaves its scar today. It is a legacy of somehow needing to expiate their sorrows from the collective memory and it is expressed in many ways, very often in the unconscious. For example, the very deeply ingrained expectation which women have in all societies to bear children is doubly reinforced in the Jewish woman in terms of the continuation of the people and the reparation of the Holocaust.

> **How do you tell children, big and small, that society could lose its mind and start murdering its soul? ... Had we started to speak, we would have found it impossible to stop. Having shed one tear, we would have drowned the human heart.**
>
>   (Elie Wiesel, quoted in Bergmann and Jucovy, 1982).

The literature on Holocaust survivors observed their compelling need to deny and repress their experiences. Later therapeutic work with the children of survivors saw a pathology handed down and expressed in terms of anxiety at even short-term separations from their parents and, simultaneously, a desire to be allowed to separate. There was also a constant need to succeed and not disappoint their parents (Bergmann and Jucovy, 1982). Whether these sorrows continue to be seen in terms of pathology in today's later generations, it is too early to say. Naomi Dale puts forward the possibility that

> the anxious, neurotic distressed Jew is the *living Jew* [her italics] – in touch with the experienced and remembered distress and pain of our history... there is no present as a Jew without the past – we have always understood this symbolically through our annual festivals of remembrance, ancient memories that are tinged with the pain of our

suffering at the hand of others and our joy at our redemption, our survival and continuity.

(Quoted in Cooper, 1988, p.74)

The Sephardim, too, of course, are the children of refugees but somehow there is a different dynamic relevant with the Ashkenazim. Cooper (1991), listening to three generations born of the refugees from Eastern Europe, notes a recurrent theme: 'Once again, the children would be the hope... The children would make it all right... But as the generations... roll on, the residue of the original deprivations remains...' (pp. 19–20). Ambition, success, guilt are, he suggests, ever-present; the unconscious need to repay the sacrifices is always there and the feeling that Jewish survival depends on staying close, with the inevitable ambivalence about breaking away.

How these expectations are expressed in everyday life is complex; there seem to be two, apparently contradictory, realities. The first is of modern Jews fully integrated into the largely middle-class way of life of the wider society; it is the assimilation-integration process, particularly highlighted by intermarriage. Simultaneously, though, there is an increasing emphasis in America and Britain on 'being Jewish', an emphasis not necessarily expressed only in terms of religious involvement, but equally in terms of Jewish cultural and communal identification. It is a picture of growing secularization alongside a growing identification with the religious and/or ethnic anchors of Judaism and Jewishness.

In terms of religious identification, the origin of the immigrants explained their subsequent influence in the country to which they fled. So, whilst the first wave – the relatively unsophisticated refugees from Eastern Europe – felt sustained by Orthodoxy, in contrast, the second wave – the European Jewish middle-classes who escaped from Nazism – became the mainstay of the Reform movement.

Chronicling the Jewish identification of the immigrants' children and grandchildren, sociologists observe how the second generation of the Eastern European settlers made vigorous efforts to forget their Jewishness and to become modern and integrated within the new society in which they were born.

We learned how to be modern. Now our problem is how to be Jewish.

(Rabbi Eugene B. Boronitz, quoted *Encyclopaedia Judaica Yearbook 1974* (Jerusalem: Keter) p. 396)

It took another few decades, during which many assimilated and were lost to Judaism, for this trend to be reversed and for a new generation to feel confident enough to try and retrieve what it had hardly known of its heritage. And it is their children, the children of the 'retrieving' generation, who are increasingly polarized – intermarrying or otherwise choosing to opt out or, alternatively, 'returning' to religion or to other contexts in which they can affirm their sense of belonging.

Ashkenazi Women

And what of the women? It is very striking how, with the needs specific to each generation, it is they who were – and still are – of pivotal importance. But whereas in the early period, their role was very clear – to hold together an uprooted family and help it survive economically – gradually, as men became the prime breadwinners, the woman's role had to be more narrowly redefined with family and community as her spheres, for how else could her husband's success be measured? It is a process described by many writers (and particularly well by Burman, 1986, in Britain, and Baum et al., 1975, in America).

But now, of course, new changes have taken place and whilst the most obvious change appears once more to be in response to economic reality with women, of necessity, working or returning to work, the real metamorphosis is a much deeper one. It is that, maybe for the first time in history, women are also beginning to define their own needs. The question is whether Jewish women, and specifically Ashkenazi women, are any different in their struggle for self-development than women generally. After all, the tendency to be self-sacrificing is not unique to Jewish women!

There are many answers. Firstly, it is striking how much further along this struggle Ashkenazi women are than women in the Sephardi world whose horizons are still primarily male-defined. But, also, even with the Ashkenazim, there are strong generational factors – profound differences between those who matured during the 1950s and 1960s and the generation which has followed. For women of the older generation tended to restrict their expectations: they married and their family remained their main fulfilment for many years. Then, when they eventually sought a role outside the home, they did so late in life, and were often not sufficiently determined to achieve what they wanted. For many, affluence, in cushioning them, failed to focus their objectives so that they ended up with many roles, but fragmented. It is a scenario rarely repeated by their daughters for whom self-development and career-development are much more valid and clearly defined. For the daughters, there are new choices concerning family life to negotiate and new dilemmas.

Equally, the context matters: American Jewish women were amongst the pioneers of the women's movement. They were sensitive very early to the disquiet amongst women confined to the wife-mother role, women who hoped fulfilment could come by fulfilling the needs of others. These women exposed this as an illusion and their successors in the sixties and seventies heard their message, internalized the ideals of feminism and learned to take responsibility for themselves. And the demands they made, both of themselves and of others, and the changes they achieved – both in their everyday lives and in their involvement with Judaism – have had a very profound effect within American Jewish society. But it took another half-generation till British Jewish women followed their path.

The story of this book is therefore a story of women's changing visions for themselves; it is told in terms of expectations becoming more widely defined. Often it is a story of a very complex struggle, for it takes place within a religiously-derived culture in which a particular image of oneself as a woman is formed. And, often, the struggle is accompanied by much ambivalence, for family and community symbolize security and self-definition. But ultimately it is a story of new negotiations by women within an age-old tradition, and the choices which they make are crucial ones for Jewish continuity.

DEMOGRAPHY: FACTS AND FEARS

Statistics can have a strong deterministic influence on people's attitudes and behaviours.

(Reisman, 1986)

Many fears are expressed in both Britain and the States about the combination of low birth rates, intermarriage and assimilation, and its effect on Jewish continuity. In fact, community statistics are exceedingly difficult to obtain: there is no census about religion in either country and therefore a composite picture has to be built up by extrapolating from small community surveys or from synagogue returns. On the basis of these, demographic projections are made which, Reisman warns, may become self-fulfilling prophecies.

There is a further problem: it is to do with determining who is a Jew. This is a theme throughout for, as Waterman (1989) points out, 'the *halachic* [Orthodox Jewish legal] definition, based on the maternal line or on Orthodox conversion procedures, increasingly fails to encompass all the effective Jewish population'. Inevitably, therefore, data is inadequate and particularly so on non-affiliated Jews.

Nevertheless, many valid demographic observations can be made and parallels drawn between the USA and Britain. However, there are also many differences and therefore, as in other chapters where a different scenario exists, the American and the British situations are considered separately.

The American scene

The Jews, the eternal 'strangers and sojourners', at last found permanent rest in a country where all came as strangers.

(Paul Johnson, 1987, p. 568)

The American Jewish community is remarkable not only because of its size, but because of its character. Despite the extent to which the majority of its members – in fact, all but the Orthodox – are fully integrated into American society, it is a community which retains its Jewish consciousness. Jews in America think of themselves as wholly American but as Jews, too.

It is, of course, a consequence of America's being a nation of immigrants that the immigrants' children could so easily integrate. But the other unique aspect of American society is that it is the first place in which Jews have come as settlers and have found that their religion and its accompanying observances and way of life are both accepted and respected.

The Jewish community and its geographical distribution
Estimates of the Jewish population of the United States suggest it is just under 6 million (the *American Jewish Year Book,* hereafter *A. J. Y. B.,* 1991, gives 5,981,000), a figure which includes both affiliated and non-affiliated Jews. Jews are now about $2\frac{1}{2}$ per cent of the American population: a proportion which has declined since the mid-twentieth century when it was estimated at $3\frac{1}{2}$ per cent.

The largest single concentration of Jews in the world is in the greater New York area, with almost two million. This is followed in size by Los Angeles, with half a million, then Philadelphia, Chicago and Miami, each with a quarter of a million Jews. On the eastern seaboard there are also very large Jewish populations in Boston (170,000), Washington DC (160,000) and Baltimore (92,000), as well as throughout the state of New Jersey and in areas of Florida as well as Miami. On the western seaboard, the Jewish populations are particularly clustered in California; as well as the half million in Los Angeles, there are 80,000 in San Francisco, and large communities in Orange County, Oakland and San Diego. There are also sizeable Jewish populations in both Cleveland and in Detroit, as well as in very many other urban areas of the United States.

Altogether, there are sixty-nine American cities with a Jewish population of over 10,000, with the north-eastern and midwestern regions of the
USA containing approximately two-thirds of the total Jewish population.

The birth rate, intermarriage and attrition
Despite these vast concentrations, there is great concern about an antici-
pated decline in Jewish population size. Projected fertility rates are below
replacement level and one of the reasons is seen to be the redefinition of
women's roles. On average, the Jewish woman of childbearing age in
contemporary society is well-educated and, frequently, professionally
employed. Inevitably, except amongst the Orthodox, the tendency is for
her to marry late, to delay having children and then to limit the size of her
family.

Added to this anxiety, there is great concern amongst community
leaders about increasing rates of intermarriage, with estimates of around
50 per cent of marriages being to a non-Jew. Whilst the contentious issue
of conversion is discussed in a later chapter, the particular significance of
intermarriage is to do with the children of these marriages, many of whom,
even in families where the non-Jewish partner converts, are lost to the
Jewish community.

Religious composition
Perhaps not surprisingly in such a pluralistic society, when American Jews
are asked what type of Jews they are, they invariably answer with a
denominational category. In fact, most of the community surveys suggest
that approximately three out of every four Jews identify with a denominational label (Kosmin, 1988). Whilst the meaning of each of the different
synagogual groups is much more fully discussed in a later chapter, the distribution is of interest here. The largest allegiance – 34 per cent of the
community – is to the central Conservative movement, with a further 2 per
cent of Jews favouring Conservative's split-away, progressive group, the
Reconstructionists. The second largest affiliation – 29 per cent – belongs
to the more progressive Reform group. At the other end of the religious
spectrum are the Orthodox; they claim the greatest recent increase in followers and now number 9 per cent of the Jewish population of the States.

Class and educational status
Despite the obvious variation in socio-economic status, demographers
note the high proportion of Jews with college and graduate-level education
and their middle-class background and values. In fact, Lerman (1989) sug-

gests that the Jewish community is the most highly-educated and the most affluent of all US minorities and Paul Johnson (1987) describes 'the transformation of the Jewish minority into a core element of American society... They have become an aristocracy of success' (p. 567).

And, at the other end of the spectrum, there are many 'Invisible Jewish Poor', to quote Ann Wolfe's (1971) title: specifically, there is a 'feminization of poverty', symbolized by the number of lone-mother families. This, inevitably, is the unacclaimed aspect of Jewish society and is more fully discussed in Chapter Eight.

In terms of the effect of the more predominant middle-class values on Jewish women, Fishman (1989) observes a striking contrast between women now at mid-life, who had had a liberal arts type of education, and younger women whose choice of studies and whose educational achievements are much more specific, leading to occupational goals and career objectives. As a result of these changed expectations, the majority of American Jewish women today marry later and bear children later than their mothers did, and are far more likely to continue working outside the home after marriage and even after children are born. In fact, Fishman comments that 'the late-forming, dual-career family has become the norm... in every Jewish denomination' (p.32). But, regardless of predictions to the contrary, research shows that the majority of these wives are deeply committed to Jewish life (Fishman, p.32; Schlesinger, 1987; Cohen-Nusbacher, 1987; Bunim, 1986).

Marriage and divorce

As might be expected in a community so integrated into the mores of the wider society, amongst Jews, too, there has been a decline in the numbers marrying. In the early 1990s, demographers have suggested that about 20 per cent of Jewish adults have not married at all and that only two-thirds of American Jewish households consist of married couples. Alongside this, there is a considerable increase in the rate of Jewish divorces, and the resultant single parent families are almost all lone-mother families.

Amongst the many consequences of divorce is one relating to communal involvement: American Jews generally join synagogues when they become parents and divorce often leads to a lapse of synagogue membership.

The demographic debate is bound to continue. On the one hand there are those who point with pessimism to the American scene; they highlight a trend of late marriage, of intermarriage, or of not marrying at all. They see delayed childbearing, small families and increasing divorce. Inevitably, they covertly blame women, pointing to their educational and career ambitions as being not conducive to the traditional values of family life.

But against the prophets of doom are those who paint a more optimistic picture, who see continued Jewish involvement, even amongst those who have intermarried. And, rather than indicting feminism for breaking up the family, they recognise that it has brought about a vastly increased commitment within all areas of religious life amongst women who had previously felt themselves to be only peripheral – and amongst their families.

The British scene

For we went, changing countries oftener than shoes ...
(Bertolt Brecht, 'To Those Born Later'
in *The Poems of Bertolt Brecht 1913–1956*
(ed. by John Willett and Ralph Mannheim))

The way in which the Jews in Britain established themselves was very different from that in the States. America, particularly during the periods of mass Jewish immigration, was 'a nation of immigrants'. British society, in contrast, particularly during those periods, was much more homogeneous and the immigrant frequently felt an alien. For the immigrant Jews, this perceived dislike of the foreigner had a two-fold effect. It encouraged the early settlers, those predating the vast influx of Ashkenazim at the end of the nineteenth century, to emulate the customs and way of life of the British. Such adaptation came easily to them for these early settlers were educated and wordly. However, for the poorer East-European Jews escaping persecution, safety in a foreign land lay in closeness. And even for the generations which followed, the tendency to perpetuate this separateness has remained.

As a result, the Jews in Britain, long after they ceased to see themselves as immigrants, have on the whole chosen to remain distinct from the host culture. They have also tended to live in fairly concentrated communities. For the observant, this congregating is felt as a necessary way of maintaining religious cohesiveness and exclusivity, but for the non-religious it may partly result from perceived social prejudice against their full integration into the wider society. For whichever reason, in most of the places where Jews have settled they are a distinct cultural subgroup. There has, of course, always been some merging between Jews and the wider society, mainly through assimilation, marrying out, or conversion, and this has increased strikingly in the past twenty years. Yet the majority of Jews, both as a group and as individuals, still maintain a separate identity.

Looked at objectively they may appear part of the larger society but frequently, in fact, they 'operate within their own specific minority experience' (Waterman and Kosmin, 1988).

As earlier discussed, how Jews define themselves is complex. Whilst the majority indicate their identification in terms of synagogue membership, a sizeable minority – Cesarani (1986) estimates it at 95,000 – feel their Jewishness only culturally. Inevitably, factual data on non-affiliated Jews is problematic. The British Census has no question about religion and no direct question about ethnic affinity and therefore, in studying a group that is predominantly British-born and has been so for the past two generations, researchers have met considerable difficulties (Waterman, 1989).

The statistics which are available come either from synagogue membership or from extrapolations from communities within the larger Jewish community. But, while in the past the community was relatively homogeneous and concentrated, today it is more pluralistic and there is an increasing trend towards alienation and outmarriage. 'Who is a Jew?' therefore becomes a question of concern to the communal demographers, too.

Population

British Jewry has been declining numerically for the past four decades. Whereas in the early 1950s, there were an estimated 430,000 Jews in Britain, by 1991 the community had shrunk to under 300,000 (Community Research Unit, 1991).

Approximately 70 per cent of the Jewish population lives in London, 10 per cent in Manchester, the other large communities being Leeds, Glasgow and Brighton. There are also sizeable communities in Birmingham, Liverpool, Southend and Bournemouth. The pattern of migration has been from the inner city areas of first settlement towards the suburban periphery of the major cities.

Religious composition

Although Judaism is a religion in which family observance in the home is as important as ritual in the synagogue, yet traditionally it is the synagogues which have maintained the religious and cultural cohesion of the community.

There are several synagogue groupings in Britain. At the right are the various ultra-Orthodox communities, often quite small congregations but attracting increasing numbers of followers. In the centre religiously is the United Synagogue, nominally Orthodox, although with considerable variation in observance by its members. It accounts for almost two-thirds of synagogue membership. Also in the centre are the Sephardim (Jews from

Spain and Portugal, the Mediteranean, the Near East and from India, Persia and Iraq) who, although proportionately few, have their own synagogues and distinctive style of service. Along the spectrum – nominally central in observance but philosophically more flexible – is the small but vibrant Masorti/Conservative movement. Then, to the left, and taking a less strict and more pluralist view or religion, are the Reform and Liberal (Progressive) congregations.

Whilst the spectrum of religious practice and experience is considered in Chapter Four, at this stage it is useful to attempt a statistical background. Membership of a synagogue is still the most prevalent symbol of identity for British Jews and, despite the earlier-stated lack of adequate information about non-affiliated Jews, contemporary studies suggest that 'synagogue membership covers the vast majority of identifying Jews' (Schmool, 1991). However, there has been a significant change in terms of synagogue membership, expressed primarily by the defection from mainstream – United Synagogue – Orthodoxy. Some or this loss reflects a drift away from any sort of affiliation, but many of the 'defectors' have been drawn towards both ends of the spectrum, to right-wing Orthodoxy and to Reform and Liberal Judaism. Predictions suggest the loss to United Synagogue affiliation is likely to continue (Schmool, 1991).

Comparing the distribution, whereas in the early 1980s the United Synagogue boasted a membership of over 70 per cent of affiliated Jews, a decade later that had shrunk to only 65 per cent. The Orthodox, in contrast, increased their membership over the same period from 4 to 7 per cent.

The increase in Orthodoxy is a very visible one – particularly so because many no longer live only in segregated concentrations. This high visibility applies especially to the Lubavitch Chassidim (more fully considered later) who pursue a philosophy of living amongst and reaching out to non-Orthodox Jews.

But the other groups which have attracted defecting United Synagogue members are the Progressives: in the same decade, from the early 1980s to the early 1990s, Reform and Liberal membership has increased from 23 to over 25 per cent of affiliated Jews. Only the Sephardi synagogue membership, just under 3 per cent, has remained stable.

However, alongside these statistics, what must be remembered are the very large number of non-affiliated Jews (Cesarani's 1986 figure of 95,000 is widely accepted) many of whom still strongly identify, although not in terms of religious or communal involvement, and others of whom have drifted away from or been alienated by the 'normative' community.

Social class and occupations
Surprisingly little is known about the socio-economic make-up of British Jewry apart from common assumptions about its 'middle-class' nature and relative prosperity. What is particularly noted about the descendants of Jews who arrived at the turn of the century is their upward mobility. The key to this mobility has been education 'which helped to transform *the male children* of semi-skilled and skilled workers into professionals and small businessmen, and *their sons* into politicians... and academics' (Waterman, 1989. my italics).

Available information on occupations is primarily about men. It shows an above-average Jewish representation in the professions – particularly medicine, dentistry, law, accountancy and the academic world – with younger men also moving into the 'caring professions'. Outside the professions, Jewish men tend to be self-employed and are ten times more likely to be so than Jewish women (Kosmin and Levy, 1981). Women's employment, discussed in Chapter Nine, is shifting from the traditional involvement in unpaid communal work to career and job choices similar to those of non-Jewish women of comparable age and education.

Yet, despite the socio-economic achievements of the majority of Jews, the demographic picture in Britain, as in the States, is one giving considerable cause for concern. Here, too, there is anxiety about declining rates of marriage alongside increasing rates of divorce and intermarriage.

Marriage
Marriage remains central to Jewish family life, but, except amongst the strictly Orthodox, there has been a serious decline in synagogue marriages since the early 1960s. The number of synagogue marriages carried out in the early 1960s had been almost halved by the mid-1980s. Equally worrying is the fact that only half of the children born in the late 1950s and early 1960s who would statistically have been expected to marry in synagogues in the 1980s actually did so. Factors seen as contributing to this decline include intermarriage with a non-Jewish partner, opting out of marriage, civil marriage among Jews, living together unmarried, emigration of young people.

Intermarriage and conversion are discussed in Chapter Eight. In Britain, with one in three marriages having a non-Jewish partner, 'marrying-out' is seen to be the most significant cause of assimilation. And, unless the non-Jewish partner converts *halachically* (i.e. according to strictly Orthodox requirements) – a process which demands great tenacity – there is a high probability that the children of a mixed-faith marriage will not eventually identify as Jews.

Divorce

The rate of Jewish divorces has also risen steadily over the past twenty years although its increase is not as dramatic as in the general population since the 1970 Divorce Law. Whilst exact figures of Jewish civil divorces are difficult to obtain as religion is not noted in secular divorce statistics, Waterman and Kosmin in 1986 estimated that about 400 Jewish couples were divorcing annually in Britain – a figure which has probably increased since. Contrary to expectation, they suggest that 'no real difference can be observed in the divorce figures across the spectrum of synagogue group-ings' (p.14).

The repercussions of not obtaining a religious divorce are discussed in Chapter Three. Yet community research suggests that only half of the couples who marry in a synagogue and subsequently divorce obtain a *get* (Bill of Divorce) from a *Beth Din* (rabbinic court). Many couples only apply for a civil divorce often not realising that, without a religious *get*, any subsequent partnership is not deemed a religiously-valid marriage by the Orthodox and United synagogues, and thus there are implications for any future children's religious status.

Births and Deaths

As well as divorce, non-marriage, inter-marriage and assimilation, demog-raphers note another source of attrition: the excess of deaths over births – an annual imbalance which by 1990 had reached over 1,000.

Emigration

Finally, emigration, particularly of young Jews, is seen as yet another important factor in the net annual decline of British Jewry. Approximately 1,000 British-born Jews settle every year in Israel, and at least two-thirds of these are under the age of thirty. The loss to the British Jewish commu-nity is, therefore, not only of those emigrating but also of their eventual children.

In pessimistic manner, Cooper (1991) summarises the demographic picture:

> Over the last decade the statistical litany has become familiar: one in three Jewish marriages ends in divorce; nearly 20 per cent of Jewish children experience the breakdown of their parents' marriage; one in three Jews who marry, marry 'out'; less than half the Jews who marry do so in a synagogue; each year Jewish marriages are outstripped by Jewish burials; the annual birth rate is roughly two-thirds of the death rate. Overall, British Jewry is an aging community shrinking numerically. (p.11).

Perhaps it is an irony that migration once again is a factor in changing the picture of a by-now long-established Jewish community. For migration is a theme through the story of the Jewish people. It is a story of exile, of new homelands and of diverse cultural origins. Yet in this book we are particularly considering the way in which Jews, and specifically Jewish women, have become a part of the countries which have welcomed them – and the ways in which they have remained separate. It is a narrative with two interwoven threads: that of being a woman in a religious context and of being a Jewish woman in a secular world.

Part II
Women and Judaism

2 Women's Role in Judaism

'BLESSED ARE THOU . . . WHO HAST NOT MADE ME A WOMAN.'

Jewish men who pray recite a blessing in their daily morning prayers thanking God, 'who did not make me a women'. A recently published prayer book has a little footnote; it says: 'There is no degradation of woman implied in this blessing. Men thank God for the privilege which is theirs of performing all the precepts of the Torah, many of which are not incumbent upon women' (Metsudah siddur, 1982, p.14).

There are many implications in this. Firstly, it is noteworthy that an 'explanation' is now deemed appropriate in a modern edition. Then, which is later discussed, there is reference to those commandments 'not incumbent upon women', which raises the vexed issue of where in religious practice exemptions become exclusions.

Within Jewish religious law (*halacha*) there are many areas in which women are disadvantaged. The Orthodox – men and women – deny this to be so; in reply they glorify the role of women as different from yet complementary to men's role in society and in religious law. Yet, at the same time, they acknowledge that there are difficult areas – woman's religious study, her participation in synagogue ritual, her legal status, the divorce laws.

Biale (1984) comments: 'The essence of the problem of women in Judaism is their sociologically inferior status.' She quotes Adler (1983), 'we are viewed in Jewish law and practice as peripheral Jews'. It is this peripheral status which results in women's being 'excluded from the central activities of Jewish life' and permits 'laws which make them dependent on men and vulnerable to exploitation' (Biale, pp. 262–3).

These laws, and their relevance to Jewish women today, are explored later. This chapter begins by comparing the woman's position in the two pivots of Jewish life – synagogue and home.

WOMAN'S RIGHTFUL REALM

Apologists emphasize that Judaism is a religion and a way of life in which the home is central and that in this sphere the woman's role is respected and all-important. However, there are two major areas – always esteemed by the practising Jew – in which woman's involvement is not required;

these are synagogue prayer and study of the religious law. Biale points out that the common thread uniting those areas from which women are exempt 'is that they are all obligations outside the realm of women's domestic role' (p.17).

Mead (1976) observes that status is usually attached to what the man does in a particular society. Applying this to a Jewish context, Burman (1982) considers the division between sacred and profane. When prayer, study and attending to the affairs of the community were the man's chief obligation, it was this sphere which was held in high esteem; the woman's role – that of being the breadwinner – was necessary and complementary, but it was an enabling role. With the increasing secularization of society and the separation of home and work, the division then became one between the public and private spheres. The man became the breadwinner, a role now carrying high status, and the indication of his success was to make the woman's financial contribution unnecessary. Her domain therefore became the domestic, private one; again complementary but lower esteemed.

> In each case, the activities in which women were engaged commanded little respect, yet, at the same time, they played a crucial role in enabling men to engage in their endeavours in the esteemed spheres from which they themselves were excluded.   (Burman, p. 37)

The role of woman in a patriarchal system is that of enabler; it is an altruistic role, important for the man, for the family and for the community. The Jewish woman has been glorified from Biblical times onwards in this role. The Proverbial 'Woman of Worth' freed her husband and sons from day-to-day economic responsibilities so that they could pursue sacred tasks; her modern counterpart still sees her family's needs as her highest priority, and arranges her life to fulfill them.

Rich (1977) comments on this process historically:

> Jewish women of the 'shtetl' and ghetto and of the early immigrant period supported their Talmud-studying men, raised children, ran the family business, trafficked with the hostile gentile world, and in every practical and active way made possible the economic and cultural survival of the Jews. Only in the later immigrant generations, with a greater assimilationism and pressure for men to take over the economic sphere, were women expected to reduce themselves to perfecting the full-time mother-housewife role already invented by the gentile middle class. (pp. 235–6)

The possibility that women's culture in all patriarchal societies becomes a 'muted counterpart culture' is suggested by Ardener (1975). Myerhoff (1978) discusses this in relation to Jewish women, seeing the woman's world as an alternative sub-culture with different symbols of value and success from those of men. It is a point taken up by Kupferman (1979): 'apart from religion, they had *space* as women – clearly demarcated areas where they reigned supreme' (p.111).

Jewish feminists ask whether it is not merely masking the inferiority of women to interpret their role as different from yet complementary to that of men. Ozick (in Heschel, 1983) suggests that the problem for women in Judaism is 'a social, not a sacred, question' (p.123). Similarly Adler (in Heschel) claims that the laws which exclude women from the central religious obligations of Judaism – synagogue ritual and Torah study – leave women outside, 'petitioning a system of life regulated by men' (Heschel, p.4).

Fundamental to Jewish teaching is the precept that woman and man were created as equals by God. In contrast to this, many Jewish feminists contend that 'not only do women not shape and control their own lives, but our most basic understandings of human nature are drawn primarily from men's experiences' (Heschel, xxi).

How does all of this translate into the lives of Jewish women in contemporary society? In many different ways. The ultra-Orthodox, whether born so or having become so, insist that such discussion is an irrelevance, that it indicates an understanding from outside, not from within their frame of reference. They genuinely see theirs as an equally valued and esteemed sphere of influence:

> The women's is the greatest role of all; she creates a home imbued with spirituality. To ask, for example, why a woman cannot say *kaddish* [prayers recited by mourners for a deceased relative] is no more a question than to ask why a man cannot bear a child.
> Our lifestyle is by choice. When you make a choice you know you make some sacrifices. It is, though, a one-hundred per cent choice. We are free women and we have no need of a woman's movement.
> (Chassidic women in Stamford Hill, North London.)

Levi-Strauss (1970) uses the word 'bricoleurs' to describe people who construct systems with leftover materials. Myerhoff (1978) applies this concept: 'These women have long known how to devise entire... worlds out of their peripheral status and tasks ... as complex as the external, male-dominated realm' (p. 236). Yet Orthodox Jewish women, in their homes, in the domain over which they preside and in which they transmit to their children the essence of Judaism – and in their study groups – convey a dignity of spirit which is very different from any suggestion of their feeling second-best.

Kupferman explains this seeming paradox: she acknowledges that Orthodox women are 'thoroughly indoctrinated into the dominant male ideology' (1976, p. 124) and yet, at the same time, she understands the serenity in their lives: 'They knew they were as essential in the cosmological scheme of things as men' (1979, p. 111).

There is, however, ferment even amongst the Orthodox. It is evidenced in many respects: by modern Orthodox women demanding the right to study religious sources in depth – and that right eventually being granted (Jews' College, London). Similarly, by the fact that a symposium in London in 1989 ('Traditional Alternatives'), discussing evolution within tradition, was followed a year later, *in response to demand from women*, by a conference aimed at re-evaluating woman's role in traditional Judaism. Although little real change was achieved, the energy generated – and discontent voiced – produced increasing ripples. At a subsequent gathering, a distinguished American Orthodox rabbi urged observant women to take back those *halachic* rights which had been theirs historically but which, through women's failure to exercise them, had gradually been eroded (Rabbi Saul Berman, 18.3.91). It was followed by an article in the *Jewish Chronicle* (29.3.91, p.15) by two well-educated Orthodox women, Barbara Green and Valerie Adler;

> We detect an impatience with Orthodox Judaism among ... highly-educated women.... The idea of Judaism in which the primary purpose of women is to clean house, roast endless chickens and bear unlimited children holds very little appeal.... Men are frightened of what will happen when the energy of educated Jewish women is finally unleashed.

All of this assumes some freedom of manoeuvre and the ability, money and time required to present demands for change. Much less is heard from working-class Orthodox Jewish women for whom the responsibilities involved in feeding and clothing their large families leave little energy for study, for ritual involvement or even for stating their basic needs. A traditionally-observant family therapist working with strictly Orthodox families in Stamford Hill describes how she may, in some circumstances, act as advocate for the women, going to the rabbi and making a case on their behalf as to why birth control is essential:

> You must have a full understanding of their values before you have any right to intervene. Despite the poverty, women in this culture do not feel devalued as they often do in other groups. Here, their status symbol is the number of children they have. Many of these families live on very low incomes and struggle on income support and when their children are small they are caught in a poverty trap. Yet there is a real network of practical support from the community, particularly when a mother is overwhelmed. It is only when they cannot cope with having that number of children that these women feel they have failed, that they have not lived up to their internalized expectations. I have to be very sensitive to know when to suggest that I go to their rabbi (or rebbe, if they are Chassidic) and ask if they may have a six-month 'rest'.
>
> (Hugette Wiselberg, in interview)

Whilst the lives of Orthodox women are totally defined by the requirements of *halacha*, the lives of the traditionally observant (the United Synagogue in Britain is more 'traditional' than the Conservative movement in the States) may be fully influenced by these laws or may be so only nominally. There is, anyway, considerable variation and compromise in what the traditionally observant actually do observe, as there is in the strength of their belief or in the extent of religious involvement which they seek. And, also, it is important to recognise that denominational labels often do not convey how a woman *feels* about religion; Reform women, for example, may well describe themselves as religious and, in fact, feel religious.

Interestingly, regardless of the community to which a woman belongs, her self-perception frequently continues to give central place to her role as home-maker, as these three very different women so strongly convey:

> (A) It's not so much a religious commitment or the ritual, but I feel a very strong Jewish identity. It is bound up with the family. If you look at Jewish history, the family was the fortress against whatever happened outside, that protected people and formed a human focal point.
>
> (B) The things I do are Jewish things. . . . I'm very, very family orientated; I'm old-fashioned in those respects. Maybe I'm lucky

because I have a husband and family who are quite dependent on me and keep me busy and I'm happy with that, so it's good all round . . . I hope it always will be my role. The kids, please God, will get married and have children and, as I adore babies and children, I hope it will just go on.

(C) I have no religious commitment based upon a belief in God but I have a tremendous religious commitment in terms of Judaism. I do not think I could have married a non-Jew. I've always accepted the importance of ritual and I wonder whether my rationalist reading of the universe really has as much validity as I thought it had and yet I cannot in honesty go against it. . . . At the same time Judaism is possibly one of the most important influences in my life.

The complexity of a woman's feelings about her Jewishness and about her roles as a Jewish woman clearly cannot be adequately indicated by her religious affiliation alone. However, her expectations in terms of synagogue involvement and communal leadership are a very different matter and are changing most dramatically within progressive Judaism.

The Reform and Progressive communities in the States and in Britain now accept women as equal with men. They have women rabbis; women may be called up to the reading of the *Torah* in synagogue; women sit with the men in synagogue (not segregated from them as in Orthodox synagogues). The extent to which women's self-definition is changing as a result is discussed by an English Reform woman rabbi – and it is interesting to see from what she says that there is much more reticence amongst British women in Reform than with their American counterparts:

The feminist movement essentially aims to produce change through dialectic and, if we believe in this aim, we – as women rabbis – must take responsibility for the consequences of the de-stabilizing process that we set going.

There has been an assumption within the Reform movement that women are equal. In fact, though, women have not really explored their needs for themselves and made demands. Some of these demands should be to do with the very symbols of Judaism, for instance the wearing of *tallith* [prayer shawl, traditionally worn only by men]. Reform women, just like Orthodox women, haven't really attempted to make changes; for example, they assume that they will light the Shabbat candles and that men will make *kiddush* [the prayer recited before the Shabbat meal].

The fundamental question is about women's choices. Of course there are positive consequences to there being different spheres – if women are confined to the private sphere they will develop their nurturing behaviour – but we also have to give women the confidence to pursue their potential in the public sphere. A whole range of issues arise from the fact that men take the space in mixed company.

To me, feminism is not just about women, it is about a set of principles, about the democratization of knowledge. The rabbi should be a facilitator, not just a 'giver of knowledge'.

(Rabbi Elizabeth Sarah)

IMAGES AND STEREOTYPES

In an article analysing young, educated American women's 'return' to Orthodox Judaism, Debra Kaufman (1987) suggests that often 'apparent polar opposites reveal hidden affinities'. She looks at the way that, historically, women in male-defined cultures reclaimed 'the autonomous values and dignity attached to women's community'.

Applying this idea to contemporary Jewish women, although outside work roles are once more increasingly an expectation, there remains a striking emphasis on home and family. Whether their Jewishness is based within a religious context or draws on a cultural tradition, they see their roles as wives and mothers as being fundamental to their lives.

Such an attitude is predictably part of a traditionally observant woman's way of thinking:

I think if the women are not totally involved with the family, there is not much hope. All the important aspects of Judaism begin and are grounded in the home. I am worried about the next generation. Our daughters are working outside the home and at the same time trying to run a traditional home. I feel we should be happy with our role as it is and not pressurize ourselves. They will be too tired to keep everything going. My daughters would disagree, but the woman is crucial to the home and family.

(Observant woman, communal worker, husband's secretary)

It is more surprising to find a similar emphasis in a feminist:

It's this Jewish legacy of the family as all-important which was difficult to reconcile with my ideological commitment to feminism. I was a feminist when it was unfashionable for feminists to be wives and mothers. My role as mother has been all-consuming yet I have always worked and a tremendous amount of my work has been concerned with this very issue – not to have the whole identity subservient to serving the family. But the nurturant roles – you can't shed them – plus all the guilt when you feel you haven't fulfilled them adequately.... A number of my friends are amazed at the closeness of our family... It's not unique to the Jewish culture – it's central to peasant communities too – but it isn't present as far as I can see in the average middle class English family.

(Non-religious woman, academic, feminist writer)

Feminists – and Jewish feminists – emphasize the patriarchal nature of the Jewish culture. They observe women's seeming collusion but they also observe a paradox: Orthodox women's dignity and high self-esteem.

Scholars have always held that the Jewish attitude towards women is a positive one, even if Orthodox Judaism denies the woman any significant role within the synagogue or community. In fact many contradictions exist: firstly, her influence is within the home where motherhood is idealized, yet it is given little formal status. Similarly, although procreation and fecundity are highly regarded, there is much ambivalence towards a woman's sexuality. Roith (1988) suggests that, in common with other religions, Orthodox Judaism indicates a fear and an envy of the female's creative functions. In fact, her sexuality is seen primarily as the means of enabling her husband to fulfil the obligation incumbent on him to procreate (Yevamot 65b) – which, interestingly, is not an obligation incumbent upon the woman (Feldman, 1972, p. 35).

In her introduction to 'The Woman Who Lost Her Names', Julia Mazow (1980) writes that 'Jewish tradition is rich in ambiguous attitudes and ambivalent feelings towards women'. In the Bible, woman's chief function is that of childbearing (Genesis 3, 16), yet at the same time she is depicted in Proverbs 31 as being a woman of great resource and energy with an important role in the public sphere.

Similar contradictions occur in the Talmud (the source of all Jewish law and codes after the Bible) where she is portrayed as 'lightheaded' (Kiddushin 80b: 'The rational faculty of women weighs lightly upon them') and seductive to men (Talmud Shabbat 152a: 'A. Tanna taught: Though a woman be a pitcher full of filth... yet all speed after her'). Yet within the same tract of the Babylonian Talmud, there is a very different assertion: 'The rejoicing of one's heart is a wife; the heritage of the Lord is children' (Shabbath 152a) and, throughout, the woman is also accorded reverence: 'Let a man be careful to honour his wife, for he owes to her alone all the blessings of his house' (Baba Mezia 59a).

Heschel (1983) comments on the recurrence of these polar images of woman in ancient and medieval Jewish sources: she is both Lilith and the *Shekhinah*. Lilith is 'the source of evil, temptation and sin, who haunts the world, seducing pious men... The *Shekinah*, in contrast, is the gentle, loving presence of God, the daughter, queen, bride and lover' in prayer and in Sabbath liturgy (p.7). These contrasting portrayals are also, Heschel notes, evident in contemporary fiction: the mother as both nourisher and smotherer.

Throughout the literature there emerges traditional Judaism's glorification of wifehood and motherhood as woman's prime roles. Since biblical times women were referred to mostly as wives and mothers:

> Whereby do women earn merit? By making their children go to the synagogue to hear scripture and their husbands to the *Beth Hamidrash* [study house] to learn *Mishnah* [the oral code of laws].
>
> (Berakoth 17a)

And even acknowledging her historic role as earner, the woman is nevertheless defined primarily in relation to others. Solomon Maimon, an eighteenth-century philosopher quoted in Heschel, p. 23, writes:

> the wife undertakes the management of the household and the conduct of business and *is content thereby to become a partaker of her husband's fame and future blessedness.* (my italics).

Yet it has been stated so frequently as to have become almost a truism that Judaism does not view men and women as unequal, merely as different. Herein lies the tension. The fundamental theological position states that God

> recognizes no stratification of human beings, no inferiority of women to men.... On the other hand, the husband represents an attitude grounded in daily life and social reality where there are distinctions of... learning and, of course, gender. Women are inferior to men in economic power, social standing, legal rights and religious role and importance. While in ultimate moral and spiritual terms a woman's life is equal to a man's, her concrete day-to-day life is marked by subservience to men. This tension appears in Genesis in the two creation myths. In one account woman is created equally with man 'in God's image', and in the other is created to meet man's needs.
>
> (Biale 1984, p. 14)

Much of our self-definition results from unconscious processes, from messages conveyed and received. Heschel (1983) suggests that the attitudes and teachings of Judaism are perpetuated through hidden images and beliefs – images which persist even in non-religious contexts. These contradictory views are inevitably part of the internalized material, but both feminist research and feminist psychoanalytic literature indicate that internalizing a poor self-image is not specific to women in Judaism: 'The consequence of being raised as a daughter in a patriarchal society is that women see themselves as inferior' (Eichenbaum and Orbach, 1986).

> I was told I was 'University material' but I remember my stepmother saying, 'You don't do proper women's things because your nose is always in a book. If you become clever, who'll want to marry you?'... When I was twelve, someone asked me what I wanted to be. I said I wanted to be a woman M.P. and to have twelve children. The subliminal message was very strong. I didn't see the contradictions... I didn't understand why it wasn't possible. When I was sixteen, I read 'A Room of One's Own' and that inspired me, but I was sixty-five before I understood why one needed it because, in the getting of it, in the getting of the economic freedom, I'd lost myself.
>
> (Asphodel Long, secular Jew, in interview)

In contrast to the medieval world where all Jews lived under the umbrella of religion, today's Jew can choose to opt out, and many do. Yet many paradoxes remain. The first is one that is noted throughout the literature (Bird, 1974; Hauptman, 1974; Kupferman, 1976 and 1979; Myerhoff, 1978; Greenberg, 1981; and many others) – that of women's high self-esteem within Orthodoxy. It would appear that the anger ignited by feminism at woman's subordinate position in the patriarchal world of wider Christian society is neither latent nor suppressed within traditional Judaism. Commenting on this, feminists (e.g. Heschel, 1983; Swirsky, 1989), suggest that Judaism, a male-defined religion and culture, which has always seen woman's prime role as being within the home, does not give birth to the 'macho man' of other cultures. In fact, the man most highly esteemed within traditional Jewish society was the pious man and the scholar. It was the woman who permitted him to aspire to these goals. His 'power' was historically not economic, although later it became so.

There is, too, the phenomenon referred to earlier: the 'return' to Orthodoxy of a significant number of highly-educated women who have fully lived in the secular world and who now choose a strictly religious way of life. To dismiss this as a retreat into safety becomes too facile an explanation as one hears about the difficult transitions these women have pursued.

3 Religious Law

The women's very perception of their Jewish identity... is concerned with the domestic world.

(Webber, 1983, p. 147)

Let me begin by dispelling a few myths. Judaism has often been accused of subjugating women to their husbands and of giving them a legal status inferior to that of men. Both of these statements are only partially true.

(Neuberger, 1983, p. 132)

In order fully to understand the influences on Jewish women's lives in the present, it is necessary to understand something of the context from which normative expectations were derived. There is a vast literature on the subject of *halacha*, the Jewish religious law. This chapter begins by considering briefly the historical origins of this law. It will then discuss woman's status within *halacha*, focusing particularly on those areas in which she is disadvantaged. There are, however, aspects of this law in which evolution has in the past taken place and these are indicated and the circumstances which made it necessary. The chapter will then look at contemporary debate within traditional Judaism concerning *halachic* change. Finally, some observations are made concerning the disparity between the legalistic ideals and the reality of day-to-day life. (A note about definitions: the words Orthodox and non-Orthodox are used throughout not in any perjorative sense, but to indicate those who are committed to full observance of *halacha*.)

Halacha, the religious law, consists of detailed rules, given as divine commands in the Bible and subsequently expanded in the Talmud and in later rabbinical works. The Talmud is composed of two parts, the Mishnah, which is the codification of the law completed during the second century CE, and the Gemara, which is the subsequent rabbinic commentary on the Mishnah. The Talmud was written in two versions, the Jerusalem Talmud and the later Babylonian Talmud, during the first five centuries CE, and it is this later version which is the source of all Jewish law and codes after the Bible, including those relating to women.

In the early period, there is strong evidence of there having been discussion, flexibility and development in the *halacha*, but over the last 1,500

45

years religious law has changed very little. In our own time, this rigidity is seen as 'the response of...Orthodoxy to secularism' (Biale, 1984, p.5). Yet the system need not be as immutable as is believed. From within tradition, the voice of Orthodox feminism suggests that 'where there is a rabbinic will, there is a *halachic* way' (Greenberg, 1981, p. 43, and lecture, London, 13.6.90).

However, *halachic* authorities have always been exclusively male and women have always effectually been denied access to the study of *halachic* sources and interpretations. Therefore, being uninformed, they have been unable with any depth of understanding to dispute rulings which nevertheless intimately affect their lives.

In seeking to understand why woman's legal status in *halacha* appears to be lower than that of men it is necessary to consider the post-Biblical period during which much of religious law was consolidated and codified. Neuberger (1983) suggests that the position of women in Biblical times was a visible one within society; they could voice their opinion, they could act as judges and prophetesses, they could even inherit property. However, by Mishnaic times, possibly as a result of the Hellenistic influence on Jewish society, women were less well-educated than they had been in the earlier Biblical period; they had also gradually became excluded from public life and less important in the structure of society. Consequently they now had a lower legal status than that of men. Despite this, the legal standing of Jewish women was

> never as low as the status of women in other contemporary societies, particularly the Hellenistic, and at no stage was the status of Jewish women as low as that of Christian women under mediaeval canon law. Women in Judaism were never chattels. They always had specific rights.
> (Neuberger, 1983 p. 136)

Equal but different

> Although the whole Torah is written in the masculine, woman is equal to man, save for certain precepts where, because of specific teachings or other reasons, she differs from him.
> (*Encyclopedia Talmudit*, quoted by Feldman, 1972, p. 85)
> Different roles may occupy the same rung in the ladder of status.
> (Rabbi Dr. Jonathan Sacks, 1990).

Underlying women's seemingly disadvantaged position in *halacha* is the belief that their roles and realm are different from those of men. Webber (1983), from the viewpoint of an anthropologist, observes that 'Judaism is in practice a male religion, a male culture, a male-dominated social system' (p. 143). Throughout there is a paradox; it is to do with the fact that Judaism is, undeniably, a male dominated religion and yet, equally undeniably, the lives of Orthodox women are enriched by a very apparent inner peace.

> Orthodox Judaism gives a woman a sense of being *more* in touch with herself.
>
> (Discussion with Orthodox rabbi's wife, who is a *Ba' al t'shuva* [one who 'returns' to religion])

The paradox suggests one of two possibilities: either that the strongly internalized value-system of the strictly Orthodox precludes their questioning or, alternatively, that questions grounded in understandings outside the strictly-religious framework are just not relevant to the Orthodox woman's *chosen* 'Torah-true' way of life.

Halacha is, however, important not only to the strictly Orthodox: its rulings also affect, or potentially affect, all those within the 'traditionally observant' groupings – specifically, the majority United Synagogue group in the UK and, although with increasing modifications, the Conservative movement in the States. Therefore, these Biblical and Talmudic laws inevitably still influence the religious rights and duties and the religious status of this majority, particularly in relation to marriage and divorce. And in these latter areas and in the laws pertaining to conversion, the religious status of their as-yet-unborn children may also be determined, even to the extent of whether or not they may eventually marry within the religiously-observant fold.

Biale (1984) points out that 'law sometimes lags behind social reality and sometimes anticipates it' but 'its fundamental impetus is to preserve the customs of the past' (pp. 4–5). Because *halacha* is based on the concept of appropriate – but separate – gender roles, non-Orthodox Judaism, in its ideological commitment to equality, has chosen to reassess and reject laws which maintain sexual divisions. A discussion of gender-based religious differentiation therefore indicates how women are viewed *halachically*, together with the rationale for the perpetuation of the system.

Women, Prayer and Study

Fundamental to traditional Jewish practice are the *mitzvot*, divine commandments. These are both negative (the 'thou shalt not' laws) and positive (the situations in which one takes on obligations). Whilst men and women are equally bound to observe all the negative *mitzvot* and all those positive *mitzvot* which are not 'time-bound', women are exempt from observing the 'time-bound' positive *mitzvot* (i.e. those for which there is a fixed time.)

The debate around inequality in this area focuses on the implications of this exemption. The exemption was based on the traditional view of woman primarily as housewife and mother, roles which were deemed to have priority over, for example, the need to pray at set times. But its effect was to exempt women from any role in public religious life.

Women were also exempted from the study of the Torah, which is the entirety of Jewish law and ideology. Torah study is, in fact, a positive *mitzvah* which is not bound by time and is regarded as one of the highest forms of worship, and yet women are exempt from it. A distinction is made in Orthodoxy: women are required to know the laws – for how else could they fulfill them? – but they are not required to study their sources or the subsequent rabbinic debates upon the laws. Women's Torah study has traditionally been looked upon with great disfavour (and even in our own day, the Orthodox young woman intent on studying *gemarah* (the rabbinic commentaries) may well find that she is prejudicing her chances of a 'good *shidduch*' (arranged marriage).

PRAYER

There is a quiet acceptance in woman's morning prayer: 'Blessed art thou, O Lord, our God...who has made me according to thy will.' Prayer is required of both men and women and is central to the life of every religious Jew. Yet in public prayer the Orthodox woman has no role; she has neither responsibilities nor rights. Women, in fact, are not obliged to take part in synagogue services and, in both Orthodox and traditionally observant synagogues, women are separated from men, usually in an upper gallery, with the Orthodox screened off by a curtain (*mechitzah*).

The woman in Orthodox Judaism is affected by both exclusions and exemptions. She is excluded from forming part of a *minyan* (ten adult males must be assembled as a quorum for public prayer). She may not be called up to recite the blessing over or to read from the Torah. She is not permitted any leadership role in the synagogue. In fact, in Orthodox communities, men perform all the liturgical roles, even those which women are permitted, such as the blessings over wine. And other exemptions became exclusions: women are excluded from wearing *tefillin* (the phylacteries used in morning prayer) or the *tzitzit* (fringed garment worn by the Orthodox) or the *tallith* (prayer shawl) – acts which link men intimately with prayer.

Underlying these are, of course, traditional expectations regarding woman's primary role as mother which, during a period of her life, prevents her from undertaking those commandments to be fulfilled at a certain time. But Biale points out that there are two other considerations: one is to do with women's voices, which are 'considered a sexual provocation ... so that a woman may not read or recite before men' (Biale, 1984, p. 26). The second is the concept of *kvod ha-tzibbur*, respect for the community: 'that women reading the Torah put men, and the congregation as a whole, to shame' (Biale, p. 28).

Apologists (e.g. Meiselman, 1978) explain these exclusions in terms of women's essentially private nature. However, Berman (1991) emphasizes how, historically, through not exercising their permitted rights, women allowed them to lapse, so that possible exemptions within *halacha* became exclusions. Whatever the theoretical premiss or historical process on which these exclusions were based, they underline the fact that 'Women are second best in public prayer ... public ritual life is the province of men' (Biale, p. 28–9).

In effect, the exemptions which became exclusions limited the religious life of women to the home in which the Orthodox – both men and women – insist that the woman's role is given equal esteem to that of the man in synagogue life.

That remains the position for the Orthodox and traditionally observant and, despite the occasional women's prayer group or *Rosh Chodesh* group (which celebrates the new month), women within these communities exert little pressure for fundamental change. Indeed, one Orthodox woman, commenting on women's prayer groups, wrote: 'I cannot avoid the sneaking suspicion that the feminist movement and its desire for *identical* rather than *parallel* roles for the sexes has played no small part in promoting such activities' (Reif, *Jewish Chronicle,* 10 May 1991). Yet at the same time, under pressure from educated Orthodox women, a seminal decision was recently reached in Israel confirming women's right to be elected to religious councils (*Jewish Chronicle*, 19.8.88).

Barbara Amiel, in *The Times* (5.8.88), notes that: 'Historically, the rites and methods of worship as well as inclusions, exclusions and theological adjustments to changing social conditions have been the hallmark of virtually every religion since time immemorial.' In our own time, within Orthodox Judaism there has been little change in woman's position in public prayer except for the covert accepting of girls' *bat chayil* ceremonies (which usually take place not in the synagogue itself but in an ancillary room). Whilst an important innovation, they in no way parallel the boy's *barmitzvah*, which is a ceremonial acceptance of his assuming the obligations of Judaism.

It has inevitably been the leaders of the Reform and progressive movements in Britain and the States who have initiated the redefinition of woman's role in the synagogue and, gradually, some of their innovations have been introduced into Conservative, Reconstructionist and Masorti synagogues.

Change concerns not only ideological commitment but also people's inner readiness for new ways. That is why, in any consideration of the process of evolution, ambivalence is also felt. Sometimes it comes from within the very group which brings about innovation, as if there is an innate conservatism, a fear of where change may lead. In modern society, where both family breakdown and individual anomie are increasing threats, tradition represents stability. So that, possibly alongside the desire to embrace the wider options which evolution brings, there are older values coming from religion which remain an unconscious force in women's lives.

RELIGIOUS STUDY

Rabbi Eliezer said that he who teaches his daughter Torah is considered as if he had taught her *tiflut*. [*Tiflut* may be translated as either frivolity or immorality]
(Quoted from the Mishnah (Talmud Sotah 20a) in Biale, 1984, p.33)

You see for me the spirit of Judaism has come from studying, from learning. Maybe I am atypical, because I had access to sources and traditions which taught me about mysticism. Women are hungry for knowledge.
(Chani Smith)

Knowledge is power. Many women feel alienated from the central avenues of power, and that power can only come from learning
(Rabbi Dr. Jonathan Sacks, in *The Guardian*, 25.7.90)

There is a paradox. Jewish women, even from Orthodox backgrounds, have often received a good secular education and been cultured in terms of their accomplishments, but until recent times they have been allowed only very limited access to Torah study.

The question of women and Torah study is a particularly sensitive issue. Firstly, of course, it concerns power: without adequate knowledge of the sources of religious law and the complex rabbinic debate on it, women are ill-equipped even to discuss those areas of *halacha* in which they are disadvantaged. Secondly, the discrimination that continues even today in Orthodox circles against women's Torah study in-depth denies them status, for in Judaism esteem has always been accorded to talmudic learning. Thirdly, effective exclusion from the intricacies of talmudic reasoning prevents women from being able to approach contemporary issues with valid religious understandings.

As with prayer, there is also continued debate about women and religious study, about whether *exemptions* have over time become *exclusions* (Meiselman, 1978; Biale, 1984; Weissman, 1986/7). The debate centres around whether women were not *obligated* or whether they were not *permitted* to study Torah. Rabbi Saul Berman, a provocative Orthodox American rabbi, insists that women were never excluded from learning but that, over time, the privilege – being not exercised – was taken away (1976; 1991).

Chaim Bermant, discussing this issue, suggests that the problem is less to do with the content of Torah study than with women's acquiring the tools of the dialectic process. In other words, he is suggesting there are dangers inherent in women's becoming acquainted with the methods of the *halachic* process – the complex rabbinic debates through which, over time, the religious law is *re-interpreted* (for it cannot be changed) to accord with contemporary needs.

In this section of the chapter, we shall see how attitudes towards women and religious study have been modified by the rabbinic authorities to correspond with the needs of the time, just as rigidly defined gender roles in relation to work outside the home have also always been relaxed (and then reinforced) according to male definitions of appropriateness.

In the Bible, women are given equal status with men; both are created in the image of God. Yet for men the study of Torah is parallel to prayer as a form of worship of God, while women were exempted from this responsibility. The reason given is that in the Bible it is stated: 'And you shall teach your children' (Deut. 6,7) – which the sages took to mean 'your sons'.

Yet even the sages of the *Mishnah* (the oral tradition) disputed this issue. On the one hand, Ben Azzai stated: 'A father is obligated to teach his daughter Torah' (Jerusalem Talmud, Sotah, 20a; Biale, p. 33). Against him, Rabbi Eliezer, earlier quoted with his prejorative remark about *tiflut*, insisted: 'Woman's only wisdom is in the loom' – and when questioned by his son on the prudence of such a reply, asserted 'It is better that the words of the Torah be burnt than given to women' (Sotah, 3, 16a. Biale, p. 35).

Needless to say, it was the negative view which held sway except for a few exceptional women who since biblical times onwards have became scholars. The consequences were far-reaching. They resulted in study – which in Judaism is equally esteemed with prayer – becoming the realm of the man whilst the woman's role became that of 'enabler'. Her place in heaven was assured if she made it possible for her husband and sons to study the holy books. She did, of course, have to learn how to observe the laws of *kashrut* and the Laws of Family Purity, how to run a religious home and how to teach her children: but nothing more.

Interestingly, other than the biblical reasons, no adequate explanation appears ever to have been given for this. Maimonides, the distinguished twelfth-century sage, suggested that the majority of women were not prepared to dedicate themselves adequately to such study, therefore they would gain only superficial knowledge (Meiselman, p. 34). But it was a circular argument: if women did not have the opportunity to study, they could hardly be expected to study in depth.

A century later, the *Sefer Hasidim* (Book of the Pious) stated that girls did not have to study the profundities of the *halacha* or to be trained in the primary sources of the Talmud and *posekim* (dialectic), since women *were axiomatically excluded from positions of cultural or political leadership.* Consequently, as Roiphe (1986) observes, 'Jewish women were trapped in a social and religious tradition that directed them away from learning and simultaneously valued learning above all else'.

Yet gradually, as the ideas of the Enlightenment spread, Orthodox girls and young women, despite being excluded from religious study, were frequently given a liberal education. They became accomplished culturally whilst remaining unschooled for roles of communal responsibility. And, for a while, the force of social norms continued to restrict their expectations.

Eventually, what gradually permitted women's access to religious study was not greater rabbinic enlightenment: it was, rather, the needs of the time. During the nineteenth and early twentieth centuries, economic and social factors resulted in an increasing defection of boys and young men from Orthodox Judaism. Because of this, responsibility for much more adequate religious instruction in the home was conferred on wives and mothers. And, in response, there came a new emphasis on the importance of a girl's being educated religiously as well as in secular studies. Significantly, though, education for women was not being advised for its intrinsic worth or for its value in terms of their intellectual development, but in order to stem the risks of assimilation.

So, in 1844, the first edition of the *Jewish Chronicle* called for the religious instruction of females, asking 'for how is a mother enabled to engraft in the heart of her tender offspring dogmas strange to herself?' And, in similar vein, in 1852, the *Archives Israelites* wrote: 'The health of our religion depends henceforth above all on the education of girls ... The women is the guardian angel of the house; her religiosity, her virtues, are a living example for the children whom she has constantly under her eyes. *Man exists for public life, women for domestic life.*'

There was also increasing concern about the woman herself. The Chofetz Chaim, writing early in the twentieth century, says:

> Formerly, when a women lived in her father's home ... there seemed to be no necessity to teach her Torah; but nowadays when women are no longer confined to the home and secular education is open to them, one should teach them Torah to prevent them from leaving Judaism and forgetting their traditional values.

But he did not suggest that they be trained in the intricacies of talmudic reasoning.

Weissman (1986–7) comments wryly on this evolution: that something which had been considered forbidden was now deemed a *mitzvah*; that learning could now be permitted to all women, not only to exceptional ones; that the innovation was legitimated on historical–sociological grounds; and, above all, that the change remained of limited scope. What was happening over this period was a contingent response to increasingly worrying circumstances. The woman now had to become knowledgeable in order to become a religious mentor. Through her elevation to the status of primary religious influence on her home and children, she was at last permitted a more thorough Jewish education. But there remained – and still remains – much male ambivalence attached to this new status; there was a covert assurance that the women was certainly not in any way being prepared for spiritual or communal leadership. And the underlying attitude had changed little: 'A man's ultimate task is an all–engrossing involvement in the study of Torah. A woman's ultimate task is in another area and another direction' (Meiselman, 1978, p. 40).

Religious learning has always been highly valued in Judaism. In the past, it has been almost exclusively man's realm: his responsibility, his privilege. But women have begun to understand that expectations are formed and status conferred through education and they are increasingly demanding it on equal terms. The implications of this in terms of leadership are enormous.

DIVORCE

> When a man hath taken a wife, and married her, and it come to pass that
> she find no favour in his eyes ... then let him write her a bill of
> divorcement, and give it in her hand, and send her out of his house.
>
> (Deut. 24, 1)

Contrary to popular belief, divorce has always been permitted in Judaism
and regarded as an accepted part of human life. However, the laws pertaining to divorce particularly support Greenberg's (1981) view of *halacha* as
representing 'the religious institutionalization of sexual and social status'.
Biblical law was grounded in the male–oriented culture of the Near East.
As originally codified, divorce was unilateral; a wife could not divorce her
husband, although a husband could divorce his wife relatively easily.

By Talmudic times, however, the rabbis showed their awareness of
woman's vulnerability under the existing law and steps were taken to
protect her. Legislation was enacted and written into the *ketubah* (mariage
document) laying down financial settlements to be paid to the divorced
wife out of the husband's estate. At the same time, the legal procedure by
which a husband could serve a *get* (bill of divorce) on his wife became
more complex. The other important talmudic innovation was to make it
possible in certain circumstances for a woman to approach the rabbinic
court with a valid case against her husband; he would then be ordered to
initiate proceedings against his wife. Yet grave anomalies remained; in
neither biblical nor talmudic law was there any provision for the wife to
refuse the divorce or to initiate one herself.

It was not until the Middle Ages that her disadvantaged position in this
respect was addressed. A ruling attributed to the eleventh-century Rabbi
Gershom of Mainz decreed that a husband could no longer divorce his
wife without her consent unless she was guilty of a matrimonial offence.
Having the power to refuse a divorce, the woman was now theoretically
better able to negotiate favourable terms. Commenting on these changes,
Biale (1984) writes:

> The talmudic prescription for compelling a man to divorce his wife in
> certain cirumstances and the medieval ban on divorcing a women
> against her consent are two fundamental changes in the laws of divorce.
> The first balances the power of a man to divorce his wife for practically
> any cause by allowing a woman with 'good cause' to seek a divorce
> through a court. The second curbs the unilateral power of a man to
> divorce his wife at will by requiring her consent to the divorce. Yet

neither innovation fully solves the problem of inequality of power between men and women in divorce. (p. 100)

There is, of course, often a disparity between a legal ruling and the reality. For instance, in practice the husband may override his wife's refusal to accept a divorce if her refusal is seen by the *Beth Din* (religious court) as being unreasonable. In such circumstances, the *Beth Din* may appoint an 'agent' to accept a *get* (bill of divorce) on behalf of the unwilling wife. It is a legal device to which the wife cannot resort in reverse circumstances – i.e. where her husband refuses to grant a divorce.

In Jewish law, marriage and divorce are not sacraments, as in Christianity; they are viewed as contracts: marriage is thus a contract entered into by mutual consent. However, divorce may be enacted only by the husband. This therefore creates a fundamental imbalance, one grave consequence of which is that the woman may become an *agunah* (an 'anchored woman'), a status exemplifying her disadvantaged position.

There are, indeed, grounds on which a wife may request that the *Beth Din* asks the husband to issue a *get*, but he remains the one to initiate – or withhold – a divorce. Herein lies the imbalance of power to which Biale refers. The woman may appeal to the religious court for their intervention:

(1) When her husband is afflicted by physical conditions or undertakes an occupation deemed unendurable for the wife

(2) When her husband violates or neglects his marital obligations

(3) When there is sexual incompatibility or when there has been wife-beating.

Within these three categories there are guidelines based on talmudic definitions; there is also dispute in their interpretation. The 'marital obligations', for example, include two aspects – appropriate financial maintenance and, the wife's fundamental right to sexual relations with her husband.

The major problem, however, remains that women are relatively powerless in the matter of divorce. Although theoretically the religious court may compel a man to divorce his wife, the procedure for so doing is beset with difficulties. There is, first, a fundamental contradiction for 'a man can give a divorce only with his full consent' (Yevamot 112b) which is questionable if he deems that he is being compelled by the court. Moreover, in practice the court is not infrequently unable to enforce its mandate to compel the man to divorce his wife.

The situation is complicated by the fact that the civil court may grant a divorce yet, if a recalcitrant husband refuses to give his wife a religious divorce, it is impossible for the wife to remarry according to Jewish religious law for, according to *halacha*, she still has the status of a married woman. This situation, of the woman's remaining tied (an *agunah*), affects all divorced woman in America and Britain who may eventually wish to remarry within Orthodox Judaism and also includes all those in Britain within the traditionally observant (United Synagogue) group.

In the States, there have been initiatives by progressive rabbis within the Conservative movement to find a *halachically*–acceptable way to prevent the status of *agunah* occurring. One of their proposals was to insert a condition in the *ketubah* (marriage document), empowering the *beth din* (court of law) to grant religious divorces to women abandoned by their husbands – a proposal provoking much opposition from traditionalists within the Conservative movement and from the Orthodox. However, two crucially important changes have been introduced; one is the addition of a pre–nuptial clause to the marriage contract obligating the groom to accept the judgement of the *beth din* if in the future it instructs him to grant his wife a *get* (a change questioning definitions of the 'full consent' required of the man according to *halacha*). A second innovation – and one which is *halachically* acceptable – has been to empower rabbis to declare the *nullity* of a marriage if a husband inappropriately refuses to grant a *get*.

Such difficulties do not confront Reform Judaism in Britain and America or Liberal Judaism in Britain, for they do not recognise the status of *agunah*. In the USA, the Reform movement has abolished religious divorces altogether, declaring that a civil divorce can terminate a Jewish marriage. Reform in Britain, whilst not abandoning the need for a *get*, has found its own solution: faced with a totally uncooperative husband, the Reform *Beth Din* will issue a document which will release the wife in terms of Reform religious jurisdiction. In this, Liberal Judaism in Britain is, in fact, closer to American Reform: it, too, has abolished the *get*, viewing it as violating the fundamental principle of equality before the law.

Reform and Liberal Judaism have therefore enacted a vital change. Yet problems remain concerning the woman who is deemed by Orthodoxy to be 'unfree'. She, herself, may be unaware of – or unconcerned about – her *halachic* status. She may, anyway, belong to a Reform or Liberal congregation. Or, being impossibly restrained by both a recalcitrant husband and a compassionate but inflexible Orthodox *Beth Din*, she may choose to remarry under Reform or Liberal auspices. But, in any of these situations, for her to remarry without an Orthodox *get* is a decision beset with difficulties, because *halachically* she is still tied to her first husband. There therefore remain possibly unrecognised serious concerns, not only in terms of her personally ambiguous religious status but, even more, in terms of religious implications for the children of her second partnership. One further disparity needs to be mentioned before a discussion of legal issues; after an Orthodox *get*, a man can remarry immediately; in contrast, a woman must wait ninety days to confirm she is not pregnant.

Grave inequalities remain within the religious law relating to divorce. Firstly the woman released from her marriage according to civil law but who remains 'tied' according to religious law is not free to remarry religiously. Children of a subsequent partnership (which may be valid according to Reform and Liberal jurisdiction) will, according to Orthodox law, earn the religious status of *mamzerim* (illegitimate) and will never themselves be permitted to marry in an Orthodox or traditionally observant synagogue. They are effectively excluded from religious Judaism.

The second area of injustice concerns the right of refusal to accept a *get*. As has been noted, the right to refuse a divorce is not only the man's. However, even in this, there is an inequality in its exercise for, where a woman refuses to accept a divorce, the man can, in the last resort, remarry – sometimes even in the Orthodox synagogue – *and no stigma is attached either to him or to any children of the marriage*. If, however, the man should withhold the *get* and the woman remarries, she is stigmatised as an adulteress and her children as *mamzerim*. Moreover, a *Beth Din* can, in certain special circumstances, override the wishes of a recalcitrant wife and accept a *get* on her behalf, but not on behalf of a recalcitrant husband.

The relationship between civil and religious jurisdiction is at its most sensitive in this area of divorce, for there are conflicting pressures. Biale (1984) writes: 'The need to ensure a way to compel a stubborn husband to divorce his wife overpowers the rabbis' reluctance to open the door to power and authority outside their control' (p. 98). Yet, in practice, the use of civil courts continues to be problematic. Despite proposals that the force of their authority should be enlisted to enforce the will of a Jewish religious court, 'none of the proposals or actual cases gained sufficient rabbinical approval or recognition to serve as a general precedent and guideline' (Biale, p. 99). It is therefore of great significance that in 1983 the New York legislature, on the urging of Orthodox groups, enacted a law designed to require a Jew seeking a civil divorce to give his wife a religious divorce. The constitutionality of this law has been questioned, but it has yet to be tested in the courts. Similar legislation has subsequently been enacted in Canada and Australia, and is pending in South Africa. No comparable law has yet been enacted in Britain.

There is great complexity in these issues as, indeed, there is in the earlier innovations. For example the concept of a conditional clause in the marriage document is seen as being incompatible with the contractual assumption that Jewish marriage is an unconditional commitment by each party to the other.

Meiselman (1978) suggests that, so far, legally acceptable solutions have been rejected by the rabbinate because they are 'inconsistent with *halachic* requirements'. Nor does the Orthodox rabbinate have adequate scope to make changes, for 'the legislative prerogative granted to rabbinic authorities came to an end with the termination of the talmudic period ... subsequent to the talmudic period no *Beth Din* was universally accepted by all Jews, and universal acceptance is a *sine qua non* for legislation' (p. 103).

Whilst legal and rabbinic authorities argue proposals, the issues remains unresolved and injustice continues. Invariably it is the women in these situations who suffer, particularly if they are the ones wanting a divorce for, as has been seen, a husband has the power to prevent his wife from remarrying religiously by refusing to grant her a divorce. She thereby becomes an *agunah*, 'anchored' in every way.

AGUNAH, 'THE ANCHORED WOMAN'

The *agunah* is bound to her husband as long as he has not divorced her or died, even if he is gone from her life forever.

(Biale, 1984, p. 119)

Although the misfortune of being placed in this religious status is relatively infrequent, when it happens there is little that the Orthodox rabbinate can do to remedy the situation. The woman is tied to a husband who is no longer with her, yet she is not religiously free to marry another. As earlier stated, it is not only the strictly Orthodox who could potentially be affected; the large numbers who are traditionally observant are equally under the jurisdiction of the *halachic* rulings on this issue. Even women who do not see themselves as in any way affected by Orthodoxy, remain *halachically* unfree. There are several categories of agunah:

(1) The 'forsaken wife' whose husband is missing. This may be through his disappearance without trace or, as at times of war, through his presumed death. In religious law, a woman is not free to remarry unless a valid witness can be brought to testify to the death of her husband (a prohibition which does not apply to a husband in a comparable position).

(2) The wife whose husband refuses, despite the order of the *beth din* that he should do so, to grant his wife a *get* (bill of divorcement).

(3) The wife whose husband is legally incompetent to grant a divorce. This usually refers to cases of insanity.

(4) The *yevamah*: the widow of a man who had died leaving her childless but who is then bound to her late husband's brother unless he ritually releases her from this bond.

There has always been much concern about the tragic problem of the *agunah*. Since talmudic times it has been debated but even till the present the rabbinate see a conflict between the need to find a religiously accept-able way of releasing the woman and the corresponding fear of inadver-tently permitting her to make an adulterous marriage. Each of the above situations will be discussed in turn.

The 'forsaken wife'

It is a striking disparity which the rabbinic authorities attempt to redress by permitting women to be witnesses – and this in itself reveals another legal inequality for, according to *halacha*, women are not n(ally permitted to testify in a religious court. (Nor are minors, slaves or non-Jews – and the historic attitudes implicit in this ruling are clear.) However, in the case of an *agunah*, testimony from the missing man's wife and from all but his closest female relatives is accepted as legitimate (Biale, 1984, p. 105).

Although the rabbis show compassion, there inevitably remain cases in which the 'forsaken wife' remains tied, especially where the husband has disappeared without trace. Presumption of death is not acceptable as proof of death and there are stringent standards requiring direct evidence of death. The particular problems created by this requirement were tragically highlighted after the Holocaust. It is also an issue very relevant in Israel and two legal devices have been proposed there to avert the risk of a wife's becoming an *agunah*. There are the 'pre-battle divorce' and the 'conditional divorce'. Yet both are legally and *halachically* problematic and have not as yet been implemented (Biale, 1984, p. 109).

The wife of an uncooperative husband

As discussed earlier, one of the most grievous situations in which a woman can find herself is of her husband's refusing to release her from a marriage which has incontrovertibly broken down. Again, many legal solutions have been proposed, such as writing preemptive conditions into the *ketubah* (marriage document) and, again, these have been pronounced *halachically* unsound. So far, it seems that the most acceptable formulation may be along the lines of the 1983 State of New York legislation which permits no civil divorce unless the person seeking the divorce has removed all barriers to his former partner's remarriage. Yet even this is inadequate, for a man may not seek a civil divorce, or may be willing to issue a *get* only upon payment of extortionate sums by his wife or her family or upon her agreement to unacceptable conditions.

As long as women are *halachically* denied the power to initiate divorce, and as long as religious courts remain unable to enforce their authority over an uncooperative husband, 'anchored wives' will remain. Each is an individual tragedy and, as Biale (1984) writes, 'since the cases of *agunot* are addressed . . . out of the public eye, it is difficult to ascertain what the dimensions of the problem actually are today' (p. 112).

The wife of a legally incompetent husband

Similar problems apply in this situation (usually in cases of insanity or mental deterioration). Proposals permitting the rabbis to annul a marriage which is inappropriate (Yevamot 110a) or after a specified period of the husband's illness both again incur *halachic* difficulties.

The childless widow

The special category of *yevamah* refers to the widow whose husband has died leaving her childless, without an heir to inherit his estate. It harks back to the biblical law of levirate marriage. The *halachic* requirement is that the deceased husband's brother or nearest unmarried male relative is obliged to marry the widow. He may, however, release her from the obligation through a ceremony known as *chalitzah* (in which the widow spits in a shoe and throws it at him, thereby releasing him from his obligation). However, in occasional cases, the very law which was designed for the protection of women may result in their being exploited, by the late husband's brother or relative making financial demands before agreeing to go through the *chalitzah* ceremony. The woman is thus effectively forced to buy her freedom.

In the context of Jewish women in contemporary society, it is important to acknowledge that the status of both *agunah* and *yevamah* are relatively infrequent. Yet it does – and may – affect women who come under the jurisdiction of religious law. They are thus doubly bound; trapped in a situation beyond their control, and dependent on the efforts of a rabbinate whose authority they respect and yet who may themselves have little room for manoeuvre. Inevitably divorce, more than any other area, has been seen to highlight the injustice to women in marriage laws dating back to biblical times.

CAN THE LAW CHANGE?

God enters society in the form of specific ways of life, disclosed by revelation, mediated by tradition, embellished by custom and embodied in institutions. . . . But one of the most powerful assumptions of the twentieth century is that . . . religion and society are two independent entities . . .

(Rabbi Dr. Jonathan Sacks, 1990, p. 27)

The whole body of *halacha* is an inspired body of wisdom and understanding from the past, but we have a responsibility to connect it to the reality of our lives in the present. Judaism historically has always evolved; it is only in our recent history that it seems to have ceased to do so. If we cannot evolve, it suggests that God is not speaking to us any more.

(Chani Smith, musician, student of Jewish philosophy and kabbala, and Reform rabbi's wife, in discussion)

Herein lies the tension. Sacks, representing modern Orthodoxy in Britain, notes that religious law was 'mediated by tradition', but in no way suggests the possibility of future *halachic* change. For *halacha* is not simply a collection of laws; it is a fully prescribed way of living. Whilst Greenberg (1981) and Biale (1984) both observe that historically *halacha* was characterized 'more by disagreement than by consensus, more by mechanisms of change than by forces of rigid conservatism' (Biale p. 5), yet Meiselman (1978) emphasizes that 'the legislative prerogative granted to rabbinic authorities came to an end with the termination of the talmudic period' (p. 103).

The Orthodox stance seems to suggest a finality about *halacha* in which looking at historical evolution becomes an irrelevance. Yet, ironically, in the past rabbinic scholars were responsive to society and often incorporated external social norms into religious law. Even post-talmudically, the position was not static; specifically, the laws concerning women underwent considerable modification and in certain areas were influenced by the status of women in the surrounding cultures.

Evolution during the Middle Ages saw changes in the divorce laws empowering the woman to withhold her consent, and in the laws pertaining to polygamy – and this latter is an interesting example of how Jewish law was influenced by the law of the wider non-Jewish society. Polygamy was *halachically* permitted in the postbiblical period. By the Middle Ages, however, for Jews living in Europe under Christian rule there was an increasing adaptation to its being unacceptable, as it was in Christianity. This aversion 'began to take the form of prohibitions set in community practice and rules' (Biale, p. 50) until, eventually, a *herem* (writ of excommunication) was introduced forbidding its further practice. (The eleventh-century Rabbi Gershom of Mainz is believed to be the instigator of this definitive order, as he was of the ban which prevented a man's divorcing his wife without her consent, although Heschel, 1983, p. xxxiv, quotes Falk, 1966, in suggesting that monogamy found its way into French and German Jewry by slow degrees, and not as a result of a single legislative act.)

Change came about not only by the introduction of bans but by re-interpretation of existing laws, as is exemplified in the laws of inheritance. Jewish women do not inherit property equally with Jewish men, for they are denied the status of heirs. A distinction however, was made – again attributed to the legendary Rabbi Gershom – between inheritance and support and it is in the latter area that the woman was given preference, for her 'essential task is to be found in the building of a family and in the private sector of life' (Meiselman, p. 95).

Laws conceived in the distant past and still perceived as binding by the Orthodox today could, in theory, be compartmentalized by the non-Orthodox to a sealed-off area of understanding. After all, we live in a pluralistic society and Jews have choices whether or not to adhere to these rules. But it is not as simple as that; many women who, through their religious affiliation, come under the jurisdiction of *halacha* may be unaware of their potentially vulnerable religious-legal status under certain circumstances.

Secondly, feminism has reached women who do feel committed religiously. It makes them think about their role and status within Jewish law; the claim that they are equal to men in spiritual value leaves unanswered the anxieties about their disadvantaged position in areas potentially affecting their personal life. Underlying the frustration is the basic fact that because, until now, only men have had access to *halachic* study – both to its primary sources and the subsequent debate, legal commentaries and interpretations – men have remained the *halachic* decision makers.

In Britain in the 1960s, Rabbi Louis Jacobs' iconoclastic view about the nature of revelation – whether biblical rulings were divinely commanded or accessible to re-interpretation – caused a grievous split within traditional Anglo-Jewry. In the States, similar arguments have made the gulf between Orthodox and Conservatives an irreconcileable one. The fundamentals of that conflict concern the possibility – or the impossibility – of *halachic* change. For the purpose of *halacha* is to specify how a presupposed divinely prescribed guide to life can infuse day-to-day practical concerns; the rules are intended to guide behaviour rather than behaviour modifying the rules. Webber (1983) writes, 'To say that the *halacha*... should codify Jewish social realities existing at a particular moment in historical time... is not [compatible with] a traditional mode of explanation, which sees biblical commands as timeless and eternally valid' (p. 145).

Whereas we may observe how actual ethnographic practice adapts the rules of normative Judaism, nevertheless, '*halacha* remains permanently lurking in the wings'. Webber illustrates the differences that may exist between religious law and actual practice but warns against assuming that these adaptations have any *halachic* meaning.

> Jewish feminist writers, in the attempt to provide *halachic* justifications and historical precedents for a more active female role in Jewish ceremonial and public life, often take as their starting-point the obvious contrast between the apparently negative attitude of the *halacha* towards women with Jewish ethnographic practice of a distinctly more positive character. But... a selective, *ad hoc* presentation of material from both sources... is methodologically unsound... (p. 145).

Questions arise. Are Jewish women being alienated from *halacha*, seeing it as rigid and unyielding? To the casual observer it would seem that a polarisation is taking place, that they are being increasingly drawn either to a strictly *halachically*-bound way of life or otherwise to abandoning such strictures, choosing the more rational adaptations of a non-Orthodox approach or opting out altogether. Yet this is not an accurate picture, for amongst religiously-committed Jews more debate than ever before is taking place and it is happening within the strongholds of tradition and not without conflict. For example, a capacity female audience at Jews' College, London, heard Judge Myrella Cohen detail the injustices to women within halacha. 'The word "*halacha*" has the same root as the verb "to move", she emphasized. 'Movement is possible given the rabbinic will to move' (16.1.89). They also heard the inhibiting response by Lady Jakobovits, wife of the then Chief Rabbi.

In Israel, civil and religious law are one; conflict therefore focuses on the issue of their separation. In the USA and Britain, however, no such overlap exists and women who see themselves as free of *halachic* restraints are, in fact, free; divorce can be granted by civil courts and, according to non-Orthodox reformulations, when this has taken place under no circumstances does the woman remain tied to her husband. But the tie to *halacha* may indeed remain and manifest itself tragically in the next generation if children of her subsequent marriage wish to return to Orthodoxy and find themselves *halachically* excluded by their religious status.

Yet, to the background of increasing defection from religious identification, debate intensifies amongst leaders of the traditional community. It intensifies partly in response to women's increasing learning and knowledge which, in itself, symbolizes progress. So that, whilst some amongst the Orthodox rabbinate insist that '*halacha* is a self-contained system which follows its own internal logic and is always in conflict with "reality"' (Bleich, 1980), others, equally scholarly, suggest specific *halachically*-feasible areas in which injustice can be rectified (Berman, 1973 and 1991).

Women wanting evolution yet who remain with a traditional framework take muted hope from modern Orthodox leaders such as Rabbi Sacks – and yet they note the caveats: 'Halacha is clearly not static . . . However, particular care is needed for any innovation. Two criteria must be satisfied. First its *content* must be appropriate . . . Second, its *motivation* must be unimpeachable' (*L'Eylah*, September 1986, p. 54). And they reserve judgement.

4 The Religious Scene

Religion is not a Jewish concept; there is no word for religion in
Judaism; it is not a thing apart.... We have a life given to us by God
which we live in every way religiously.

> (Strictly Orthodox woman, living in Gateshead)

Being Jewish in Beverly Hills was no big deal. Everyone was. And
everyone we knew was the same kind of Jew that we were – went to
classes, went to synagogue on important holidays and on Friday nights
from time to time... Perhaps there was some religious emotion but my
memory is more of a social occasion rather than an important ritual
event.

> (Reform American woman)

There are many, many contradictions in Judaism: maintaining a Jewish
home is the responsibility of the woman, yet praying – or, at least, synagogue prayer – is traditionally the man's realm. Then, again, women
are *halachically* exempted from synagogue attendance yet the more
Progressive the affiliation, the more it is the woman who takes the lead in
encouraging her family's synagogue-going.

Many writers comment on Jewish women's greater religiosity. Kaplan,
1986, for example, explains that 'women, for whom religion was less for-
malized and more internalized, ... found in Jewish family rituals a sense of
importance'. Similarly, Kosmin and Levy (1983), whilst highlighting 'the
dominant role played by men in both the religious and communal arenas',
emphasize the higher commitment of Jewish women. They were observing
the British scene. In contrast, in the States it is no longer an assumption
that men hold a dominant role in both arenas; in communal affairs it is
often women who are to the fore. Yet, in the religious sphere, even in
America, despite the fact that women have been ordained as rabbis since
1972 in the Reform movement and since 1985 in the Conservative, and
despite the assumptions of full egalitarianism, most congregations still rel-
egate women clergy to subordinate positions.

Being Jewish is, at root, both an ethnic and a religious identity. For
many, in our largely secular world, the religious aspect is no longer relevant – or, at least, not at a conscious level. Yet for the majority of Jews in
both America and Britain, although they may differ in their degree of
active involvement, 'a sense of belonging' still means identifying with a
synagogue. Interestingly, there is much evidence that, to non-Jews, Jews
irrespective of their piety or non-piety continue to be perceived primarily

as a religious community based around the synagogue. And, in fact, orga-nized religious life remains the foundation of Jewish communal identity in both countries.

As might be expected, the spectrum of religious observance in American has many parallels in Britain, particularly within Orthodoxy. But there are major differences in the majority group in both countries. This divergence – between Conservative Judaism in the States and United Synagogue Judaism in Britain – is not only to do with degrees of obser-vance, it is much more fundamental: it concerns the immutability or other-wise of *halacha*, the religious law. Whilst Conservative Judaism attempts to combine tradition with progress, United Synagogue Judaism maintains the Orthodox position – that *halacha* is divinely commanded and therefore cannot be changed.

Many issues divide Jews religiously, particularly attitudes towards and interpretations of *halacha*. However, one of the most contentious issues in modern times, resulting from the increased frequency of intermarriage, is conflict over the basic question of 'Who is a Jew?' The *halachic* (i.e. Orthodox) definition, based on matrilineal descent or Orthodox conver-sion, increasingly fails to encompass all the identifying Jewish population. Indeed, the conflict surrounding this issue is so great that an Orthodox American rabbi (Irving Greenberg) has predicted that by the end of the century there will be half a million children in American, born to mothers converted by Reform rabbis or accepted as Jewish under patrilineal definition, whose Jewishness will not be accepted by other Jews.

Depicting the religious scene is a daunting task, for it is a composite picture in which immigration and culture of origin are interwoven with contemporary issues – and underlying it all is where it began, with biblical law and rabbinic interpretation. This chapter focuses on the different reli-gious groupings and, in particular, their evolving attitudes towards women's participation. And, as with the earlier discussion of immigration, here, too, it feels more natural to look at the situation in American and Britain separately.

AMERICA

Population studies suggest that the majority of American Jews continue to identify with one of the denominations of American Judaism, although in declining numbers. The spread of affiliation is estimated as being Orthodox 9 per cent; Conservative 34 per cent; Reform 29 per cent;

Reconstructionist 2 per cent; 'Just Jewish' 26 per cent (North American Jewish Data Bank, 1991).

The Orthodox

The type of Judaism brought to America by the vast majority of immigrants pouring in from Eastern Europe between 1880 and 1920 was Orthodox. It is from their religious way of life that other types of Judaism evolved or broke away. But, gradually, Orthodoxy itself has evolved and, because of its importance both as the source and as a continued current in Jewish thought, it is considered more fully in a chapter of its own, as is the *'ba'al t'shuva* phenomenon' – the return to Orthodoxy of many previously uncommitted Jews. *Halacha*, the religious law on which Orthodox Judaism is based, also has its own chapter, for it is central to our understandings of the questioning, re-interpretations and rejections which have always been a dynamic part of Jewish existence. This section of the present chapter therefore briefly depicts something of Orthodoxy's background and contemporary relevance in America.

The Orthodox Judaism of their immigrant parents was seen by the next generation as being unsuited to a more dynamic lifestyle in American society. However, whilst the second and third generation were defining themselves in a more 'modern' way religiously, or rejecting religion altogether, Orthodoxy itself was being revitalised. Ironically, its new energy came from the refugees of Nazi Europe amongst whom were Orthodox scholars and *chassidim* (literally 'pious ones') bringing diverse understandings from their countries of origin – Lithuania, Germany, Hungary, the Balkans – and a new ferment. As a result, in the post-war years there was a tremendous new impetus, finding expression in growing enclaves of Orthodox families, particularly in Brooklyn and the Bronx, and a burgeoning of synagogues, *shtieblach* (small synagogues favoured by the *chassidim*), religious day schools and *yeshivot* (schools for advanced talmudic study). Gradually, Orthodoxy was no longer seen as a vestige of the Old World, it was no longer only the religion of poor immigrant Jews: increasingly it also began to attract educated business and professional men and their families.

The contemporary picture is one of growth, with many followers amongst couples of childbearing years who amply fulfill the biblical injunction to 'be fruitful and multiply' (Genesis 1: 28). An added source of strength are the *ba'alei t'shuva*, the newly Orthodox. But it is easy to exaggerate the size of the Orthodox community. Its greatest allegiance is still in New York, in Brooklyn and the Bronx, where over 25 per cent of heads of households identify themselves as Orthodox. And it is precisely this concentration which can be misleading for, as Wertheimer points out, 'the numerical strength of Orthodoxy in the largest Jewish community of the United States gives that movement a visibility that belies its actual size' (1989, p. 80). Numerically the Orthodox represent only about 9 per cent of the American Jewish population but in the past two decades Orthodoxy has achieved an unprecedented revival and popularity. The accompanying confidence has led to a shift to the right – a greater emphasis on the most punctilious observance of ritual commands. It has also, sadly, resulted in greater intolerance of the other religious groupings, the Conservative and Reform, and their leaders.

The initiative encouraging Jews back to Orthodoxy came from the *Lubavitch Chassidim* (who are discussed in the next chapter) and from the 'modern Orthodox' – both groups convinced, especially in the face of dramatically increasing intermarriage amongst the non-Orthodox population, that Orthodoxy is the only avenue for Jewish survival. As a result of their 'outreach' programmes on university campuses and in public gatherings they have attracted a significant following. For the 'returnees' (*ba'alei t'shuva*), popularly known as 'b.t.s', Orthodox Judaism was – and continues to be – seen as giving rootedness and meaning to their lives. Also, at a time of high marriage breakdown in the non-Orthodox population, the comparatively low rates of divorce within the Orthodox world encouraged would-be returnees to see it as a source of stability. The phenomenon of 'returning' – 'I found what I was searching for in my own back yard!' as one 'b.t.' said – is explored by Aviad (1983), Kaufman (1987) and Danzger (1989) and is more fully considered in the next chapter.

It seems a paradox that a group attracting increasing numbers of adherents should become more rigid and far less tolerant of deviance than in the past. Wertheimer (1989) suggests two explanations: firstly, it offers explicit guidelines for behaviour to people who no longer want the burden of autonomy (cf. Eric Fromm's 1941 'fear of freedom'). Secondly, in sharpening the group's boundaries, Orthodoxy provides its members with a strong feeling of community and belonging: and there is much evidence that integration within a group provides a support system.

But the increased right-wing tendency must also be understood in the wider context, for many Orthodox parents, themselves integrated within American society, fear that their children may join the slide into assimilation. So, to avoid this, they inculcate in them, first in strictly Orthodox schools and then in *yeshivot* for the boys or seminaries for the girls, a

Judaism that is far to the right of their own thinking. One result of this increased fundamentalism has been a deliberate segregating of the Orthodox from the non-Orthodox. It is a gulf which may, anyway, have gradually become unbridgeable as the Conservative movement increasingly moves away from rigidly-defined *halachic* rulings.

One of the most complex issues within Orthodox Judaism remains the status of women. It is particularly complex because the majority of Orthodox women deny that they feel any inequality: they point to 'equal but different' spheres and emphasize that they are respected in a way that women in the non-religious world rarely are.

Even so, there are two areas in which Orthodox women have tried to reconcile their commitment to Orthodoxy with their increasing feminist consciousness – religious study and public prayer. And, whilst introducing change, they have taken great care to avoid conflict. So, for example, they have expanded what they study and yet have made no demands to be educated in the methods and sources of the law. Similarly, they have developed women's *tefillah* (prayer) groups, particularly in New York, and yet meet only monthly so as not to separate themselves from their families in synagogue-going. With equal concern, they have scrupulously omitted from their prayers those sections of the service which may be recited only by a *minyan* (a quorum of ten men). And, despite their care, they have still incurred rabbinic disapproval, for their motives are regarded as not unimpeachable!

Conservative Judaism

The Conservative syngagogue group is the largest in the United States, with 34 per cent of American Jews identifying with it. It began in 1887 as a reaction not to Orthodoxy but to Reform, which was increasingly felt to be abandoning too many of the tenets of traditional Judaism. One of its early leaders, Solomon Schechter, recognised that the American-born sons of Eastern European Jews, who were settling in the suburbs in non-Jewish areas or in areas of the States with only small communities, were looking for a safe compromise between both extremes of Judaism. Conservative Judaism could offer them this and, as a result, it became increasingly popular. However, the time of its greatest expansion was during and after the horrors of World War II which led many Jews to want to re-identify with some form of religion.

From its earliest days, the Conservative movement showed a willingness to respond to contemporary issues, and this attracted increasing numbers of followers, the majority of whom were not committed to the rigid observance of *halacha*. They felt easier with Conservative's ideology of 'Tradition and Change' – a pragmatic approach epitomized in the 1950s by its decision to allow driving to synagogue on Shabbat.

Committed to a more egalitarian form of worship, it gradually introduced mixed seating, mixed choirs and *bat-mitzvah* ceremonies for girls (which correspond to the boy's religious induction at thirteen). But these were changes which led to increasing conflict between the traditionalists and the progressives, who were drawn to a Reconstructionist ideology.

This internal dissent took place during the 1970s at a time of increasing religious polarization. Orthodoxy was attracting more adherents; the Reconstructionists had broken away from the Conservative movement; and many former Conservative members – especially if they had intermarried – were turning to Reform. At the same time, many younger members, feeling alienated in the large Conservative synagogues, were forming small independent *Havura* groups for prayer and study.

The conservative movement was no longer 'Americanized Orthodoxy' and was increasingly snubbed by the Orthodox. Not too surprisingly, one of the issues which widened the rift was the question of women's status in synagogue worship.

The Changing Status of Women in Conservative Judaism
Although mixed seating and *bat-mitzvahs* had long been allowed in Conservative synagogues, there was increasing ferment amongst women for more substantial change. This ferment found voice in a pressure group, *Ezrat Nashim*, ('helpers of women') started in 1972 and committed to equality. It demanded that women should be counted in a *minyan* (the religious quorum); be allowed to participate fully in religious observances; be recognized as witnesses before Jewish law; be allowed to initiate divorce; be encouraged to positions of communal leadership; be permitted to study for the rabbinate and be ordained as rabbis and be trained as cantors.

These demands divided the Conservative leadership. The split was heralded in 1973 when its Rabbinic Assembly proposed legislation to allow women to be counted as part of a *minyan*. This and other 'egalitarian' proposals were bitterly opposed by the traditionalists, committed to role differences between men and women in the synagogue and to upholding *halachic* objections to the ordination of women. However, although in the face of great dissension, change took place, culminating in 1983 with the admission of women students to the Conservative rabbinic seminary and, two years later, with the ordaining of Amy Eilberg, the first Conservative woman rabbi.

The struggle over women's ordination highlighted the conflicting positions within the Conservative movement, with the traditionalists emphasizing the 'indispensability of *halacha*' and the progressives seeing *halacha* as amenable to re-interpretation. But the die was cast and further innovations included the introduction of a new *siddur* (prayer book) in which there are blessings for women to put on the *tallit* (prayer shawl) and *tefillin* (phylacteries worn for morning prayers) and for women to be called to read the Torah (the scroll of Law). In defiance of the traditionalists, an increasing number of Conservative congregations began to elect women as officers and to count women in the *minyan* and as equal participants in all aspects of religious services. These are changes inconceivable within Orthodox Judaism and, in fact, they continue to be opposed within the more traditional Conservative congregations, particularly in Brooklyn and Long Island.

Despite divisions over the status of women, there are two issues over which the majority leadership within Conservative Judaism remain firm. They are questions of descent and conversion. Their position is that only matrilineal descent is acceptable. They also affirm the need for conversion as the only way of the non-Jew being accepted as a Jew.

Reconstructionism

The split away from the Conservative movement took place in 1968. However, as an ideology Reconstructionism began in the early 1930s. It had both Conservative and Reform followers and even attracted some secular Jews. Essentially it saw Judaism as an evolving religion and, after the split, it made changes which were problematic for the Conservatives, with their nominal allegiance to *halacha* (religious law).

In four areas in particular this new movement totally rejected the *halachic* position. Firstly, they recognised as Jewish the children of mixed marriages in which the mother was non-Jewish, as long as the parents reared the child as a Jew – (*halacha* recognises only matrilineal descent). Secondly, they permitted their rabbis to participate in civil marriage ceremonies between a Jew and a non-Jew. Their third area of innovation concerned the status of women: since 1975 women have been ordained as Reconstructionist rabbis and a decade later their rabbinical college began admitting openly lesbian students. The movement also allows women full participation in synagogue services; it accepts women as legal decision-makers, as witnesses and as members of the movement's *beth din* (the religious court of law). Women are also permitted to initiate a divorce. A more recent initiative has been the preparation of a new *siddur* to eliminate a male-dominated liturgy.

Reconstructionism views Jewish ritual not as law but as a means to the spiritual growth of the individual Jew. Towards this aim it encourages both men and women to study the Kabbalah (the mystical teachings, not traditionally accessible to women) in *chavurot* (small study groups).

Yet, despite all these changes, the Reconstructionist movement has remained small, even in Philadelphia where it is at its strongest, and its estimated following is only 2 per cent of identifying American Jews. It is, in a way, in an ambigious position between Conservative and Reform and, whereas its original members were Jews rejecting Orthodoxy, now its members are primarily newcomers to Judaism.

Reform

Reform Judaism was introduced into America by German Jews arriving in the 1830s and 1840s. They brought with them a rational, anti-fundamentalist approach to religion and soon greatly outnumbered the long-established Sephardim whose Judaism had been much more traditional.

Early Reform Judaism in the States was radical: it totally rejected the Orthodox view that the Bible was divinely inspired and therefore also rejected traditional practices, including the laws of *kashrut* (the dietary laws) and the laws of Shabbat. All ritual incompatible with a modern way of life was abandoned and Reform's new prayer book introduced a logical, humanistic type of Judaism. By the 1870s and 1880s, Reform Judaism was almost synonymous with American Judaism.

However, as earlier described, the third wave of immigration between 1881 and 1924 brought to America over two million Jews escaping from economic pressures and pogroms in Eastern and Central Europe. They came from countries in which the Jews lived in ghettos and this new inpouring either clung to the certainties of Orthodoxy or, at the other extreme, were idealistic Socialists rejecting religion altogether. Reform once more gained ground with the children and grandchildren of these immigrants and, in the 1930s, with the refugees from Nazi Europe.

Ideologically there have been interesting changes. Reform began its life with a commitment to rid Judaism of anachronistic ceremonies. Increasingly it aimed at winning the unaffiliated and by the mid-1960s had over 600 congregations. But it has been sensitive to a growing desire amongst non-Orthodox Jews for some traditional practices and, responding to this, has re-introduced ritual into its synagogue services and into home observance. As a result, many former Conservatives have joined Reform, which now has an estimated membership of 29 per cent of identifying Jews.

Reform and Mixed Marriages

Reform has the highest level of mixed marriages and, although it emphasizes its preference for the non-Jewish partner to convert to Judaism, in 1983 it finally rejected the *halachic* requirement of matrilineal descent and since then has accepted as Jewish a child who has only one Jewish parent. It also no longer places sanctions on rabbis who officiate at mixed marriages and increasingly recruits new members from amongst mixed-marriage couples.

Women in Reform

> Feminism questions any definition of 'normative' Judaism that
> excludes women's experience.
>
> (Judith Plaskow in *Tikkun*, 1987)

From the beginning, feminist aims and ideology have found acceptance in Reform Judaism and, as a result, within Reform women have made themselves central to the public functioning of religious life. It is a supreme irony that when, except for the Orthodox, most American Jewish men are drawing away from ritual observance, women have become increasingly involved in a leadership role in synagogue worship.

Unlike Conservative, Reform resisted none of the demands of feminism. In the late 1960s it began to enrol women in its rabbinic programme. Its first woman rabbi was ordained in 1972; its first woman cantor in 1975. Reform synagogues have mixed seating and include women in a *minyan* (the necessary quorum for prayer). Women are called up to the Torah reading; they give sermons, open the ark and recite *kiddush* (sanctification prayers) and *havdalah* (the ceremony ending Shabbat). Also, as well as the long-established *bat-mitzvah* ceremony, in which girls, too, are called to the Torah, women in Reform are introducing many other life-cycle celebrations, such as the *Shalom Bat*, the welcoming of a daughter.

It is in religious study, most of all, that women have become newly-empowered for this, the most highly-esteemed sphere of Jewish life, used to be the prerogative of men. And, resulting from this learning and involvement in public ritual, a new awakening of women's spirituality has come about based on women's feeling included – rather than excluded, as in Orthodoxy – from involvement in all aspects of prayer.

A further radical departure which Reform has made is in welcoming homosexuals. Gay synagogues started to be formed in the 1970s and were eventually accepted as members of the Union of American Hebrew Congregations which also, in 1987, passed a resolution aimed at including homosexuals into all aspects of congregational life. It is an awareness which epitomizes the story of Reform's success, for it has increasingly appealed to groups who have been made to feel disadvantaged in Orthodox or Conservative congregations – mixed marriage couples, feminists and homosexual men and women. But its challenge now is seen to be a different one: to find its own version of authentic Judaism.

The *Havura* Movement

This small movement began in the 1960s and 70s as a Jewish counter-culture, created by the grandchildren of immigrants from Eastern Europe. They formed groups for study and prayer, alternative to the established synagogues, and in which gender equality was a fundamental principle. They have grown as young communities not bound by *halacha* and in this way have encouraged a more spontaneous expression of Jewish involvement.

> What is most troubling is that when we come together as Jews, it is the Orthodox who set the terms, as though they have beliefs and principles that cannot be compromised, while the rest of us do not. Our principles, as religious Jews who are Conservative or Reform or Reconstructionist, our commitments as feminists to the human dignity of all persons, are regarded as personal and we are expected to compromise and accept Orthodox standards.
>
> (Susannah Heschel in Dialogue on the Role of Religion, p. 9, *Congress Monthly*, March/Apr. 1991).

It is a theme throughout. Judaism in the States has questioned and evolved, and particularly so in the roles and participation of women. Yet in this process of selecting, rejecting and retaining, *halacha* remains immutable, with its upholders upholding it as the only authentic Judaism. And the more change takes place, the more irreconcileable seem the different ideological positions. Yet, despite this, Jews continue to redefine their Judaism, surely suggesting a healthy dynamic.

BRITAIN

The Orthodox

Strict Orthodoxy is an all-embracing way of life. How it is lived both by those born into it and by those later drawn to Orthodoxy (the *ba'alei t'shuva*) is the subject of Chapter Five. In terms of Orthodox Judaism in Britain, there are so many parallels with Orthodoxy in the States that a separate discussion is unnecessary, except to comment here, too, on its increased allegiance which, in terms of synagogue membership, represents a threefold increase over twenty years. In London, particularly, the strictly Orthodox are 9 per cent of affiliated Jews.

United Synagogue

However, the vast majority of British Jews are neither right-wing Orthodox nor Reform or Liberal. The majority (about 65 per cent over the UK as a whole) belong to what is called in the statistics 'Central Orthodox'. They are traditionally observant, primarily members of the major United Synagogue grouping which first established its Ashkenazi roots in 1870. Although nominally Orthodox, in fact they vary enormously in their degree of religious commitment and in the extent to which they fulfill all the requirements of *halacha*. Social pressure often strongly influences conformity to rules which are externally visible, not driving on Shabbat or festivals, for example. But what happens within individual family walls may be different: members may or may not fully keep the laws of *kashrut* and the Laws of Family Purity; they may or may not fully observe the Shabbat, with no work of any sort, and all the two-day festivals. And, much more intangibly, they may or may not be able to create *shalom ha bayit* – a peaceful home – the idealized norm which, it is always hoped, children will reproduce in their eventual marital home with a Jewish partner.

'Mainstream Orthodox in decline, new study shows.' (Jewish Chronicle, 11.10.91)
There have been two trends over the past twenty years: firstly, a defection from United Synagogue-type Judaism (a male membership of 72 per cent in London in 1970 had dropped to 58 per cent by 1990). Secondly, amongst those who have retained their United Synagogue allegiance, there has been a movement towards greater religious observance, thereby accelerating the defection, either to the left or to the right, either to Masorti, Reform or Liberal, or to ultra-Orthodox. The malaise is particularly expressed by one traditionally observant woman:

> We belong as a family to a United Synagogue, which I attend as rarely as possible. I feel very out of tune with what is going on there. If I weren't married to D., I'd go to the Reform, there's no question about it . . . One of my biggest difficulties is people's expectations of me; they ask me, 'Why don't you come to *shul* [synagogue] with D. and the

children?' or 'Why don't you come to the Ladies Guild?' Other people's expectations – that's one of the things I have spent most of my time discussing in therapy.

What is most noticeable for women in United Synagogue is an uneasy acquiescence. They sit in synagogue in a Ladies' Gallery where they can see and be seen but take no part in the service. They are decorous and decorative. They may *daven* (pray) – and increasingly do so with knowledge and fervour – but they may not be counted as part of the necessary quorum for prayer (*minyan*). Their main role, all acknowledge, is in the home. Traditionally they extended this nurturing to the synagogue and came into their own after the Shabbat service with the provision of *kiddush* – wine and cake served in the synagogue hall, celebrating Shabbat and *barmitzvahs* and *aufrufs* (when a bridegroom is called up to the reading of the Law on the Shabbat preceding his wedding). More recently, a quiet mutiny has undermined these 'Ladies' Guild' expectations and women have increasingly begun seeking more political roles in terms of synagogue Boards of Management, even aspiring to the Board of Deputies, which is the lay leadership of Anglo-Jewry. But it is an uphill struggle in the face of the male establishment, as Joy Conway described:

> I was appalled at the lack of respect given to women at Board meetings . . . We were not allowed to vote and . . . the men thought we were there to participate only if matters concerning catering arose. I felt I had much to contribute on concerns of greater importance.
>
> (from *Hamesilah*, 1990)

Slowly there are changes, but beset with difficulties. The *bat-mitzvah* (lit. daughter of the commandment) ceremony is a case in point. Long established in Reform Judaism where it parallels the thirteen-year-old boy's 'rite of passage' when he takes on the obligations incumbent upon a Jewish man, it creates problems in traditional Judaism, for women are not permitted to take any part in the ceremonial of synagogue services. Meiselman (1978) concedes that 'it is certainly permissible to celebrate the birth of a daughter or her *bat-mitzvah*' but continues: 'However, it completely mocks the entire structure of Judaism to invest these celebrations with specific and detailed rituals' (p. 61). Yet the (female) demand for a *bat-mitzvah* ceremony or a *bat chayil* ceremony ('daughter of worth') had somehow to be met and eventually a compromise solution was reached. In most United Synagogues it takes place by means of a special service in which several girls participate together. But, as Cooper (1991) points out 'the emotional energy surrounding tribal continuity continues to revolve around the males – and this is the case across the religious spectrum' (p. 35).

Women's Prayer Groups
The concept of *kvod ha-tzibbur*, 'the honour of the congregation', bars women from reading from the Torah before a congregation. That a woman should be needed to read from the Torah in a congregation of men would, it was argued, put the men to shame by casting doubt on their piety and learning (Biale, 1984, pp. 27–8). Reform and Liberal Judaism have long ago swept away these restrictions but – with more deference to *halacha* – 'modern' Orthodox and traditionally observant women have attempted instead to circumvent them by creating women's prayer groups. Ironically, such prayer groups are perfectly acceptable as long as they are not motivated by feminism! If the motivation for them is that women are trying to find more spirituality in an increasingly secular world, such groups can be permitted; if, however, they are being used to make a statement about women's position in the religious communal world, they are abusing prayer (Sacks, 1991).

But the fact that motivation should be questioned concerns many participants for 'men's motives remain unquestioned as they take part in the highly fulfilling rituals which form part of the religion's basis.... it is an example of social double standards which have become accepted as Jewish law' (Melissa Nathan, 1991). In fact, the women's prayer groups slowly evolving within the world of traditional Judaism are unchallenging of *halacha* and keep within specific boundaries for, in the absence of men, women may read from the Sefer Torah (the scroll of religious Law). They make no claim to be a *minyan* and forego those prayers for which that is required.

Women's prayer groups in religious circles are very new, very tentative and emerging only amongst religious woman who have exposed themselves to feminist thought. But already they are having positive consequences in women's seeking to learn more and extend their knowledge of ritual. There has always been a *mitzvah* for women to pray. Traditionally, women's prayer was private prayer. Now, modern religious women are finding new meaning in prayer, in praying with other women.

A letter to an Orthodox Jewish man from a Jewish woman
On Saturday night I had a dream. I dreamed I was in *Shul* [synagogue], but a hurdy-gurdy was playing.
I rose above this surreal scene and was bound in tapes and cloths like

a mummy until I was drowning and fighting for breath. I called 'help' but no sound emerged. I knew that if I didn't wake myself, I would die.

The nightmare wasn't difficult to interpret. The hurdy-gurdy was the organ I had heard in a Reform synagogue twenty years ago.

I can still hear you shouting 'the Masorti is absolutely *treife* [forbidden] – it's worse than Reform' and telling me that 'women don't need to go to *Shul.*'

I'm writing to you because I thought you were a man of humanity. It's not enough to cry *'treife'* – you have to listen and you have to hear what I and other women are saying.

You may feel it's not your problem, but then who is going to listen? Who is going to hear and who is going to wake me from the bonds of suffocation?

(Sharon Lee)

Further notes on what it means to me to be an observant Jewish woman

I think in terms of continuity of a people and ask who am I, and what gives me the right to break that continuity? I feel it a privilege to be born a Jew. By not practicing the edicts of the religion I would be breaking the links between the past and the future and I could not bear that responsibility.

I feel I must continue with the traditions of Judaism, keep a kosher home, etc, and pass these on to my children because I do not believe the Jewish people can survive for many generations without the actions. The outside influences of the general society we live in would be too great if there were not the positive actions of being a Jew to counteract those exterior pressures.

To this end, I will lead a traditional Jewish life and teach my children how to be good Jews.

(Susie Kleiman)

Masorti

United Synagogue ministers appear increasingly inflexible, alienating rather than accommodating their members' spiritual needs.

(Joshua Rozenberg, *Jewish Chronicle*, 18.10.91)

Central Orthodoxy, 'United Synagogue'-type Judaism, is losing members alarmingly. But the intellectually-vibrant Masorti movement represents not a drift to stricter Orthodoxy or to greater Reform; it represents a schism about fundamentalism.

In Britain, Masorti did not evolve: it erupted from a conflict within United Synagogue about belief. The catalyst was Rabbi Louis Jacobs' 'heretical' book, *We Have Reason to Believe* (1957), which questioned whether every word of the Torah had come directly from God. Whilst fully accepting the Torah's divine inspiration, Jacobs argued that the whole Bible, including the five books of Moses, had always been and should always be open to contemporary discussion and interpretation by rabbinic scholars. His claim was antithetical to Orthodoxy: from the Orthodox viewpoint, to admit the existence of human intervention and historical development would render the whole body of *halacha* invalid. The *mitzvot* (divine commandments) would lose their sanction. Ironically, 'Masorti' means traditional, but it suggests that throughout Jewish history *halacha* has developed in response to the spiritual needs of the people.

As an intellectual movement, Conservative/Masorti Judaism traces its origin to mid-nineteenth century Germany. It was one response to the challenge earlier posed to European Jews by the Emancipation. Subsequently, this form of Judaism was introduced into the United States by Solomon Schechter and today it is the largest Jewish religious movement in North and South America.

In Britain its membership is small but growing. Its first synagogue, following the split from United Synagogue, was the New London, begun in 1964. A few years later, a sister congregation began in North London but it was not until the mid 1980s that a formal Masorti movement with constituent synagogues began. There are now six congregations – although still only in and around London – with a total membership of approximately 2,500 (1991 estimate).

Women in Masorti: areas of uncertainty and areas of change
In terms of women's religious experience within the Masorti movement, what is surprising is the differing attitudes within its different synagogues: some do and some do not have mixed seating and the same lack of consensus also applies as to whether or not the constituent synagogues call up women to the Torah or count women in the *minyan*. All are sensitive issues. However, in one area there is consensus: women in Masorti *are* permitted to recite *kaddish* (the memorial prayer for a close relative) and, of all the changes, this is probably the one of greatest emotional significance. Just how important it feels for a woman to say kaddish is movingly described by Sara Reguer (in Heschel, 1983, pp. 177–81).

With its emphasis on the compassionate nature of Judaism and on the validity of reinterpretation of *halacha* to have relevance to modern life, it would seem likely that the woman's position regarding the *get* would be improved. In fact, unlike Reform, Masorti has not yet taken a decisive stand. Masorti's position, faced with the impasse of a recalcitrant husband refusing his wife a religious divorce, is that 'if persuasion failed, one would do one's best to use the *halachic* system – and any religious loopholes possible – but, if the husband remained intractable, then the rabbis may endeavour to annul the marriage. If that were not possible, sadly, no, – in terms of marriage without a *get* – no, we couldn't do it' (Rabbi Jonathan Wittenberg, personal communication, November 1991).

There is indeed a *halachic* ruling which permits the rabbis to annul an 'inappropriate' marriage, but it is a difficult procedure to sustain. Biale (1984, p. 58) explains that it is a religious-legal option very occasionally used to ease the trapped status of the *agunah*: the halachic authorities try to find a 'technical point' allowing invalidation of the original betrothal: 'the rabbis have the power to declare retroactively that the act of intercourse was an act of mere sexual promiscuity (*be' ilat zenut*) and not an act of betrothal' (p. 58). However, cancelling an inappropriate marriage by divorce is still regarded as a preferable way. This therefore remains within Masorti as problematic as within Orthodoxy.

The fundamental issue of conversion is amongst the most difficult which Masorti has had to face. Like Reform and Liberal Judaism, it recognised the distress suffered by would-be converts denied this possibility by the Orthodox *Beth Din* if marriage were the motive. The Orthodox refusal to accept intending marriage to a Jewish partner as a sincere motivation for conversion led to much alienation. Masorti reversed this view, seeing marriage as a valid reason for wanting to convert; they quote from the Talmud, 'out of doing something from impure motives one comes to do it for its own sake' (Pesachim 50b). However, like the Orthodox, Masorti retains as a prerequisite to conversion the need for rigorous learning and preparation, followed by the *mikvah* ceremony of ritual immersion. Yet, despite the strictness of Masorti's own requirements, Orthodox Judaism – including the majority United Synagogue – refuses to recognises Masorti converts as *halachically* Jewish. As a result, a Masorti convert (and the children of a female convert) may not marry in an Orthodox synagogue.

As in Reform and Liberal Judaism, the implications for the convert's religious status of these divergent viewpoints are profound. The Orthodox insist that a convert must take on the full yoke of *halacha*, a responsibility not only within his or her lifetime but for their children yet unborn. In a time of increasing intermarriage, they insist that only the safety of their way of life can keep Jews truly within the fold. The justification for such exclusivity can be questioned on many levels, yet in terms of preserving Jews for Judaism, their claim is a valid one. A Reform rabbi, Barbara

Borts, acknowledges it to be so: 'The only ones who could say with more certainty than anyone else that their grandchildren will be Jewish are the extreme ultra-Orthodox.' In reply, the iconoclastic movements would stress the vitality of their form of religion.

The question inevitably arises as to whether the woman's religious experience in Masorti is very different from that within traditional or Orthodox Judaism. The changes there are may be partly felt in tentative ways in public ritual:

> The overwhelming feeling was one of gratitude at being included. I, too, could be involved in the service when, always before, I'd felt an onlooker. In Masorti, I was part of it and not 'other'.
>
> (Sharon Lee, November 1991)

Listening to women in Masorti, what emerges is that being part of a vibrant movement gives freedom to question and to initiate. Amongst these innovations are women's *rosh chodesh* groups, celebrating the new month. They reclaim a ceremony, lost over many centuries, which had long ago been a festival for women. Waskow (in Heschel, 1983) explores its origins and symbolism. Inspiring these groups has been the desire to give expression to women who have felt excluded and whose life experience has been ignored. In the moon, with its ebb and flow, is seen a symbol of woman's creativity.

> Once a two day holiday, the most sacred stretches
> in the slow swing of the epicycling year;
> then a remnant, a half holiday for women,
> a little something to keep us less unsatisfied; . . .
> Let the half day festival of the new moon
> remind us how to retreat and grow strong, how to
> reflect and learn, how to push our bellies forward,
> how to roll and turn and pull the tides up, up
> when we need them, how to come back each time
> we look dead, making a new season to shine.
>
> (Marge Piercy)

Reform Judaism

Reform Judaism was introduced to Britain by enlightened German immigrants, men whose energies were no longer devoted solely to Torah study. In one way it was a negative reaction to the rigidity of Orthodoxy and the centrality of Torah (religious law). More positively, it claimed that

Judaism was not just a collection of outdated laws and rites, but a rich cultural and ethical tradition. Yet, although the first Reform synagogue was founded in 1840, it did not represent a fundamental intellectual or theological break with tradition. Established British Jewry remained essentially traditional in the nineteenth century and Reform Judaism did not spread widely. Nor did it have any appeal for the impoverished immigrants from Eastern Europe who entered Britain in the 1880s and 1890s, for they clung to the certainties of Orthodoxy. It was not until the influx of the Central European Jewish middle classes in the 1930s and 1940s – refugees from Nazism – that Reform began to gain real influence.

After the war, Reform Judaism became more popular and, particularly over the past twenty years, has drawn many of those defecting from United Synagogue: its 12 per cent of affiliated Jews in 1970 had grown to 18 per cent by 1990. Brook (1989, p. 119) suggests that one reason for its increasing popularity is as a reaction to what many perceived as the hypocrisy that infuses many United congregations.

> I consider myself quite a religious person.

> (Reform woman)

There is a mistaken tendency to confuse freedom from *halachic* restraints with lack of religious conviction. Reform is not concerned only wiht the abandonment of 'inconvenient' rules and seemingly archaic requirements – observing *kashrut*, not driving on Shabbat, etc. – and, in fact, many Reform Jews do keep some of the dietary laws, many observe Friday night, attend synagogue and celebrate the festivals, albeit in a different way from the Orthodox, but no less meaningfully. Their homes, too, retain a Jewish atmosphere. But whereas in the early days Reform Judaism was essentially a negative reaction to Orthodoxy, its present-day appeal is of a greater vitality in religion, less repetition and more use of English in its services and a feeling of welcome in its synagogues – which is present only for the 'in-group' in Orthodox or United synagogues. Also, Reform, by its nature, re-evaluates and is prepared to change; its attraction is in its willingness to combine aspects of tradition with an adaptation to contemporary life. In stark contrast to Orthodoxy, Reform rejects the concept of *halacha* as a monolithic and immutable body of law. It believes that divine revelation is continuous and that religious law is always open to study and reinterpretation.

Many of the seminal changes in Reform Judaism are to do with women's participation in public worship and in religious affairs. Firstly, women are permitted to become rabbis (and half the current enrolment for rabbinic training within the Progressive movement is female). Secondly,

Reform synagogues have mixed seating, as distinct from the segregation of Orthodoxy where in United Synagogues women are in a gallery and in ultra-Orthodox congregations they are behind a *mechitzah* (curtain). Thirdly, women in Reform Judaism can be honoured in the synagogue and called up to read from the Torah scroll. Girls have *bat-mitvah* and *bat chayil* ceremonies, women may wear the *tallit* (prayer shawl) and be included on synagogue boards of management. To Reform, these represent a re-interpretation of *halacha* within the changing realities of existence. For the leaders of Reform seek to redress the inbalance which reflects a historically-rooted male-female hierarchical status.

Yet, ironically, these innovations are not greeted with unanimous approval – not even by women. Charles Emanuel, formerly an American Reform rabbi and now the rabbi of a London Reform congregation, comments on the reticence of many women to participate in those synagogue honours which, in Reform, they are entitled to do: 'Many of them feel uneasy, as if they are held back by *halachic* constraints of which, consciously, they are unaware.'

A similar anxiety is expressed by Judy Blendis, a Reform synagogue member. She talks of 'the Yentl syndrome', in which a woman emulates a man:

> It has caused disquiet amongst many Reform women. It seems a sort of zealotry, bordering on fundamentalism . . . Often mothers and daughters, often consequent on divorce, put on a *tallit* [prayer shawl] and a *cappel* [skull cap] and persuade other women that they should do so too. They kiss the *sefer torah* with a fervour which has elements of histrionic passion in it.

How prevalent this reaction is, it is difficult to ascertain. It certainly contrasts with the attitudes of other British Reform women as they describe their joy at involvement in synagogue ritual.

These are not the only contentious areas. Two major concessions made by Reform and in conflict with the Orthodox *halachic* position are in relation to religious divorce and conversion. These are more fully considered in Chapters Three and Eight. Basic to the difference with divorce is that the Reform *Beth Din* will intervene if, in its judgement, a husband withholds a *get* on unreasonable grounds. In such cases, it will issue a document dissolving the marriage and freeing the wife to marry again without the fear that any children from her subsequent marriage will incur the religious status of *mamzerim*. This *get* and its accompanying 'freedom' are, however, valid only within Reform and Liberal jurisdiction. As earlier discussed, in the eyes of the Orthodox *Beth Din*, the *get* not actually granted by a woman's husband is not *halachically* acceptable; her re-marriage without it is *halachically* forbidden and the children of this forbidden union become *mamzerim*, themselves forbidden ever to marry in an Orthodox synagogue.

Similarly with conversion, Reform's attitude expresses more compassion and leniency. Yet it is in conflict with the Orthodox rabbinate who see as a prerequisite to conversion the need severely to test the world-be convert's motives. They are, for this reason, unsympathetic to any applicant whose desire to convert is secondary to his or her desire to marry a Jewish partner. In reply, Reform claims that its more accepting approach lessens the effect of out-marriage on the Jewish community. It is a polarization of attitudes.

Liberal Judaism

It was a woman, a Reform Jew, who was one of the founders of the Liberal movement. At the beginning of this century, Lily Montague, whose father had been president of the United Synagogue, together with the biblical scholar, Claude Montefiore, and several concerned Orthodox rabbis, recognised that the Reform synagogue movement was not preventing a worrying defection from Judaism. This led in 1903 to the first Liberal synagogue. There are now twenty-six in Britain. Brook (1989) describes the evolution of Liberal Judaism as being an even more heretical defiance of Orthodoxy than the 'iconoclastic movement' of Reform Judaism

Its philosophical beginnings were, however, different from Reform: it questioned the value of much traditional home-based ritual, seeing Judaism not as obedience to a set of rules but rather as an ethical imperative about how to act in the world. It therefore stressed one's duty to care for the welfare of others – Jew and non-Jew alike – rather than formal practice and observance.

Like Reform, Liberal Judaism refuses to accept that *halacha* is unchangeable. Unlike Reform, it is also prepared to reject the definition of 'Who is a Jew'? as being dependent on matrilineal descent. It insists that upbringing, rather than paternity or maternity, is the decisive factor in the determination of the status of children of mixed marriages. By this definition, the child of a non-Jewish mother and a Jewish father, who would *halachically* be regarded as non-Jewish, is accepted as fully Jewish if he or she is raised as a Jew.

> Being Liberal is a very thought-out way of being Jewish and I feel part of a community which believes in equality right the way through. Women take part in everything. We are people; we are not only women, we are people.
>
> (Liberal woman, in interview)

In terms of synagogue life, the Liberal movement very early redefined women's roles. Women were first permitted to preach in synagogue in 1918 and, since Lily Montague's historic challenge in 1928, 'The women must come down from the gallery', it has been normal in Progressive communities for men and women to sit together, for women to serve on synagogue councils, to conduct services, to be called up to open the ark and read from the Torah, although it was not until the mid-1970s that the first Liberal and Reform women rabbis were ordained. A more recent innovation is a baby-naming ceremony at the end of the Shabbat service, when both parents are called up to the ark. It contrasts with the Orthodox practice of giving that honour only to the father.

Perhaps surprisingly, in terms of liturgical and ritual practice, both Reform and Liberal Judaism have gradually become more traditional. They have, of course, retained the fundamental changes they introduced: particularly women's full participation in synagogue ritual and the use of English as well as Hebrew in their services. Yet there is a curious irony: the more Progressive the synagogue, the better the decorum and yet the less vibrant the atmosphere feels. Commenting on this seeming lack of vibrancy, Brook suggests it may be to do with one's need to respond to ritual 'and to action that does not have a rational meaning' (1989, p. 134).

Liberal Jews do not interpret their Judaism as a religion of 'Thou shalt not'. For example, they drive on Shabbat and festivals. Very few keep the rules of kashrut. But regarding ritual in the home, although it is very different from the stringency of Orthodox observance, many Liberal Jews now observe more than their parents or grandparents did in terms of celebrating Shabbat and festivals and especially in celebrating the Seder meal on Passover.

There is, however, an unbridgeable gulf between Liberal and Orthodox Judaism based on Orthodoxy's understanding of *halacha* as God-given and immutable. There are three major contentious areas. They concern divorce, conversion and Jewish status. All profoundly affect women and, although they are more fully discussed in other relevant chapters, they are summarised here:

Divorce

At the same time as having abolished the *get* in its own jurisdiction, Liberal Judaism recognises that a woman may want to remarry in an Orthodox synagogue, for which a *get* is necessary. It therefore requires a divorced man, before allowing him to remarry, to offer a religious divorce to his former wife.

Conversion

Right along the religious spectrum, there is great consternation at inter-faith marriage. In no synagogue is a Jew permitted to marry a non-Jew, nor will any British rabbi solemnize the wedding of a mixed faith couple. But, in relation to conversion, Liberal – like Reform – will not deny the non-Jewish partner the right to study and convert. It contends that, if con-version is denied to the non-Jew, the result will be the Jewish partner's rejection of his or her Judaism. It also points out that Talmudic law made specific provision for the admission of proselytes and, contrary to the Orthodox *Beth Din*, refuses to impose obstacles to the sincere would-be convert.

Jewish status

In Orthodox, traditional and Reform Judaism, the child of a mixed faith marriage is regarded as *halachically* Jewish if the mother is Jewish. Liberal Judaism contends differently; it claims that the child of a mixed marriage is Jewish as long as he or she has received a sound Jewish upbringing, regard-less of whether the mother or the father is the Jewish parent.

One further point needs making: the children of a *halachically* Jewish couple who marry in either a Reform or Liberal synagogue are in every way *halachically* Jewish – i.e. the synagogue's stance does not in any way detract from their religious status and, if the eventual partner of these chil-dren is also *halachically* Jewish, they may marry in an Orthodox syna-gogue.

RITUAL

Ritual, in any religion, is an important aspect of shared group life. Bernice Martin (1981) writes: 'rituals operate so as to affirm common belonging... ritual always performs the same miracle of symbolically banishing differ-ence and distance and manifesting commonness'.

In the Jewish religion, the ritual which takes place in the home and with the family is as important as that which takes place in the synagogue and it is in the area of religious practice within the home that the woman's role is central (Kobler, 1953; Meiselman, 1978; Greenberg, 1981). There is, of course, a significant link between type of affiliation and the observing of ritual, with the Orthodox seeing it as all-important and the non-Orthodox seeing it more in terms of family togetherness.

The fulfilling of ritual practice within the home carries with it many related expectations; for example, the Shabbat candles – which, in

Orthodox Judaism, must be lit at sunset – can be kindled only when the home is completely ready to welcome the Shabbat, when all the preparations (cleaning, shopping, cooking) have been done.

> I have a real creative joy in bringing in Shabbat, making the table beautiful, preparing for it.
>
> (Orthodox woman)

Yet it is not only for the Orthodox that it has importance; for many women ritual in the home has a personal meaning, often intricately bound up with roles and identity:

> The ritual fulfills for me a personal need of homemaking and mothering.
>
> (Traditional woman)

The Orthodox usually enact home ritual in all its detail. So, too, may the traditionally observant – the Conservatives in America, the United Synagogue in Britain – although many modify certain aspects of it; for example, although the candles will be lit on Friday evening in nearly every observant home, not all 'traditional' families will conclude the Shabbat on Saturday evening with the beautiful *havdalah* ceremony, which separates the sacred from the profane, the Shabbat from the workaday week.

For non-Orthodox women, too, ritual in a 'modernised' form often has both symbolic and family significance, – although interestingly these two women quoted below both felt the need to compare their practice with the Orthodox:

> A relationship with God is central to my life. I was brought up without ritual, starved of it ... and now, although it's not the way the Orthodox do it, I feel it as having a symbolic meaning for me – for us – part of our identity as Jews. It affirms the value of carrying Judaism on to our children and they to their children.
>
> (A convert to Reform Judaism; father was a Liberal Jew; mother was non-Jewish; husband Jewish).

> I come from a totally non-practising family so, compared to the Orthodox, the ritual must seem unimportant in our home. We don't keep a kosher home, for example, but we do keep Shabbat and the festivals – but not like an Orthodox shabbat. Ritual is important to us, but it wouldn't be thought of very highly by a really Orthodox family.
>
> (Parents Liberal 'but very assimilated'; husband from traditional family; now both turning to Reform as being more religious than Liberal)

In fact, one of the interesting trends in both Britain and America is a revival of the home rituals within the Reform movement. Sklare (1971 and

1989), writing in America, suggests that for the non-Orthodox the rituals most likely to be retained or returned to will fulfil some or all of five criteria:

(a) they will be capable of redefinition in modern terms
(b) they will not demand social isolation or adoption of a unique life-style
(c) they will accord with the religious culture of the wider community, while providing Jewish alternatives when such are felt to be needed.
(d) they are centred on children
(e) they are performed annually or infrequently.

Not surprisingly, the extent of ritual observance is strongly associated with denominational self-identification. However, a desire for ritual is not necessarily absent from women who define themselves as 'non-affiliated':

> We don't belong to a religious community or worship with them. But we have a home religion. It's trying to get to the source of all truth and approaching that source by means of ritual and customs and repetition.
>
> (Naomi Stadlen, in interview)

So, whilst ritual is formally defined in terms of shared expectations – and, for the Orthodox, in terms of the minutiae of performance – rituals nearly always have personal meaning, too. Myerhoff (1978) describes the lighting of the Shabbat candles, suggesting a sometimes almost mystical experience:

> Literally and figuratively, her kitchen becomes a sacred place and her most trivial, repetitive tasks . . . are sanctified. Appropriately, the Sabbath is female, the Bride who comes to the people of Israel, and it is the woman, now Queen of the home, who brings this blessing to her family. . . Barely audibly, she says the short Hebrew prayer . . . She lights the candles, bows her body forward over the flames, then circles her hands over them three times, drawing their holiness toward her face . . . as she silently . . . prays to herself.
>
> (p. 221).

The interview which follows similarly conveys one woman's Shabbat feelings:

To pray with a purpose: one woman's account

Late in life I have begun to have a dialogue with God. Let me explain. For years I lit the Shabbat candles and recited the blessing. But it was in a language that had no meaning for me. Week after week I repeated the alien words in parrot-fashion and it was a duty performed.

Then, recently, I felt able to talk to my son about prayer, to admit my feelings of hypocrisy and contrast them with his powerful beliefs and his ability to share his concerns and hopes with God. For him, prayer has become a message of purpose; he has experienced affirmations, insights.

My son responded by suggesting something so simple: that I talk to God, voice my frequently-expressed despair and in the process share my most profound feelings. 'Treat your candle-lighting as the time to pour out your soul and express your inner needs in a language that will feel true for you.'

The first moments of my attempt to speak before the Shabbat candles felt unsure but gradually I began. I told God what I longed for most, that my daughter – after all these years – should be blessed with a child. That one-sided dialogue with God was overwhelmed with tears as I questioned, explained, pleaded. No mystical experience, just my inner pain poured into my prayers, into my attempt to reason with God.

Now I speak to God first in my own words before blessing the candles in Hebrew. It has become essential for me. Prayer gives me an inner peace which surpasses all understanding; joy and sadness together.

(Sheila Kustow)

Public Ritual

Non-Orthodox feminists have targeted their objectives on the synagogue – from mixed seating to women rabbis. But the synagogue is *not* the focus of Judaism or of Jewish self-respect, except for those whose Judaism outside the synagogue is limited and secondary.

(Rabbi Dr. Jonathan Sacks, *L'Eylah*, 23, 1987)

Shul (synagogue) is a man's world.

(Orthodox woman)

Ritual – the woman in her home – that was the traditional association. Yet, in a contemporary gathering of Jewish women from many backgrounds the theme that emerges is of a polarity of views. Whilst the Orthodox and traditionally observant still speak of the home as their focus – 'the synagogue has never been all that important to us' is a sentiment often expressed – in contrast, as one moves progressively along the religious continuum, other women talk with emotion of their involvement in synagogue ritual.

The position of women in public ritual was initially a fluid one but, over the centuries, those *mitzvot* (commandments) – particularly in public ritual – from which women were exempt came to be interpreted in Orthodox Judaism as exclusions. What characterised these particular *mitzvot* was that they were 'time-bound' – i.e. had to be performed at special times – and women's prior commitment was seen to be with their children. But Meiselman (1978) suggests another reason, too: women were exempt from those rituals which entail public appearances and 'the merging of the individual self with the communal self'.

The value system of Orthodoxy profoundly influences a woman's expectations for it emphasises that it is in the home, not in the synagogue, that the woman fulfills her central and exalted role. In fact, there are three *mitzvot* (positive commandments) which are women's special province and they are all home-based: *niddah* (regulating the rhythm of marital relations), *hallah* (symbolizing her role as nurturer) and the lighting of the Shabbat candles. It is a value system which strikingly separates Orthodox from non-Orthodox women, not only in their options but also in their thoughts.

Progressive Judaism – Reform in America and Reform and Liberal in Britain – in freeing itself from the belief in *halacha*'s immutability, recognised from its earliest days the rightfulness of women's participation, if they wished it, in synagogue ritual. Women in these synagogues have therefore gradually taken on obligations and privileges in all areas of observance. Many now wear the ritual garments – the *tallit* and *tzitzit* and *kippah* – with all their connected symbolism. Women are called up to the reading of the Torah, they perform the ceremony of binding and lifting the scroll, they may lead the congregation in communal worship.

> I began to wear a *tallit* . . . with pride and joy . . . it has come to symbolise . . . a bringing together of mind and body to the oneness of prayer.
>
> (Dee Eimer, in Borts, 1987, p. 13)

However, even within the Progressive movement, there are contrasts between the feelings of British and of American Jewish women about the 'appropriateness' of performing these public rituals. Rabbi Charles Emanuel, earlier quoted, comments on the frequent reluctance of his English women congregants to accept the *aliyot* when they are called up to the reading of the Torah.

Rabbi Elizabeth Sarah, a London Reform rabbi, confronts the personal dilemma:

> As I see it, the Progressive debate on the performance of *mitzvot* seems

strangled in a false dichotomy. On the one hand, there are God's commandments – the preserve of the Orthodox, for whom they are binding on all Jews (unless they are public, time-bound ones, in which case Jewish women are exempt ...) On the other hand, there is 'personal choice' – the privilege of the Progressive Jew: each individual (and that includes female individuals too) is in a position to choose what she or he will or will not do Jewishly-speaking. But what does 'personal choice' mean? ...

Personal choice assumes personal gratification. Am I simply gratifying personal needs when I choose ... to make *kiddush* [the blessing over the Shabbat candles, traditionally recited by the husband] and *havdalah*, to wear a *tallit*?

There has to be more to it than this. But the 'more' is complicated by the implications of being a Progressive Jewish *woman*. As a woman I am aware of the extent to which the *mitzvot* defined as God's commandments have been mediated and interpreted by men who have devised special provisions to ensure that God's commandments don't conflict with the domestic and nurturing obligations they have assigned to women ...   (Borts, 1987, pp. 16–17)

Evolution in roles rarely takes place without ambivalence and this was particularly so within the Conservative movement, with its avowed commitment to *halacha*. The changes which were eventually introduced (described earlier in this chapter) came about as a result of much questioning and ferment and women's realization that their desire for involvement in synagogue worship was a legitimate one. But no single issue caused as much debate in the Conservative movement as that of women's greater participation in public ritual.

However, despite the debate, women in Conservative synagogues gradually achieved their aims. In contrast, Orthodox Judaism – faced with much more moderate requests – responds by discussing what is *halachically* possible in the context of why it should be wanted. Rabbi Kimche, a 'modern Orthodox' rabbi, writes:

Judaism has always sought to protect women's dignity and welfare. The Torah, while patriarchal and consigning women to a supporting role, is not unbending, otherwise it would have collapsed as a source of religious authority centuries ago. The *halachic* system must respond to feminism by looking for places where we can and where we cannot adapt to changing modern realities.

(Brook, 1989, p. 188–9)

He continued by considering two contentious areas; the first was whether women should be taught Torah, for which he found no contra-indications in today's climate of thought. The second concerned the time-bound *mitzvot* – for example, women wearing *tallit* or *tefillin* – where he presented the conflict: although there was no overriding *halachic* objection to their doing so, one should not undertake extra *mitzvot* until the obligatory ones had been fulfilled.

> To go beyond the call of duty is to invite close scrutiny of one's motives, and the suspicion would be aroused that one is wearing *tallit* for political or provocative reasons. The centre of a Jewish woman's life must be the home.

It is irrelevant for feminist logic to wonder that men's motives remain unquestioned in the same context. The world of *halacha* is, after all, a man's world.

THE SECULAR JEW

> And so, a most curious phenomenon has emerged. Jewishness without Judaism, or at least Judaism as traditionally conceived.
> (Rabbi Dr. Jonathan Sacks, in *L'Eylah*, 27, April 1989, p. 6)

> Religion is a very painful thing for me because two of my daughters have converted to Christianity. I feel such anger that my children, whom I've tried to bring up as humanists, have had the need for religion and then that, needing religion, they couldn't choose Judaism ... Being Jewish is a very great part of my identity.
> (Jewish agnostic woman)

Alongside the statistics suggesting that 'synagogue membership covers the vast majority of identifying Jews' (in Britain, Waterman and Kosmin, 1986; in America, Goldscheider, 1986) there are nevertheless many who identify as Jews – who feel Jewish – yet have no religious affiliation. Cesarani, for example, (1985–6, pp. 50–4) estimates that in Britain there are almost 100,000 Jews – a third of the community – who do not belong to a synagogue or to a major Jewish organization. Kosmin (1987) suggests a similar proportion of 'secular Jews' in America.

Many of these non-affiliated Jews may be loosely associated with the established community through participation in Jewish political organizations, particularly the Jewish Socialist movement. Others have points of contact through student politics, Jewish history groups or adult education

classes, or through social and cultural events. Often, for women, their connection with other Jewish women is in feminist groups, by involvement in
radical politics, the Women Against Fundamentalism movement, or in
Jewish gay and lesbian groups.

The point that Cesarani makes – as do other writers from outside the
'normative community' (eg. Bard, 1988) – is the secular Jew's perception
of being excluded by the established, affiliated community. Many feel
unequivocally Jewish but may have been excluded after 'marrying out'.
Others are the children of mixed marriages. Whatever their background,
they often feel that the 'establishment' (particularly the religious establishment, for there is also a communal establishment) refuses to validate those
outside its definitions. Cesarani writes: 'The Jewish community has a
system of discourses which marginalize and de-judaize these groups: they
are dissidents, intellectuals...they are "lost and searching for an
identity"...they don't belong to synagogues and therefore can't be Jews.'
Bard (1991) similarly observes:

> The communal leaders use political and religious orthodoxy to define
> the limits of the community and the limits of Jewish identity. Jewish
> children are brought up to believe that breaking ranks...brings trouble
> for all Jews...dissenting adults are told that they have no place in the
> community despite anxiety being widely expressed about Jews being
> 'lost' through assimilation. (p. 68)

Yet, even with the alienation felt by Jews who do not formally 'belong',
there remains a difficult-to-define sense of group awareness: a shared
history, shared understandings, a Jewish ethnic identity. It is defined by
Herman (1977) as a 'peculiar interweaving of both religious and ethnic
elements'. Erikson (1960) in a different context very aptly describes this
ambivalent sense of belonging: it is 'the reflection in the individual of an
essential aspect of a group's inner coherence'.

There is endless debate in both America and Britain about Jewish survival, with high intermarriage rates and declining religious affiliation seen
as the most worrying warnings of increased assimilation. And, against
these predictions, there are those who observe that the non-affiliated retain
links with Jewish family and friends and concern themselves with Israel
and Jewish culture (Goldscheider, 1986).

There are, after all, apart from religion, two most central and sensitive
areas which deeply concern both the involved and the seemingly-unin-
volved Jew: they are to do with anti-Semitism and with feelings towards
and about Israel, its problems and its politics.

What public opinion should understand is that anti-Semitism begins to kill with words.

(Serge Klarsfeld, *Washington Post*, May 1990)

The lessons of the Holocaust remain. Cooper (1991) tautly writes: 'Those who persecute us do not discriminate between us' (p.138). It is impossible to refer to so profound and emotional a subject in a few lines; its analysis still compels historians and psychologists; its effects still permeate the group unconscious.

Needing to defend against anti-Semitism has never been the privilege only of the religious (although they maintain that by assimilation and intermarriage Jews give Hitler a 'posthumous victory'). Anti-Semitism is a prejudice so deeply-rooted that it equally confronts the secular Jew with an awareness of his or her culturally distinct identity.

Although equating it with anti-Zionism blurs the dividing line, it is exactly that which became a raw issue in the late seventies. Paul Johnson (1987) details how the 1975 session of the United Nations General Assembly came close to legitimizing anti-Semitism when it passed a motion condemning Zionism as racism (pp. 578–9) – a motion only eventually rescinded in 1991. The repercussions of this 'Zionism equals racism' motion caused a deep rift in the feminist movements in both Britain and America and a seemingly irreconcileable conflict: 'a sudden realisation that there were only two ways you were allowed to identify as Jewish: religious or Zionist. And I was neither' (quoted in Cooper, 1991, p. 136). It seemed an impasse for the secular Jew and 'forced many into a re-evaluation of their own identities and beliefs as Jews. In re-examining Jewish history and culture they found rooted values which could stand up to the . . . propaganda coming from extremes of right and left' (Cooper, p. 136).

Julia Bard (1991) discusses the dilemma, a particularly painful one for the secular feminist Jew. She asks how, as members of a doubly oppressed minority, Jewish women can opt out of the struggle on behalf of other oppressed peoples. From such a perspective, to remain silent about Israel's policies in relation to the Palestinians seems an ideological betrayal. At the same time, to denounce Israel provokes different emotions. She suggests a partial resolution to this cognitive dissonance by questioning the apparent consensus in the diaspora of unconditional support for Israel's policies.

I've come from a position of freedom and what I want to put back into my life is the 'shamanism' – the candles flickering, etc., – the 'hocus pocus' which somewhere is in my roots. I want my children to know they're Jews.

(Sandar Warshall, secular Jewish woman)

Hers seems an increasingly expressed view. It is a strange irony that, particularly in American society where religion has become so secularized and so confined to a diminishing portion of life, there is a reaction. Huberman (1991), interviewing a large cross-section of Jews in Los Angeles, sees it as a reaction to the 'anything goes' philosophy. People are once more seeking roots, commitments, a meaning to life, and in this context, religion (mostly re-interpreted to accord with modern society) is seen as offering a value system, as being a way of making sense out of the world.

It is an immensely complex understanding – what it is to be a secular Jew. For some, especially those alienated by a Jewish community perceived as rigid and judgmental, it may lead to assimilation within the more pluralistic wider society. Yet many critical commentators (e.g. Glazer, 1987) believe it unlikely that the majority will abandon their Jewish identification because, especially in America – a nation of immigrants – 'ethnic identity and religious identification have become in large part expected norms of individual identification'. They see that 'there is amongst most Jews a real desire to maintain identity and continuity' (Glazer, pp. 17–18). Huberman agrees: 'Ethnic identity is, today, "in" among all age groups'.

How this Jewish awareness is felt, how deeply the sense of belonging has been internalized and in which way expressed, is explored in the two interviews which follow. The first one particularly highlights the truth of Melanie Kaye/Kantrowitz's observation:

The individual is profoundly connected to the community, so profoundly that separation is not truly possible without extreme loss.

(Melanie Kaye/Kantrowitz in *Jewish Women in Therapy*, 1991, p. 13)

WHAT DOES IT MEAN TO YOU, BEING JEWISH?

One woman's view

It is often assumed that a conscious awareness of one's Jewish identity is defined, at least partly, by some sort of religious affiliation or observance. But this assumption overlooks other complex issues, such as how we defend against prejudice: issues which are raised in the interview which follows.

I've always wanted to belong but I don't believe in God, so I feel excluded from the Jewish community. I belonged when I was young: to a Zionist, non-religious youth movement. But at University I felt unable to join the Jewish Society: prayer seemed so much part of being Jewish.

Yet I married a Jew; we were both programmed to marry someone Jewish – although he, like me, has no religion. We had a synagogue wedding to please our parents. The other thing is that we had our sons circumcised so they had options. When it came to Jewish education we said to the grandparents – 'if it's important to you, you do something about it.'

I consider myself English and Jewish although I probably have more in common with my non-Jewish friends than I have with Jewish women who keep religion. There are times when, sitting with a group of Jewish women talking about religious issues, I sit there thinking I have nothing in common with these women *on this level*. It is the religious part of Judaism that alienates me; in every other way I feel Jewish.

Being Jewish is relevant to me in the way that being a woman is and being English is. It is not a conscious part of my daily life; I become aware of those identities only in reaction to provocation. Intellectually, I'm not sure that I would be more outraged by anti-semitic remarks then I am about other racist remarks. But of course emotionally, it depends on the particular trigger; for example, when during the time of the Lebanon crisis a friend likened Sharon to Hitler, I was deeply, deeply shocked. After all, I was brought up knowing about the Holocaust, about the concentration camps. That is a part of my heritage.

Regarding intermarriage, it could easily happen in my own family; the fact that my son's girldfriend is not Jewish doesn't bother me one bit; the fact that she is not white doesn't bother me either. As long as they are happy, that's what matters. In fact it might be more difficult for him if one of my sons were to marry a Jewish girl from a religious background where keeping kosher, etc., was important. Marrying out doesn't bother me but I think it would be sad if the special cultural characteristics were to disappear.

When I die, my Jewishness will die with me. Any continuity I shall have with the future is determined by what my sons decide to carry on from the legacy we have given them; for example, I would like their homes always to be open and welcoming. But that's not specifically Jewish.

There are real contradictions in what I feel. In a way I think that marrying out is a good thing – it does away with the barriers – and I think that religion has a lot to answer for in terms of intolerance. I feel alienated – not only from the Jewish religion but from other religions, too, in terms of their exclusivity and sense of superiority. Yet I miss the structures of religion and the traditions that go with it. They are very comforting; it's like Mummy tucking you up in bed.

There are lots of inconsistencies: I am Jewish. Most of our friends are Jewish, but they're Jewish like us, completely non-religious. Being Jewish is not an issue for me, but it would become an issue if anti-Semitism re-emerged. At the same time I want to work towards a more tolerant society which, I believe, is better achieved by doing away with the barriers – 'you're a black, you're a Jew, you're a woman' – than by the other way, the sticking together in case of anti-Semitism.

If we want to prevent anti-Semitism or any other form of racism, then perhaps it's wiser for us to mix more rather than less – although I know that was not the experience of assimilated German Jews under Hitler. It's hard to argue the point. I can only do what feels right for me.

(Sally Malnick)

Discussion group

Rosalind Cole, Toni Fine, Juliette Joffe, Susie Kleiman, Sharon Lee, Sandar Warshal

Sa. I addressed the fact of being a secular Jew and I've thought about it in terms of;
my connection with Judaism, by which I mean the observing Jewish community.
my connection with God, and how God is seen from my perspective – which is certainly not to do with having different kitchen sinks.
my connection with the tribe.
my connection with our shared history.

J. My relationship with God has nothing to do with having two sinks.

Su. No, except that you can't feel part of that particular Jewish community which depends on those values unless you also observe them.

T. The conflict only arises when you cross boundaries between communities. In the States, I had no problem; I knew where I belonged and felt accepted there.

Su. Therefore you can't be part of a community where there are those requirements if you don't conform.

J. My feeling is that you are a Jew and proud to be a Jew. To me, the religious aspect, keeping kosher, etc., is secondary. Yet I belong to a more traditional Reform *shul* than most; we observe two days of all the

yomtovim; our service is 75 per cent Hebrew. But there are contradictions: for example, lighting the Shabbat candles is important to me – it
is part of my Jewishness – but I don't feel that in winter I have to light
them just at 4 o'clock or just at 3.30, when it gets dark but when my
family are not yet home. It matters more that I light them when my
family are with me. So I guess that's not what an Orthodox person
would see as acceptable.

Sh. The reason for the ruling is that you can't make fire – strike a match –
after Shabbat has come in. Judaism concentrates first on the 'doing':
the idea is that you should do the things you are supposed to do first
and then think of what is behind them.

J. But I feel we're looked down on by the Orthodox.

T. Then the answer is not to go to the Orthodox and ask them for their
approval.

Sh. But we do stick together as Jews; we're here in this group as Jews.

T. We should be looking for tolerance, searching for shared experiences,
not differences.

Sh. That's what happens now in Rosh Chodesh groups where women are
able to enlarge boundaries. I'm very excited about this because, as you
know, I'm full of religious conflict. I'm not happy with the synagogue
to which we've always gone. There's no opportunity for real dialogue;
often it's as if you've been asked to keep your brain at home. Yet I
want to pray and to practice. Maybe as a woman in Masorti I can also
keep my intellectual awareness alive. The Orthodox wouldn't allow
me to ask questions – or at least, the answers would be very circumscribed.

T. I wonder how much the individual interaction with God is defined by
your community.

R. We've actually changed our degree of Orthodoxy; we had to learn
more when we adopted children and now observing has become comfortable.

Su. Observance is not something you think of: it is just part of a way of
life – you don't question.

T. My interaction with God is very personal yet it's without the structure
of a *Shul*. I don't even go to synagogue on Yom Kippur yet I fast and
think very deeply.

Sh. I know that when I went to Masorti, it was a spiritual experience; we
were praying as a community. I don't know if it was a personal God.

T. It's a sense of belonging. I know if I went to a synagogue where they
sang the songs of my childhood, I'd be overwhelmed.

Sh. What sort of God are you praying to?

T.   I can't answer that but, for example, on Yom Kippur – that's a day of reflection for me about what is right and wrong, about what sort of a person I am.

J.   So what is the answer to the problems of right and wrong?

R.   It's not to do with expiating sins.

Su.   If you think about religion as a framework, then if you keep within this framework – you don't work on Shabbat, you don't eat bread on Pesach, etc., etc., – then it's a discipline for all of life.

Sh.   We've discussed this before: what we do we especially do for our children: we want them to stay Jewish; we want Judaism to survive.

T.   I have two sons. To one of them, having Jewish friends is important; he feels more comfortable with them. The other son doesn't seem to label people as Jewish or not.

R.   The first memory I have of childhood is to do with anti-Semitism, someone tried to pull off my *kemaya* . . . [religious symbol on a necklace].

J.   My memory is also of anti-Semitism: being on a bus when a Jew was beaten up. I learned you have to stand up for yourself as a Jew. I feel great peace in going to *Shul* yet my husband, who feels very Jewish, is alarmed at my wanting to become more religious. I've actually always wanted to live in Israel, but when we applied to go – with a baby and twins due – we were dissuaded from going. They advised us not to go then. So I felt that I should be more religious here.

S.   I want to know how you feel about the attitude towards women in Orthodox Judaism: that you are not regarded as fully-entitled, whole people.

R.   I personally don't actually want to take advantage of the possibility to *daven* [in this context, it means to pray as part of the required quorum]. But I would like the option.

Sh.   My daughter had a *bat-mitzvah* and it didn't compare with a boy's *barmitzvah*; it was second best. I find it disconcerting that a little boy can sing '*Anim Zmirot*' [a hymn concluding the shabbat service], etc., and a daughter can't.

Su.   You see I'm very happy with the woman's role in the home. I don't need the spiritual side, but I'm very lucky that I haven't had a crisis when I've needed to turn to God.

Sh.   I have no parents and my husband has always said *kaddish* [the memorial prayer for parents which a woman may not recite in an Orthodox or United Synagogue] for me. But this year I've joined Masorti and I have the option to say it – and I don't know if I shall exercise it.

Su. I don't know if I get the spiritual satisfaction for myself. What I do is part of a framework of expectations – but I get the spiritual satisfaction from what other members of my family do.

T. I bring in Shabbat; we keep it in our way; we're together as a family; we never go out on Friday nights. I need and like Shabbat; we need that division from the rest of the week.

Sh. Sometimes I feel Shabbat is a taskmaster – I don't want to clean out another bloody chicken! It's relentless: I don't want to look at another chicken's cavity! You can't opt out of it. The whole week leads towards Shabbat; you do your baking on Wednesday, your chicken soup on Thursday . . .

R. I enjoy Shabbat because I enjoy a day of rest. It's the one day I really relax.

Sa. To come back to the minute details of what's supposed to be religion: my God would not notice what is happening in my fridge on Shabbat [reference to the light which may not be turned on on Shabbat]. My God is *the* God. My God is to do with happiness and joy, with the 'flame' that is life. He is the God whom we exalt. I've been taught you must add to life – bring people forward and lift the shackles. That is what my God is to me. My friend is dying just now of cancer and she and I can talk: she is Sikh; we can talk about eternity and about the eucalyptus growing in her garden. Judaism for me is to do with celebrating life – *l' chayim* – to life! – like in Fiddler on the Roof: not to do with the light bulb in my fridge.

R. For me the most terrible prayer on Yom Kippur is the one in which we atone for our sins and the curses which follow – and one of them is the sins for which we should bear the curse of barrenness.

T. Then isn't that a reason for changing the structures of religion, the way things are?

Sh. You pray on Yom Kippur that if you repent you will be forgiven – and yet the righteous suffer. How can we explain that?

Su. I don't feel that when you leave this world, that is the end of things.

Sa. My friend said last night 'I can't think of you now; I must turn towards my after-life'. Yet I don't think I am ready to let her go.

T. There is a link with previous generations.

Sa. The mysticism was lost in Reform Judaism. That was a big loss. The realisation of the Holocaust is very strong for me. I put my arm around my son when he goes on the train and I think of how other women then, during that time, must have put their arms around their sons . . .

T. When I look at the documentaries, I realise the similarities.

J.   I think the Holocaust is what we've always known about. I had a nanny once who, when I was speaking about it, said: 'Oh, nonsense; it never happened'.

S.   I have one friend who, I felt, could have betrayed me. I mistrust her at such a deep level.

T.   That's to do with our feelings about belonging – the tribe.

Sa. I've been involved in some controversial situations politically, where I had to show my moral stand. But I would not like to test my morality if what I had to do (for example, hiding Jews during the war) were to threaten my children.

T.   My mother still won't talk about it. She left Czechoslovakia and lost many of her family. I wonder if that is what has prevented her from observing religion.

Sa. The Jews were murdered simply because they were Jews. This had nothing to do with God; it was people who committed the crimes. mostly men. God to me is the flame. It's what you do with it which matters. I think Orthodox Judaism is a distortion of the celebration of God.

Sh. I can't look at any of the laws and think they're bad: I'm talking about the basic tenets of the Torah. But we respect them within a framework.

Su. We have conflict because we have options. And sometimes people whom we hold in high esteem may not act well and that, too, is a conflict. If you have certainties, you have no conflict.

J.   I think there is a God and I actually pray. I need to pray.

Sa. We have a common history and we have always been a despised minority. We have a shared wit, a shared past, shared feelings about the Holocaust.

T.   When you put the religious expectations aside, there is something shared. We're a family: you fight within it, but should anybody be against any member of my family...

5 Aspects of Orthodoxy

THE ULTRA-ORTHODOX

> Being an Orthodox woman is *the* most creative task; we create children; our children are our *mitzvot* [commandments].
>
> (Ruth, Gateshead woman. Mother of fourteen children and wife of distinguished talmudic scholar)

> Let these matters that I command you this day be upon your heart. Teach them diligently to your children and speak of them while you sit in your home, while you walk along the way, when you lie down and when you arise.
>
> (The *Shema*, part of the morning prayer)

How does one begin to describe a way of life in which every thought, every action, is 'Torah true' – religiously inspired? There is a gulf of understanding between the woman who is fully a part of a religious community and the woman from outside who questions the values and assumptions, the structures and hierarchies of such a community. The difficulty in understanding is compounded by the need to recognise that not all the strictly Orthodox were born so; many choose to become Orthodox – the *ba'alei t'shuva* – and these are often educated, successful men and women, often previously little involved with religious belief and observance.

This chapter will try to glimpse what it means to be an Orthodox woman. It begins, briefly, with the factual picture in the States and Britain. Then, it looks at the specifically woman's world – her home, the shops, the *mikvah* (ritual bath), the all-women's study groups, – both literally and metaphorically the other side of the *mechitzah* (the curtain separating men and women in prayer and public celebration). But as well as the beauty and dignity, what else? We must also look beyond the idealized view to the sometimes bleak realities of belonging to a closed community in which birth control is viewed with disfavour and in which problems are denied.

The second and third parts of this chapter are more specific. Firstly, it contemplates the chassidic world and considers some of the differences between the *chassidim* – particularly the Lubavitch – and the non-*chassidic* Orthodox. Finally, the chapter explores the '*baal t'shuva*' phenomenon.

The factual picture

> Society can affect one. You can be unsettled by the suggestions of the
> outside world. But if you are living a full Torah life, you will not be
> unsettled.
>
> (Hadassah, mother of eight.)

Creating their own safe world separate from outside flux and turmoil
ensures stability. In fact, the tight-knit apect of the Orthodox way of life
with its shared values provides a chosen insulation against the 'contamina-
tions' of secular society. Not surprisingly, therefore, the Orthodox – in
whichever country they settle – live in concentrated areas. In the past
twenty years in the States and in Britain, there has been an unprecedented
increase in the strictly Orthodox. In the USA they now represent 9 per cent
of the Jewish population (*A.J.Y.B.*, 1991). They live in segregated communities, clustered around *yeshivot* (talmudic colleges), with concentrations in
certain areas – in Boro Park, Crown Heights and Williamsburg in Brooklyn,
in New Skvare in Rockland Country, New York. There are dense enclaves
too in the Bronx, as there are in other parts of the USA – Scranton, Pa.,
Baltimore, Seattle, Pittsburgh, Rochester, Miami, Cleveland. Sometimes
there are communities within communities; for example. Sometimes there
are communities within communities; for example, Lubavitch are concentrated in Crown Heights, with estimates ranging from 20,000 (Halevi,
1992, p. 32) to 35,000 (Stern, 1991, 12), whilst Williamsburg is settled by
an estimated 30,000 Satmar chassidim (Stern, 1991, ibid.).

In Britain, the ultra-Orthodox represent 7 per cent of affiliated Jews,
although in London the figure is 9 per cent. There are four major ultra-
Orthodox concentrations: in London they are primarily in Stamford Hill in
the north-east and Golders Green and Hendon in the north-west. There are
also strong enclaves in Manchester and Glasgow. Above all, there is
Gateshead – an otherwise ordinary northern English town with a Jewish
community which is totally ultra-Orthodox.

Women in the ultra-Orthodox world

Many writers, both from within and from without, have been intrigued by
women's experience in Orthodoxy and by the 'return' to Orthodoxy. They
all (Aviad, 1983; Kaufman, 1987; Loewenthal, 1988; Danzger, 1989;
Kupferman, 1976 and 1979) note the sense of fulfilment and dignity which
Orthodox women convey. Regardless of her objectively-speaking disadvantaged position within *halacha*, despite her lack of role in synagogue

ritual, the Orthodox woman finds her satisfactions in uniquely female spheres – the family, the home. But looking at the way in which (in this male-defined system) women create their 'counterpart culture' (Ardener, 1975) with symbols of success different from those in the dominant group, it is a valid question to ask whether they are, in fact, reinforcing the status quo (a situation comparable to Gluckman's 1964 'rituals of rebellion'.)

Let's begin at a wedding: the wedding of my friend's *ba' al t'shuva* daughter. Come with me to the women's side of the *mechitzah*. Dancing. The sweet-sad sound of *klezmer* music. A swirl of women dancing joyously in a circle around the bride – her mother, her aunts, her cousins, her friends, the entire community, it seems – circling her with ribbons. Women only – and yet, I wonder aloud, how coquettishly some of the younger ones dance. 'Of course,' my own daughter, who is now part of that world, explains, 'they're dancing for the *shadchanot* (matchmakers)'. So, we've touched on two themes: the women separated from the men in public gatherings (for the *mechitzah* is a screen hiding them away), and the young women seeking a *shidduch* (a 'match').

The *mechitzah* is both real and symbolic and can be understood only within the framework of traditional perceptions. It represents a need to separate women (seen as a sexual distraction) from men in prayer and public worship. Meiselman explains: 'The sex drive is a very powerful ... aspect of the male personality ... The presence of women prevents him from attaining the ... intense concentration necessary for ... prayer' (1978, p. 142). To the objective thinker such a view is offensive but, for women in Orthodoxy, it is one based on the distinction between the intimacy of marriage and the superficiality of relationships in the public world, and therefore a view rarely questioned.

So what, then, is this woman's world? It is her family, through which she enables her husband to fulfill the command to be fruitful and multiply; the shops, through which she defines herself as nurturer and keeper of a kosher home; the *mikvah*, in which she maintains the purity of the marital relationship; and her study groups in which, ideally, she finds reinforcement. Kupferman lived in and studied this world and came away with a conviction of its special quality:

> In spite of very large families, relatively bad housing, frequently low incomes ... there was an unusual cheerfulness ... about the women ... they laughed often and easily and for women who ... were restricted in everything they did, from how they dressed ... to the rigid dietary restriction ... and who were never once able to stray from their 'woman's space' in this sexually segregated society, they showed a

remarkable energy... I remember one woman who... forty-eight hours after the birth of a fifth child, came rushing, dishevelled into a study group, having stayed up the night before between breast-feeding to study the text. Wig askew, leaking milk, she looked radiant.

(1979, p. 110)

Each day has a meaning. Living religiously gives me the fortitude to face the vicissitudes of life and to gain perspective in terms of my relationship with God.

(Rivka, Gateshead woman)

Problems

But it is not all such an idealized picture. Wolf (1982) identifies the '*Baruch Ha'Shem* Society'. *Baruch Ha'Shem* means, literally, 'blessed be His name' – a response implying all is well. She speaks of a 'pseudo-intimacy' based upon a conformity to norms, denying that all may *not* be well. For, she suggests, the risk of self-disclosure is too great. Within this expectation, 'women felt torn between an attitude which values questioning and doubt as growth-producing rather than threatening, and simple faith in which incongruent issues tend to be avoided rather than wrestled with' (p. 48). The dilemma is expressed simply by one Orthodox woman:

Years ago, I thought that I had to be the perfect wife, the perfect mother, homemaker, worker in the community, support to my husband – and what happened? Bang into depression. It took me a long, long time to learn that you don't have to be perfect.

Kate Loewenthal, in preliminary research into well-being and depression in Anglo-Jewish women (1989) suggests that for the ultra-Orthodox woman, happiness seems to depend on her role and identity as wife and mother and her integration into and status within the community. 'The ultra-Orthodox woman lives in a tiny subcommunity, with separate social worlds for men and women... If she is integrated, then people can know if she has difficulties. Help is forthcoming without her having to ask.'

There are, of course, many individual realities within this Orthodox world. For the majority, religion probably does give a sense of dignity and worth so that their most banal tasks become imbued with spiritual meaning. And, of course, having enough money for everyday needs and for security helps. But there are others – women whose tasks concern the basic struggles of daily survival. There are, inevitably, many social problems in a closed community where the families are large and many are poor. Brook (1989, p. 65) quotes the director of one of the welfare agencies working in the Orthodox community as saying 'when a rabbi tells you there are no problems in that community, it means he is sitting very firmly on the lid'. Commenting on this, one of Jewish Care's social workers lists four main areas of concern: (a) poverty and sometimes even malnutrition; (b) the widespread occurrence of hereditary diseases, intensified by constant inbreeding; (c) a higher than average incidence of mental and physical handicaps, which are often hidden so as not to spoil the arranged marriage prospects of siblings; (d) neglect and abuse, and a reluctance to seek help from outside agencies. Women marry young and are often 'totally drained just producing kids'. But Brook also quotes one of the social workers: 'From our enlightened viewpoint, the women get a hard time. But I don't think they see it that way themselves.'

Wiselberg, involved in this community as a family therapist, is aware of much secrecy and denial. She describes how religious observance may mask family dysfunction:

> The defence mechanisms are enormous. The community supports a family in keeping the denial going as long as they are observing all the external requirements – the children attending [religious] school, the husband and sons going to synagogue. The child will often be sacrificed for the needs of the group. Unhappy marriages may stay together. The fifth commandment – 'Thou shalt honour thy father and thy mother' – is so often a barrier to exploring difficult and sensitive areas in the parent-child relationship. The interface of psychopathology and religiosity is a complex area.

Affirmative literature on Orthodox Judaism inevitably portrays a system of values and practices creating family harmony and making for inner peace. So, too, do the 'women of worth' who come forward to talk about their way of life. The community closes ranks on dysfunction – ostensibly, it does not exist. Women who are not coping with their large families, who are living on income support in poor housing, who are weary, unable to provide adequate food for their children: these lives are not often depicted. When they appear at all, it is within the confidential records of Jewish Care and, often, not even there. For there is great reluctance in the Orthodox community to admit of problems, even greater reluctance to take these problems outside their close-knit society, and a virtual taboo on its members approaching non-Jewish agencies for intervention.

It is a complex situation: the leaders of the ultra-Orthodox sects fear giving 'ammunition' to the outside world, anti-Semitism being the implied reason. At the same time, powerful communal pressure rarely permits a family to speak outside the community of things going wrong. To be labelled a *moisser* (informer), as one mother was during 1991, is tantamount to being banished.

To comment on that world is to comment only on the externals. There is, of course, economic and personal hardship and family dysfunction – and denial. But, equally, there is a degree of communal support and care rarely so readily given in more sophisticated communities. At every rejoicing and at every sadness, at every birth and at every illness or trauma, the women of the community come together to shop and cook and care for each other. A characteristic of all Orthodox communities is the extent of mutual support. There is a very alive, informal network of voluntary organisations in which all the women, particularly as their children become independent, are involved. The Jewish concept of *chesed* goes beyond good deeds; it is more 'loving-kindness'.

And, despite the differences, for the women there are many areas of shared understandings which concern their most profound values, which influence every aspect of their lives. So, for the interested visitor to such a community, there will be very striking indications of these values – the high proportion of pregnant women, the extreme modesty of their dress, their hair coverings.

Many daughters have done worthily, but thou excellest them all.
(Proverbs XXXI, 10–31: prayer recited by husband on Friday evenings)

In discussing women within Orthodox Judaism, there are so many contradictions. Several of them have been explored earlier in the discussion of *halacha* (religious law) – for this is the area *par excellence* in which, despite all the pronouncements of the apologists, women are denied access to knowledge, status and power. Feminist writers such as Friedan (1963), Greer (1970), Millett (1971), Figes (1978), Dally (1982) were not, of course, considering Jewish women when they asked whether women in patriarchal societies unknowingly help to perpetuate a deeply-entrenched system of male privilege – but it would have been a valid question in this context.

The very large families are a case in point. The *mitzvah* of procreation is discussed in Chapter Seven. An additional comment is relevant: Sarah Bunim's (1990) work with American Orthodox women suggests that, even when they receive rabbinic permission to use birth control, many wives feel ambivalent about it, as if its use implies their inadequacy as mothers.

On the other hand – as the traditional form of reasoning goes – Orthodox women seem, on the whole, happy with their lot, and more and more women are even choosing it. In relation to childbearing, it is difficult to disentangle perceived religious expectations and peer group pressure from the individual woman's intense conviction that having many children is her way to serve *ha kodesh, baruch hu* (the Holy One, blessed be He), and that each child is a blessing. Other areas also differentiate the Orthodox from the non-Orthodox. Modesty, *tzni'ut*, is basic to Orthodox women. Literally it refers to 'that which is concealed'; it is a striving to preserve the inner life from the constant preoccupation with outer appearance. Therefore, in terms of dress, high necks, sleeves to below the elbow and longish skirts are the imperatives and the wearing of trousers is forbidden, for that is regarded as emulating a man. Finally in terms of externals, married women cover their hair. In the Code of Jewish Law a man is forbidden to 'gaze at a woman's hair' (vol. 4, CLII, 8) and it is written that 'Daughters of Israel ... should not go into the street with hair uncovered'. (Kitzur Shulchan Aruch, pt. 4, p. 416,5). Whilst, for the 'modern Orthodox', the hair covering may be a scarf or snood, for the 'ultras', nothing less than a wig (a *sheitel*) will suffice and at the extreme there are even women whose heads are shaved beneath their wigs. It is an issue not without controversy in which *halachic* concerns and social custom are involved.

It is a safe, curious, shut-away world – and yet, surprisingly, not a totally homogeneous one, for there are internal divisions. They are all strictly Orthodox, but there are the *chassidic* and the non-*chassidic* ultra-Orthodox. In terms of externals, it is the men who indicate to which world they belong, for the *chassidim* wear a distinctive garb. But the distinction is even more an internal one, to do with approaches to prayer, through the intellect or the soul.

THE *CHASSIDIM*

The Hebrew word *chassid* means, literally, 'pious one'. Not all the ultra-Orthodox are *chassidim*, although all *chassidim* are strictly Orthodox. As a modern movement, *chassidism* began in the eighteenth century but its roots go back as far as biblical times. The Middle Ages saw the brief flowering of *chassidism* in twelfth-century Germany and its ideas were carried to Poland by Jews fleeing the anti-Semitic campaigns of the Crusades. In Poland, too, Jews suffered persecution and pogroms but, although *chassidism* declined, a pious fervour remained which even survived the discrediting of the false messiah Sabbatai Zvi in Turkey in 1666.

The messianic fervour had symbolised a hope of redemption for the poor Jews of Easten Europe who were aware of their inadequacy in relation to their scholarly rabbinic leaders.

Modern *chassidism* thus developed as a reaction against the intellectual emphasis of the rabbinic scholars, an emphasis which conveyed the feeling that only the learned could be devout. Its founder, known as the *Ba'al Shem Tov* (the Master of the Good Name), was himself a man of the people with little formal learning. But he was a mystic and had great charisma. Basic to the movement he inspired are two concepts: the first, an ancient idea, is that of the *tzaddik*, a wise man, who can bless, comfort and enlighten and who acts almost as an intermediary between God and the members of the community. The *tzaddik* remains today for each *chassidic* sect; he is the *Rebbe*, whose dynastic role is usually passed on to his son or son-in-law.

Equally central to *chassidism* – and again inspired by the *Ba'al Shem Tov* – was the realisation that prayer could allow even simple people to reach into the divine world. It was an understanding drawn from the teachings of the *kabbalah*, the Jewish mystical tradition. To reach this union with God, man must pray with his whole being. This fervent prayer, usually accompanied by swaying and chanting, is characteristic of *chassidic* prayer; in fact, sometimes, at weddings or on *Rosh Chodesh* (the New Moon) or *Simchat Torah* (the Festival of the Rejoicing of the Law), prayer is also accompanied by clapping and singing and dancing. There is also *klezmer*, a lovely, haunting celebratory *chassidic* music.

The core of *chassidic* belief emphasizes the mystical presence of God in all things and strives to imbue all aspects of life – eating, praying, love-making, social relationships – with holiness and joy. In its early days it shocked the Orthodox establishment who tried to ban it. Despite this, it spread and established itself as a seemingly vital part of Ashkenazi Judaism. The conflict between the non-*chassidic* ultra-Orthodox and their *chassidic* brethren is essentially one of approach to God: for the former, it is through Torah study and prayer; for the Chassidim, it is in the intensity of their prayer that they reach God.

In terms of externals, the ultra-Orthodox anyway are set apart. Their separateness is deliberate, to avoid any possibility of their merging with the wider society with its potentially corrupting influences. But the *chassidim* are doubly set apart and most strikingly in the men's dress, which strongly resembles that of eighteenth century Polish merchants. Interestingly, the women dress less distinctively than their menfolk, although what they wear is dictated by considerations of *tzniut* (modesty) and, like all ultra-Orthodox women, they cover their own hair with a wig.

There are several major Chassidic sects – Satmar, Lubavitch (the two largest); Bobov, Belz, Vishnitz, Sassover, Gur and other smaller ones. Each sect follows its own venerated *tzaddik* and each has a distinctive style of prayer, of dress, of attitude, depending on their specific origin – Poland, Hungary, Lithuania, Russia. There are, of course, similarities between them and, as with all the ultra-Orthodox, they all have very large families. But there are also differences and even hostilities between the different sects – for example, regarding attitudes towards Israel.

The Lubavitch

Of all the *chassidic* groups, it is the Lubavitch who arouse the most interest and provoke the most emotion. They are differentiated from all the others because they are consciously inspired by an evangelical philosophy. Their members – intelligent and dynamic – believe that they most appropriately perform 'the Rebbe's work' by reaching out to previously uncommitted Jews. To fulfill this *mitzvah*, Lubavitch families frequently go to live in areas where Orthodoxy is weak. There they convey a Judaism which offers joy and vitality and, not surprisingly, their flock is increasingly significantly, with many new followers drawn from amongst those who had felt uninspired by any of the formal synagogue groups. The *ba'alei t'shuva* are more likely to join Lubavitch than any other *chassidic* group, for this is where they feel welcomed and not judged. As a result of this missionary zeal the Lubavitchers have – again, not surprisingly – been likened to the Moonies. In Britain anxiety is even being felt that their crusading rabbis may be gaining influence in United Synagogue congregations.

The unease about Lubavitch comes from both directions – from other ultra-Orthodox who are wary of the Lubavitch ideal of bringing wayward Jews back to religious consciousness and, equally, from the less Orthodox who fear its charismatic attraction. The latter see that 'young men and women, often highly educated and with excellent career prospects, have suddenly abandoned their secular life and disappeared into *yeshivot* and seminaries to emerge soon after with all the trappings of the ultra-Orthodox Jew' (Brook, 1989, p. 62).

The reality, of course, is usually less extreme than the fears. There is nothing in ultra-Orthodoxy or in Lubavitch to exclude work involvement in the outside world. On the other hand, it is interesting that the Lubavitch – who both live and work in the non-Orthodox world – feel the need for what Shaffir (in Cohen and Hyman, 1986, ch. 13) calls 'insulating mechanisms' to offset 'the assimilative tendencies of the larger society' (p. 190).

They very much see the forces of the secular culture as detrimental and potentially contaminating and shield themselves – and particularly their children – from these influences as much as possible. For example, they will not have television in their homes and would certainly not attend places of entertainment. Education is seen as all-important and 'children are repeatedly taught that what is out there is not for them' (Shaffir, p. 189). But education is by no means restricted only to the young; the Lubavitch way of life is conveyed in frequent lectures and seminars for men and women, in weekend gatherings and in their publications.

Like many other *chassidic* sects, Lubavitch began in the eighteenth century. Its particular philosophy is drawn from an inspirational volume known as the *Tanya* – a guide to religion written in the late 1790s by the founder of Lubavitch, Schneur Zalman. It was written for 'seekers' and the 'perplexed' – but not the sophisticated perplexed for whom Maimonides wrote his *Guide* six centuries earlier. The *Tanya* is a synthesis of mystical and rational currents of Jewish thought; it teaches a way of prayer and contemplation and holds that by searching the depths of their own souls people can come to understand all the dimensions of the world. From this developed the '*chabbad*' philosophy underlying Lubavitch, *chabbad* being an acronym of the Hebrew words for wisdom, understanding and knowledge (Harris, 1985, ch. 4).

Lubavitch began to establish roots in both the States and in Britain in the early 1940s, although its expansion has been particularly important since the Arab-Israel 1967 Six Day War which was a turning-point for many who were, possibly unconsciously, seeking a deeper meaning to their Jewish identity. Lubavitch responded to their search. Lubavitch is part of a world-wide movement, headed by its New York-based *Rebbe* and aimed at reaching out to other Jews and bringing them back to their religious roots. The Lubavitchers achieve this aim very effectively by sending *shelichim* (emissaries of the *Rebbe*) to schools, universities and youth clubs, to adult education courses and to towns with small communities. Most of all, they reach other Jews by the informal contacts they make in Jewish districts and by the warmth and hospitality they then offer.

It is, of course, the very seductiveness of what they offer which provokes the most concern in their detractors: 'Posing as an alternative to the alienation and identity crises experienced by many Jews, born again Judaism offers a warm secure setting where a troubled, lonely search for understanding can be replaced by a set of moral certainties' (Bard, 1990, p.20)

Unlike other ultra-Orthodox groups, Lubavitch do not have an 'all or nothing' approach; their apparent open-mindedness – and the eloquence of their members – is one of their strengths. At the same time, they are undoubtedly religious fundamentalists and, as a result of their evangelical zeal, they are accused of breaking up families by drawing adult children away from their less religously-observing parents. They are also much criticised for appearing to present themselves as *the* authentic voice of Orthodox Judaism. There is thus, and understandably, much opposition to what they do, to their consciously high profile and to their techniques. But the opposition is confronted by a wealthy and sophisticated organisation – and, significantly, much of Lubavitch's financial support comes from non-religious Jews.

Women within Lubavitch
Quite often, women marry men more Orthodox than they are and then rise to their husband's level of Orthodoxy. This pattern is paralleled in the *chassidic* community where not infrequently non-*chassidic* women marry *chassidic* men (Danzger, 1989, p. 195). A similar phenomenon occurs when wives, of necessity, follow their husband's lead into Lubavitch.

The fact that women seem to derive a particular fulfilment from Orthodox Judaism has earlier been noticed. Confronting it, an urgent voice of warning has arisen from within the feminist movement: Women Against Fundamentalism. Amongst its members are many Jewish women endeavouring to challenge fundamentalist approaches. They ask, in particular, why do women become attracted to 'patriarchal institutions which define and confine them' (Bard, 1990). This is a curious paradox, discussed in the context of Lubavitch by Kupfermann (1976) and Loewenthal (1988). Within that world, Loewenthal sees three types of women: firstly, those 'inspired' towards Orthodoxy as a result of a crucial experience; a second group consists of those who, after initial resistance, take their husband's lead; then, thirdly, there are those born into Orthodoxy but who, nevertheless, make a conscious choice to re-think its beliefs and practices for themselves.

Uniquely amongst the ultra-Orthodox, Lubavitch places special emphasis on women's ability in the spheres of leadership and education in the wider community, as valued role-models for uncommitted Jewish women. They accompany their husbands to non-Orthodox communities and show the way, not only as exemplars of family life but as able scholars. The task bestows a sense of purpose and self-esteem. 'This dual process, in which the intellectual input, the transmission of the *Chasidic* ethos by means of ideas and teachings, is translated into activist organizational power, increasingly became part of the normative life of the *Chabbad* woman' (Loewenthal, 1990, p. 204).

Looking at the Lubavitch literature aimed at non-Orthodox women,

Bard (1990) observes its familiarity with basic feminist texts. She sees it as being naively sophisticated but warns that the effectiveness of the Lubavitch influence 'derives as much, if not more, from the way they operate and the type of structures they are infiltrating, as from what they are saying. They know how powerful is the image of a Jewish mother, her face and those of her ten children glowing in the light of the Sabbath candles' (p. 20).

Similarly, but from a less polemical stance, Rapoport-Albert (1988) notes Lubavitch's understanding of feminist concerns and terminology – relevant to potential converts who have been exposed to the 'critique of "patriarchy" in both its religious and secular manifestations' (p. 525). She, too, sees their skills in exploiting areas of overlap (for example, between the separatism of extreme feminism and the traditional separation of the sexes as practised in Orthodoxy); in redefining rites (the period of *niddah* becomes 'space for myself'); and in reclaiming festivals, such as Rosh Chodesh, as traditionally women's celebrations.

Remaining Orthodox

The methods may be unsubtle, but the attraction remains. Women are drawn to Orthodoxy and so far there has been relatively little defection from it (Tali Loewenthal, personal communication). Nor has there been significant defection from the ranks of those born Orthodox. But achieving and retaining a religious identity is by no means an easy process: it involves constantly facing up the 'anti-religious forces either outside or within the individual' (Loewenthal, 1988). Wolf (1982) describes the continued questioning for the Orthodox woman who values both selfless giving and self-fulfilment: 'I love my husband and kids, but I don't know who I am any more.'

Considering Orthodox women's responses to secular influences, Cohen-Nusbacher (1987) discusses Festinger's (1957) theory of cognitive dissonance. Conflict arises when people are faced with irreconcileable perspectives. Orthodox women, she suggests, deal with this conflict by rejecting or resisting modernity, or by taking in aspects selectively and 'compartmentalizing' the self. She describes the enormous strength of communal pressure to conform and concludes that, in this context, 'observance is a major part of the woman's self-definition'. Cohen-Nusbacher quotes Kaufman's (1984) study in which newly Orthodox women talk of their increased self-esteem, feeling their role imbued with dignity and importance, part of the spiritual sphere. It is a self-perception in great contrast to that of women in the secular world.

One woman describes what if feels like to change worlds:

I was twenty-seven. I had my career, my own flat, my friends. I was drawn always to bohemian people – artists and poets – yet all along I felt their values were not my values; one thing was that they didn't believe in fidelity.

Then my closest friend came to stay. I remember it so clearly: we went . . . to Crown Heights to see Purim. When I got there I saw a joy which was sobering, a beauty from which I felt excluded. During the evening I spoke to a young woman with a baby in her arms; she had a *tichul* [scarf] on her head. I guessed I knew her background: Orthodox – we make such assumptions – and couldn't believe it when she said 'Haight Ashbury'. She invited me back to their home for Shabbat . . .

Sometimes somebody breaks your *kali* [vessel] – your preconceptions. I was a 'hedonist'. My philosophy had been 'go out and try things and when the shoe fits wear it'. Till then I had not yet found a particular point of meaning.

Then my friend moved into Crown Heights and that was a bridge for me. I started learning more about Judaism; I learned about the concept of soul and that was the starting point. I had been searching for a meaning, a poetry in life and within Judaism I found a poetry which elevated: not a poetry which hurt, as there was in that bohemian world . . . I felt, in T. S. Eliot's phrase, 'I have measured out my life with coffee spoons.' Judaism asks you to do something very different, to stretch every aspect of yourself.

What clinched my Judaism? I was sent on a business trip to Brazil. People invited me to eat with them; the *kashrut* went by the wayside and I remember when I came back I had an argument with my father who said 'Judaism is not something which you turn on and turn off.' Later I was in Australia and was to fly to South Africa to meet the man who was to become my husband. The airline could offer me only a Saturday flight. I wouldn't take it, to fly on Shabbat. I went another route. The following year I became observant, I went to study and I became observant. . . .

There is part of me still which is existential, which asks where I should give my energies. I recognise the evil inclination within me which descends into the blackness. But also I see that I do not have to be the victim of experience; I can make the experience.

(Arlene (now Chana Shaindl) Sidelsky, in interview)

THE *BA'ALOT T'SHUVA*: WOMEN WHO 'RETURN' TO STRICT ORTHODOXY

While I was at University, studying Philosophy, I became very unhappy at the inconsistency between the ideals of these thinkers and the reality of their lives . . . I wanted to find a philosophy which was consistent with a way of life rather than an intellectual system that wasn't really working. It was this disquiet which made me look into Judaism deeper . . . I met my husband-to-be at about this time and he was religious. Then a Lubavitch emissary came from London and I responded very much to the Chabad philosophy. So, slowly, not without doubts and not without great upheaval in my whole life, I became committed. It took me about two years. It wasn't easy. It was opposed by my parents, but it seemed a way of life which made tremendous sense because . . . the action reflected the philosophy. . . . I have always been a spiritual person, looking higher and higher for some kind of spiritual satisfaction . . . Certainly it forced me to think at a far deeper level. And it just seemed to make a lot of sense in its ethic and its morality.

(Lynndy Levine)

Two interwoven themes run through women's reflections on becoming Orthodox. Whether they came from 'traditional' Judaism or from little or no religious involvement, their 'return' is to do with a renunciation of a lifestyle increasingly felt as being empty of real meaning and a search for values.

This '*ba'al t'shuva*' phenomenon is inspiring a 'literature of return' (Aviad, 1983; Kaufman, 1987; Danzger, 1989; Dansky, 1991) because, at a time of increasing 'marrying out' and defection from Judaism, to become Orthodox seems to be 'swimming against the tide'.

Usually there is not one particular catalyst which starts the process of 'return'; there are, rather, what Kate Loewenthal describes as 'inspirational experiences' (1988, p. 11) – a seemingly chance invitation to spend Shabbat with a religious family, a deep discussion with an Orthodox person who may later become a mentor. The change process is always a gradual one, a growing awareness; it involves a period of guided but individually-pursued learning and increasing observance. What is of particular significance is that this building of a new belief system occurs not only in the mind of the *ba'al t'shuva*; it occurs within a very relevant social context, the religious community.

Understanding why a person 'returns' is complex. Both Kaufman (1987) and Danzger (1989) suggest an approach similar to Weber's '*verstehen*' (interpretative understanding); one requires not the 'objectivity' of an observer (there is anyway a questionable assumption as to whether an observer is value-free); what is needed is a sensitivity to the perception of the 'returnee'. From the viewpoint of a sociologist, Max Weber defined motive as the *meaning* that appears to the actor as the reason for his or her conduct (in Mills, 1940, p. 906); it is not the same as the *cause* of the action. Discussing this, Danzger suggests that we cannot find a motive for a person's becoming *ba'al t'shuva*: 'we must look instead towards group affiliations... or past experiences... Situational factors strongly affect a person's actions... The stated motives of people are less explanations of their behaviour than rationalizations' (p. 224) – a view similar to that of Festinger (1962).

Orthodox family life seems to have a particular appeal for women. Kaufman (1987, pp. 60–3) is interested in this paradox: after all, 'the inviolable basis of authority for Orthodox Jews is *halachah*, the code of law which requires that women adhere to a legal system created, defined, and refined exclusively by males.' Yet many of the women who 'return' are intelligent and highly educated; some are well-versed in feminist thought and their former way of life was fully-integrated – often assimilated – into the wider, non-Jewish culture; even those coming from more 'traditional' backgrounds have worked and been very aware of the increasingly wider options open to women.

Kaufman notes that, irrespective of their early background, all the women in telling their stories convey their disenchantment with secular society, seen as masculine in its emphasis and lacking in real values. 'Ironically, it is through their return to a patriarchal tradition in Jewish orthodoxy that many... claim they are in touch with... the "feminine virtues" of nurturance, mutuality, family and motherhood.'

As later discussed, observing the Laws of Family Purity (*taharat hamishpacha*) is one of the Orthodox woman's central *mitzvot*. For the 'returnee', these laws are seen not in terms of a simplified feminist perspective, as men's controlling woman's sexuality; in contrast, they are experienced as an enriching of the relationship between husband and wife and as a heightening of the woman's sense of self. At the same time, Kaufman observes, they seem to symbolize a transcending of self and an almost mystical union with the entire community.

In many aspects of their lives – and probably most of all in their observing of the Laws of Family Purity – the Orthodox woman strongly feels herself as part of the shared world, the shared understandings of other women. Kupferman (1979) particularly comments on this:

> they had *space* as women – clearly demarcated areas where they reigned supreme; they knew they were as essential in the cosmological scheme of things as men – even as they peeled the potatoes they were making something happen in heaven; they had enormous support from one another; as they were all working towards a common goal, neighbours would not hesitate to babysit, or take in and feed another child; they had that enviable thing called '*Gemeinschaft*' – a community of like-minded people; they had rituals which gave them outlets for emotion . . . (p. 111).

Shulamit Firestone – although far from commenting on Orthodox Judaism – similarly described these separate male-female worlds: 'there exists a wholly different reality for men and women' (1979, p. 151).

One of the most interesting aspects of women who become Orthodox is their re-immersing of themselves in essentially feminine values within a patriarchal context *which they no longer feel the need to challenge*. In a strange way, it is as if, through religion, they are fulfilling the ideals of the 'second wave' of feminism (e.g. Gilligan, 1982; Miller, 1986); they are celebrating women's difference and esteeming in their own lives all that stems from maternal experience. They recognise that women are central to Orthodox living and this gives them a sense of worth; it dignifies what they do. They become part of 'a tradition with a moral ordering in which women play a fundamental role' (Kaufman, 1987, p. 62).

Kaufman sees this 'return' as comparable to the 'dialectic of tradition' described by feminist historians and anthropologists: a turning-away from the male-dominated, oppressive values of the wider society and 'a quest for revalued domesticity, an emphasis on their everyday lives as wives and mothers. . . the reclaiming of the autonomous values attached to women's community' (pp. 62 – 3).

The process of becoming religious is, of course, not unique to Judaism. Early studies of religious conversion (eg. Fromm, 1941) depict the convert as a person who fears the freedom offered by a secular society. That may be so, but Danzger (1989) sees many differences between the 'return' to Judaism and the 'rebirth' to Christianity. Firstly, Christianity requires belief primarily and ritual acts only secondarily, whereas becoming Orthodox in Judaism essentially involves *acts*, the performance of *mitzvot* (commandments). Secondly, Christian 'rebirth' requires a 'leap of faith', in Kierkegaard's terms (1953), whereas the performance of *mitzvot* does not necessarily involve decisions about ultimate values. Becoming Orthodox – although an individual choice – is above all else a process of becoming integrated into a community and a way of life. Yet another difference is the fact that Christianity is practiced primarily in church; in contrast, Judaism is practised mainly in the home; its meaning, its rituals and its understandings are learned by the *ba'al t'shuva* by living with an Orthodox family over a period of time.

Judaism is both an ethnic and a religious identity. The Jews are a people and a religion with a history of persecution. In fully taking on the religious aspect of his or her identity, the *ba'al t'shuva* is acknowledging a full acceptance of the apart-ness of the Jew from other people. To become Orthodox is to estrange oneself from the dominant culture and to embrace a different set of values, rituals and way of life.

Discussing how it happens, Danzger makes an important distinction between the Orthodoxy of the *ba'al t'shuva* and that of those Orthodox (*frum*) from birth (lightheartedly the former are known as the b.t.'s and the latter as the f.f.b's). Those born into it are socialized from infancy into a set of behaviours and beliefs which keeps them within the fold; in contrast, the *ba'al t'shuva* has no 'presocialized' attitudes: for him or her Orthodoxy is a matter of choice.

Interestingly, most of the *ba'al t'shuva* are not significantly different in terms of education and social class from the general Jewish population. Nor had they previously been 'seekers' of different religions or alienated from their families before turning to Orthodoxv.

The most striking aspect of the process of becoming Orthodox is that it takes place within the context of the Orthodox community. Danzger (p. 330) suggests that what holds the *ba'al t'shuva* is the 'plausibility structure' – the network of people sharing the belief system, in which the family is the central focus. Hence the desirability of the *ba'al t'shuva's* living in an Orthodox family over a period of time (equally a requirement to be fulfilled by the *halachically*-to-be-accepted convert).

Because community plays such an important role in anchoring Orthodox Jews, 'boundary-defining mechanisms' are central, and these are evident in a multiplicity of factors, of which residential area, style of dress, type of education are only a few of the most obvious. In fact, the Orthodox are defined in every aspect of their experience, from the way in which men and women relate to each other, right through to the most everyday forms of greeting – 'How are the children?' will have the reply: '*Baruch ha shem...*' ('Blessed be His name...'). The community becomes a social anchor for the *ba'al t'shuva*: if his or her commitment begins to wane, it encourages compliance; it recognises that the returnee wants to preserve the love and approval of the community's members.

The way in which a 'returnee' explains his or her becoming Orthodox often brings in intimate and early memories, but it also fits the values and perceptions of the community of which they are becoming a part. The *ba'al t'shuva* may, for example, recall a religious grandparent, evoking a special warmth from memories of the rituals. Feelings of attachment and of separation are often relevant – 'the threat of loss of attachment, by siblings who intermarry, parents who divorce or die' (Danzger). These conscious and unconscious emotions are given expression in the process of becoming religious for, whilst study is an important aspect, the learning of Orthodoxy is imbibed firstly by fulfilling the acts and then by learning about their basis; in other words, it has an experiential emphasis in keeping with the traditional Orthodox perspective of doing first and then evaluating the experience.

Danzger suggests that the newly Orthodox tend more often to be women. His finding is consistent with other writers' observations on women's affinity to the Orthodox emphasis on traditional and nurturing roles (Kaufman, 1987; Loewenthal, 1988). Marriage is often the route through which the woman becomes Orthodox. Within marriage she creates a religious home and it is religious observance which elevates her role in the home to a crucial and idealized one. Kate Loewenthal likens the process of becoming Orthodox to the developing of maturity in an Eriksonian sense (1956). From this perspective, the *ba'alot t'shuva* have evaluated conflicting options in their present and integrated them with values from the past: eventually they achieve an identity based on this integration and on a commitment to an ideology and an esteemed occupation – that of Jewish wife and mother (Loewenthal, 1988, p. 16).

Part III
Family Life

6 The Jewish Woman at Home

The mother brings up the child .... We're the safety harbour for our
children even when they leave home. Really for religious people it's
important the mother stays home.

(Orthodox woman)

I haven't seen myself as a Jewish mother and homemaker; there's
something too patriarchal and rigid in that. I've done it in a different
way. But I think my taking on a caring profession, taking on the needs
of others, is part of my Jewish identity.

(Liberal woman)

They seem to confirm stereotypes. But are the stereotypes right? Listening
to what women say suggests differently (Baker, 1990). In a study amongst
a group of Jewish women along a religious/non-religious continuum, surprisingly little evidence was found for the assumption that the more religious woman is more home-bound than her non-religious counterpart. But
what did emerge was the extent to which women along this con   .ium
found a way of harmonising the perceived expectations which others had
of them with their own hopes and expectations for themselves. 'Their
needs *are* my needs' was expressed by religious and non-religious alike; at
the same time, alongside this traditional attitude there was also ample evidence of both religious and non-religious women working and developing
careers outside the home.

In most cultures, the care-giving, nurturant, expressive role – the family
role – is allocated to the woman. Usually it carries lower status than the
man's traditional outside-the-family role. Yet the Jewish culture, unlike
most, esteems this home role. The family, and the woman's pivotal place
within it on which the practice of religion depends, is central to Judaism.
The day-to-day concerns of women may have the same discontinuities as
in other cultures but they retain a dignity coming from this religious
legacy:

always expecting to be interrupted, never finding full closure but
hastening from one activity to the next, watching her work come
undone as soon as it was completed ... [yet] in her own miniature
world, the woman was in charge ... the women's tasks are part of
living ... they continue through the life cycle ... their understandings
are a kind of underground culture ... and they knew that without what
they did there would be nothing and no one.   (Myerhoff, 1978).

Kupfermann similarly writes, 'they knew they were as essential in the cosmological scheme of things as men' (1979, p. 111).

But, of course, the rational response to this is to examine the indoctrination process and the internalization of this idealized role. This chapter therefore begins with a historical perspective suggesting the real significance of the Jewish mother's role for the continuity of the group.

How do women learn these family roles? The next section focuses on the 'apprenticeship' of a Jewish daughter and the intensity and ambivalence of the mother-daughter relationship in this cultural context. And what of the Jewish mother? She has defied all attempts at de-mystification; we shall consider the nature of the myth, both in humour and in the hidden-away recesses of family life. The mocking stereotype depicts the Jewish mother above all else as a provider of food. In fact, food plays a central part in religious observance, expressed in the dietary laws and the festive meals. But it also plays a symbolic role: for the group, in terms of cohesion, for the woman, often, in terms of confirmation of her sense of purpose. Finally, we shall look at the image of Jewish mothers as culture bearers and the way in which, over time, this responsibility has been redefined.

THE JEWISH FAMILY IN HISTORY

In the Bible and post-biblical literature, the wife and the home were seen as synonymous. In fact, rabbinic commentary in the *midrash*, which expands on the biblical text, likens the woman to a tent, all encompassing and indispensable. Yet, historically, the lives of Jewish women have always resembled those of women of other cultures and similar social standing living around them; one important difference is that Judaism is a religion practised above all within the family and it is in the family that the woman's religious role has always been crucial.

Heine described the family as the 'portable homeland' of the Jew and Hannah Arendt noted that 'family ties were among the most potent and stubborn elements with which the Jewish people resisted assimilation and dissolution' (both quoted in Kaplan, 1986). For a people who over the ages have been forced by persecution to be itinerant, who have had to settle in foreign cultures amid different religions, the family has always had a special significance. Jews looked to it to provide the roots and security they often lacked.

At the same time, Judaism has also always provided an ethnic identity (Herman, 1977) and over the generations what was distilled in the crucible of the family was what Myerhoff describes as a 'domestic religion', linking this ethnic experience with family ritual and Jewish cultural influences.

Whilst dispersion strengthened the need for family stability, it was the gradual secularization of society and the separation of home and work-place which presented new challenges. Jewish women have worked throughout history, for economic necessity has always modified traditional gender roles. The difficulty came not in their working but in men's taking over the breadwinner role. Whereas early immigrant women in Britain and America continued to work outside the home as they had in the *shtetls* of Europe, increasing affluence resulted in women's having to acquiesce to a redefinition of 'women's place'. Within the family they had a respected position but, ironically, they became more exclusively family-centred at the very time when structural changes in society could have opened the public sphere to them.

But a parallel factor re-emphasized their importance in the home for, as men began to defect from orthodox religious observance, their wives – who anyway had only a peripheral role in the synagogue – often continued the home observances. For women, religion has always been less formal-ized and much religious feeling which is preserved in family ritual is not necessarily expressed in socially observable conduct. Whilst men's rela-tionship to religion is equated with synagogue attendance and external compliance, such as not working on the Shabbat, women's religiousness is conveyed in their preserving a feeling of 'Jewishness' in the home, both in specific practices – the observance of the Shabbat, the festivals, the dietary laws – and in creating a way of life in which family cohesion remained their responsibility.

THE DAUGHTER'S APPRENTICESHIP

My mother would have condemned me in her heart if I hadn't married and had children. I think if your daughter doesn't want to have children, it somehow reflects on you as a mother. . . I can see why a mother imposes that on her daughter, the wish to have children: it confirms her as a mother.

(Reform woman, mother of three)

I don't in any way fit the Jewish ideal yet I was brought up to know I was Jewish and to be proud of it. My mother's parents scoffed at religion in Germany but still suffered anti-Semitism. My mother still remembers someone shouting 'You bloody Jews' and her father didn't defend them and she was horrified that they were powerless.

(Naomi Stadlen, in interview)

Psychoanalytic literature explains how daughters identify with their mothers (Eichenbaum and Orbach, 1983). The mother is, of course, the first love object and the primary care-giver to both the boy and the girl but, whilst the son must separate from his mother and identify with his father to become a man, the daughter unconsciously remains attached.

The mother-daughter relationship has a special quality. Firstly, a woman's sense of identity, as well as her view of her place in society, is largely shaped in response to her relationship with her mother, who is her earliest role model. And, secondly, as de Beauvoir (1953) suggests, the mother often unconsciously hopes to realise her own unfulfilled ambitions through her daughter.

Chodorow (1978) furthers these psychoanalytic understandings by discussing how prescribed gender roles, and attitudes to one's gender, are learned and internalized at a very young age within the family. The sense of gender is woven into the fabric of a child's earliest experience. However, the family serves another function too: it mediates the expectations of the external world, of both the particular culture and the larger society. It is a dynamic relationship: the particular culture influences and reinforces what is learned in the family and, through the family, it gives definitions for living.

For the Jews, a history of exile has made the family crucial to survival and, because of this, the mother's role has always been of central importance and conveyed strongly to her daughters. The historian Carol Smith-Rosenberg (in Rich, 1977, pp. 233–4) points out that 'as long as the mother's domestic role remained relatively stable and few viable alternatives competed with it, daughters tended to accept their mother's world'. Survival also dictated those norms and values selectively chosen and legitimated from the larger society: the ambitions and self-denial necessary for attaining economic success; the drive and independence instilled in the sons simultaneously with the contradictory expectations that they will not stray too far from family ties.

The family has always been the principal sphere of Jewish women but, although their public lives were circumscribed, it is important not to underestimate their influence on other family members and, through them, on the economy and the larger society.

Throughout, there are two contrasting perspectives on the Jewish mother and therefore on the messages she conveys to her daughters. The first observes the strength and resourcefulness of Jewish women throughout the ages. Historically, they worked and earned, they ran the home and raised and educated the children. In this way, they freed their husbands and sons from practical day-to-day responsibilities, enabling them to pray and study and involve themselves in the needs of the community. These women were facilitators. Yet a feminist analysis also comments on 'the centuries of injustice built into Jewish secular and religious traditions in which women carried the full burden of childcare and domestic obligationwhile being denied the spiritual and intellectual sastisfactions that challenged and supported their menfolk' (Roiphe, *Tikkun*, 1986, vol. 1, no. 2).

Coming to our own times, there are two legacies. Each shows Jewish women's response first to economic need and then to fundamentally changing attitudes. Whilst early immigrant women worked outside the home, their more established sisters, both in the States and in Britain – the more educated, upper-middle-class Jewish women – channelled their energies into philanthropic work (Baum et al, 1975; Burman, 1986).

However, with increasing affluence and men's increasing defection from the religious world, the role of breadwinner became more widely a male prerogative and responsibility. The result was that the daughters of the working immigrant women matured with a very different set of expectations from those of their mothers. It was no longer a necessity for them to contribute to the family income, therefore it was no longer deemed appropriate for them to work outside the home after marriage. As their family needs lessened and they had more time, then they also took on voluntary work within the community.

Whilst the idealized picture depicts both the earlier working woman and her homemaking daughter as fulfilled in their allotted roles (Kobler, 1953; Brayer, 1986; Ghatan, 1986), there is also much written on the paradoxically confining effect of affluence on the scope of the woman's roles and the consequent under-development of her potential (Koltun, 1976; Rich, 1977; Heschel, 1983; Schneider, 1985; Kraemer, 1989).

But the last twenty years has been a time of change for all women; traditional roles and expectations have been questioned and often re-thought and Jewish women, too, have been affected by this ferment (Schlesinger, 1984; Cohen-Nusbacher, 1987; Baker, 1990).

Stereotypes abound, but founded on reality. The 'image of the "*yidishe mama*", the peace-making Jewish mother, pivot of domestic unity (and psychoanalytic preoccupation)' is attributed by Webber (1983) to the early immigrant generation. It was this woman's daughter who inherited all the aspirations of the self-denying immigrant parents. But the daughter, freed from the need to earn, was in a different way inhibited in her development; she was held back by the then prevailing emphasis on motherhood to the exclusion of virtually all else. As a result, she was forced to live through her husband and children. Not until the generation of daughters which followed did the real struggle begin for wider options, a struggle often causing conflict between these women's perceptions of traditional values and their desire to forge a new identity for themselves (Baker, 1990). It may take still more time to find the right, finely-balanced equilibrium but there is a backlash:

> The new generation of Jewish women in business and the professions is accused of being responsible for the low birth rate, the high divorce rate and trouble in the Jewish family. What do critics want? – A Jewish woman who has education but stays home? It seems like a simple case of entrapment.
>
> (Roiphe, 1986, pp. 70–5)

Howard Cooper (1991), whilst acknowledging the strength and tenacity of Jewish family ties, asks 'at what cost?' He suggests that 'the outer fragmentation . . . is a reflection of a deeper, inner loss' (p. 5). In examining the rates of family breakdown and marrying 'out' he finds disturbing evidence of the gulf between the idealized picture and the reality. For the traditional requirements of Orthodox Judaism, whilst restricting options, had given direction; 'they were a source of nourishment and personal affirmation' (p. 13). Greater freedom has given wider choices but has also led to a sense of anomie; there is a recurring conflict between an illusion of freedom and an unconscious desire for continuity.

Looking historically, Cooper hypothesizes that the working immigrant mother, whilst providing economically, impoverished her daughters. The daughters, the post-war mothers, gave up work to become the mothers whom they had never had – available. But they were needy in a different way: "they had few inner resources to draw upon as to what 'good mothering' might mean" (p. 18) The sons of the immigrant generation similarly lacked a role model who could adequately equip them, for their fathers had been preoccupied with their own and their family's survival or were otherwise remote, religious, other-wordly figures.

'Once again, the children would be the hope' (p. 18) and Cooper examines the legacy of expectations which these children of the post-war parents had to carry, a legacy passed on to the later generations – the necessity to 'make good', always trying to please a self-denying, judgemental internalized parent. His thesis is a feasible one but, as with Freudian theory, it is largely formulated on the understandings gained from pathology. For

Cooper is both a Reform rabbi and a psychotherapist and, inevitably, many of his conclusions must be impressionistic.

The legacies, however, are real and complex. They are first of all the legacies of the Holocaust – six million dead enshrined as part of the collective unconscious. And possibly part of this suppressed memory still expresses itself symbolically in the men's seemingly relentless drive for security and success, a conscious bid to safeguard the future.

But there are other, conflicting pressures, too, for the Jewish family is both enabling and disabling; in their expectations of their children, parents strive to quell their own inner neediness. Despite all their apparent success there seems to be a continued awareness in the generation now at mid-life of these emotional issues:

> I can still hear my mother ranting; our poverty was like a dirge, a lament. I knew I'd have to marry someone who could earn. Money became a curse.
>
> (Sixty-year old woman; mother, counsellor)

> My mother was a very positive person and overwhelmed me. I'm still struggling to come out from under her shadow. To this day she can only define success in material terms, so that she still can't recognise that I am doing anything of any value . . . I still feel the need to prove myself to her.
>
> (Researcher; wife of Liberal rabbi; mother)

Yet a generation on, and no longer overshadowed by their parents' survival needs, Jewish daughters now negotiate a new set of seemingly incompatible demands. Firstly, they are aware of their own wider potential in the context of peer-group expectations regarding career success – expectations encouraged by mothers in all but the Orthodox world. But alongside this is a persistently repeated message that they will marry and have children. It is a message which subversively redefines 'career' to mean 'job – and flexible enough to fit around family needs.' They are in a classic 'double bind' situation (Bateson 1956), a situation not unique to Jewish women in the modern world, confronted with two mutually exclusive sets of expectations, presented simultaneously but on different levels of communication. The dilemma is vividly illustrated in a discussion amongst a group of Sephardi women. An Iraqi mother and daughter were speaking:

> *Mother*: We give our children education; this is the one thing that cannot be taken away from them. I made sure my daughter had a profession. I had an education but not a career. A career wasn't possible – only poor women worked – and I was frustrated.

Daughter (stockbroker): The way we are brought up is dependent on the frustrations and expectations of our mothers. It is what my mother unconsciously wanted for herself.

Mother: My daughter says she must succeed for me!

Daughter: She says she brought me up that I could mix marriage and career but, in fact, she told me to get a career and she also told me to be a wife and a mother. I feel as if I am in the middle; there's what non-Jewish society tells me I can do and there's what Jewish society tells me I should do.

Iranian woman: The problem today is that the woman has an undefined role; she must make the role for herself. It depends on her background, her husband, etc. Women are lucky now that they have options and they are unlucky because they have conflict. Only a very wise woman can manage a career without antagonizing her husband. My husband expects me to be a good housewife, to create a home of elegance. At the same time, I should be available to bring this and that for him to the office. And if the children do anything wrong – whose fault is that? Economic power is what matters even today.

Egyptian woman: Leaving work undermines one's confidence; I gave up work when I had kids. It undermined me. I had no idea what the implications would be. When I thought I could return, I had no confidence left. I wasn't encouraged to return and I needed that encouragement.

Iranian woman: If you're a working woman, you're always compensating for guilt. When I went to work, there were commiserations. The feeling was that if I had to work, as long as I could get home quickly for the children and my husband, then so be it. When I was working full-time, I used to stay up till 2 a.m. compensating for being out at work.

So what is this Jewish mother love with its accompanying guilt? Cassie Cooper (1988) suggests that

> Jewish parents long to be seen as understanding parents and, in order to buy their love, the child has to go along with this creation.... Such parents have scant respect for themselves ... To be a good Jewish child in these terms is not to be a child. Instead, the 'children of projection' grow up quickly to become in turn the mothers, friends, comforters, advisers and supporters of their own mothers. Sometimes this is to take

over the care of other children, to throw themselves between their parents to save a marriage, to provide ... academic achievement, money, ... anything, anything for the love of one's mother. (pp. 12–13).

From a Kleinian perspective, Cooper explains how the infant needs to see its mother as all-good. Bad feelings must be split off, for neither mother nor child can accept them; after all, the mother had denied her own anger. But the daughters, too, are needy and their needs 'can only be assuaged temporarily ... in motherhood' (p. 15).

The maternal role cannot, of course, be considered in isolation. Jewish feminists and psycho-analysts see the ambiguous image of the Jewish father and suggests he both fears and envies woman's creativity (Heschel, 1983; Pirani, 1988). Roith (1988) similarly claims that Freud had to depict woman as inadequate in order to reverse the intolerable reality of the all-powerful Mother from whom the son cannot separate. The possibility is that this religion and culture which is male-defined silences women's authentic voices and denies adequate expression to women's most profound experience – that of bearing a child and giving birth – for it is significant that there is no ceremony in Orthodox Judaism in which the woman celebrates giving birth, nor one celebrating the birth of a daughter.

Pirani (1988), from her clinical experience, describes women's persistent guilt feelings which 'derive from men's expectations and rejections ... Mothers and daughters will collude in maintaining their inferior position, constantly ready to feel guilty and then use guilt subtly to control their men' (p. 54). When the archetypal all-giving, overfeeding, smothering mother and care-giver reverses the stereotype it is to male roles that she turns – the business woman, the organizer, the intellectual-academic. These, Pirani suggests, are 'daughters of the patriarch', either trying to please the internalized powerful father or becoming what the father failed to be – educated, effective, affluent.

I think the Jewish religion psyches a woman out. It separates her from her own needs. She always has to be a helpmate to the man. He never is for her. Many of women's roles are to do with being a good wife and mother. Look at what obituaries of women often say – 'she was a good wife and mother.' How many obituaries of men say that?

(Orthodox woman, mother of five)

MYTHS

Myths and stereotypes: Do they reflect reality or are they exaggerated forms of reality? The dictionary defines a myth in three ways: it is fictional; it embodies popular ideas about reality; it has symbolic meaning. Myths may become stereotypes, images constantly repeated without change. They actually have a purpose; they give concrete form to attitudes and beliefs and, by doing so, they help to preserve the status quo. In a strange sort of way they are needed by those who believe in them. Webber's earlier-quoted observation that 'women's very perception of their Jewish identity is concerned with the domestic world' (1983, p. 147) is similar to the biological myth which sees woman as primarily mother. But feminist writers are now challenging these stereotypes and asking whether they are really description or prescription (Janeway, 1972).

In fact, as discussed in Chapter Two, the woman in Jewish tradition has always been portrayed with great diversity; primarily she is mother but economic reality has frequently given her an important role in the public sphere. Similarly, throughout literature she has been depicted as both frivolous and worthy (Heschel, 1983). Historically, the image of the Jewish woman as matriarch prevailed, with her power base not only in the home but also in the world outside. Ironically, the over-protective martyr image (and the reality, see Bart in Koltun 1976 writing on depression in Jewish mothers) developed not in relation to women who struggled and toiled to ensure their family's economic survival. It came, paradoxically, as a consequence of affluence for, as men took over the economic role, the sign of their success was their no longer needing their wives to earn. Rich suggests that, in the absence of other challenging uses for her energy, 'the full-time homemaker sank into the overinvolvement, ... the possessive control, the chronic worry over her children, caricatured in fiction as the Jewish mother' (1977, pp. 235–6). And behind the caricature there was often real sadness; there was the hungry Jewish mother so poignantly described by Erika Duncan (1983), who was fearful of 'the drowning into needing and being needed' (Olsen, 1956, p. 92).

The martyr represents the self-effacement associated with the traditionally over-loving mother, whose primary role is to nurture, literally and metaphorically. The matriarch, in contrast, represents the power – a power both respected and feared. They are two aspects of the same reality.

The Jewish woman has traditionally acquired merit through her men. In the world of Orthodoxy, her place in heaven was assured if she facilitated Torah study for her husband and sons. In the secular world, she remains the enabler, encouraging her husband's endeavours and implanting her sons' ambitions. Freud held that a mother could transfer to her son the ambition which she had been forced to suppress in herself. She had little 'formal' power or status, yet within her own household she reigned supreme. The psychoanalyst, Estelle Roith (1988), writes : 'Lacking real power in the outside world, the Jewish woman made sure that she ruled the roost. Thus was born the great Matriarch.' And in the stereotype of the matriarch, the giving of food becomes synonomous with the giving of love, just as in the stereotype of the martyr, the giving of guilt becomes synonymous with the giving of self.

A sad little folk tale tells of the young man who runs to his mother and begs for her heart which his fiancée wants as a gift. She plucks it from her chest and, as he runs off with it, he falls and the heart breaks in two. 'Have you hurt yourself, my son?' she asks.

Like many fables, it is an overstatement of a partially accurate observation, for myths are composite pictures which focus on only certain characteristics of members of a group. Myths about women are nearly always created by men. They either exaggerate or, alternatively, negate an often feared or envied reality. In the seemingly contradictory myths of matriarch and martyr, the reality is woman's power as creator. Rubin (1979), analysing myths, suggests that the group which is denigrated is, in fact, feared – 'a threat to be contained' Within men, 'there are always the unconscious infantile memories of woman as all-powerful, giving and witholding her nurturing breast. Men must palliate those archaic fears by rendering woman powerless in the world of daily experience' (p. 71).

Elizabeth Janeway makes a parallel point. In her study *Man's World, Woman's Place* (1972), she writes that every positive role has a negative side, a shadow role. Negative roles support the status quo just as positive ones do; the positive ones are promises, the negative ones, threats. Jung also describes man's image of woman as two-sided: on the hand she is the pure, the good, the goddess-like figure; on the other hand, she is the seductress or the witch.

In challenging the stereotypes of women, Jewish feminists have reclaimed the legend of Lilith (Heschel, 1983; Pirani, 1991). She is the shadow side of Eve; Lilith is the woman who would not be dominated. 'The polar images of mother as nourisher and smotherer in contemporary fiction parallel the twin female figures of the *Shekhinah* and Lilith found in ancient and medieval Jewish sources. Lilith is the demon woman... The *Shekhinah*, in contrast, is the gentle loving presence of God...' (Heschel, p. 7). Both, of course, are myths, symbolic of the two faces of woman in a male view of the world. They reveal not who women really are, but how women are made to appear and function from a male perspective.

How are these myths propagated? In our own times, through literature, film and humour. A recent analysis of 'Jewish mother jokes' (Rothbell, 1986) sees the mothers as having three characteristics: (a) they attempt to dominate their sons; (b) they create dependency; (c) by their martyrdom, they instil guilt feelings.

> This control through dependency and guilt then supposedly allows Jewish mothers to manipulate their sons into ... becoming 'my son, the doctor'. The Jewish mother can then bask in the reflected glory of her son's achievements, while he spends his money on visits to the psychiatrist because his mother has made him crazy.
>
> (Rothbell, p. 123, in Cohen and Hyman, 1986)

Interestingly, the jokes are created and disseminated by Jewish men, by humorists, novelists and psychologists, and they reinforce the popular image of the Jewish mother. The psychiatrist, Theodore Reik (1962) explains. 'It is as if Jewish mothers tried to make the nutritional symbiosis of babyhood, and with it the dependence of their children on them, permanent' (in Rothbell, p. 123).

Roiphe (1986) believes that the stereotype describes a woman whose own creative energies have been stunted, misdirected, misused and wasted. 'Blocked of opportunities, she can only be a reflector.' She sees these jokes as a symptom of gender hostility. 'What is funny ... tells us also what we hate and what we fear. The Jewish male is afraid of the mother who might control his very life ... He also feels guilt ... for the sacrifices she has made for him. He wants to grow away.'

In literature, too, parallel themes can be found and possibly no caricature has provoked as much discussion as Phillip Roth's Mrs Portnoy. Bruno Bettelheim – in 'Portnoy Psychoanalyzed' (1969) – writes "Portnoy's complaint is that his mother's love for him is too overpowering, that she never lets him alone ... Yet whatever she does for him is not enough; he always wants more ... she is not permitted to have a life of her own.' Similarly, in the cinema, Erens (1984) sees the contradictory images of the suffocating and simultaneously over-demanding Jewish mother from whom the son must somehow, not always successfully, free himself.

How different is the reality? Does she exist, this Jewish mother who gives her all to her son, who imposes on him her high aspirations, who conveys to him that she herself is worth little, that her needs should be subordinated to his? As always, within the stereotype there is some truth for, whilst being a mother conveys a sense of worth in a way that few other experiences can do, being 'only' a mother can deprive a woman of a sense of self (Bart, 1976). The possibility is that these contradictions reflect an ambivalence within society – within male-defined society – about motherhood. For motherhood is simultaneously both idealized and given little formal status. Yet within Judaism, the apologists emphasize, the mother's work is held in such high esteem that she is exempt from most of the time-bound positive commandments incumbent on men (Plaskow, p. 225 in Heschel, 1983; Meiselman, 1978). Certainly, too, Jewish literature is filled with songs of praise to her virtue. But when the full-time Jewish mother is no longer needed as the everlasting nourisher, she is at risk of continuing to inhabit an obsolete role (Bart, 1976). The role which offered her early definitions for living may leave her very vulnerable at mid-life.

Of course it is not in being a mother that a woman risks her identity; it is in being a mother to the exclusion of all else (Dally, 1982). The predicament is not unique to Jewish women; it is a predicament of a generation which was privileged with affluence. Today, economic necessity, social change and feminism remove that particular dilemma but present their own problems to a generation of younger women.

FOOD

Chicken soup was the love-offering that solved everything.

(Cooper, 1991)

The giving – and receiving – of food is often unconsciously invested with emotional significance; symbolically it becomes intertwined with the giving of love. In the Jewish context, at the heart of this is the 'Yiddishe mama', stereotypically 'precoccupied with food, urging her children to eat and interpreting their refusal as a rejection of love' (Myerhoff, 1978, p. 225). Barbara Myerhoff, the social anthropologist, suggests that, in terms of the woman's role, it evokes her dominant function as a caregiver. 'Denial of this function is equivalent to denying her the major source of identity and self-esteem' (p. 225).

The ritual and the symbolic meaning of Jewish food is a subject of enormous complexity for 'food never exists in its own right. It comes in a context – social and cultural' (Myerhoff). Two aspects of Jewish food are the dietary laws and the celebratory meals. The dietary laws are an important part of Orthodox observance and, because Judaism is very much a home-based religion, the meals celebrating the weekly Shabbat and all the festivals carry significance – even for the non-Orthodox – in terms of family togetherness.

This section of the chapter therefore first studies the dietary laws and their underlying effect. It then discusses the role of food in family ritual observance. In this context, what is often overlooked is that the preparing and giving of food, probably more than any other task, emphasizes a family orientation in which little role exists for the single woman, except as a child.

Dietary Laws

For the observant Jew, *halacha* is truth set forth in terms of action in this world. Strict adherence to the dietary rules – the rules of *kashrut* – possibly more than any other observance, singles out and separates the Orthodox from both the non-observant and the non-Jew. The dietary laws were first set out in the Bible as given by God to Moses. The basis for prohibited and approved foods appears in Leviticus XI and these foods are codified in the Table of Laws, the *Shulchan Aruch* vol. 1, XLVI. The Jew may eat only *kosher* (i.e. permitted) foods, which are then prepared according to very strict rules, also specified in the *Shulchan Aruch*. Forbidden foods are known as *t'refah*.

Meat may come only from an animal which has cloven hooves and which chews the cud, hence the prohibition of pork. Permitted animals must be ritually slaughtered in a manner which is regarded as the most humane, after which the meat must be soaked and salted (*kashered*) to draw out any remaining blood. The particular method of slaughter and the subsequent *kashering* process derives from Leviticus XVII, 11 and 12, forbidding the eating of blood, for blood is seen as the life of the flesh.

Regarding food preparation, there are many and complex requirements. One of these derives from the injunction in Exodus XXIII, 19, Exodus XXXIV, 26 and again in Deuteronomy XIV, 21: 'Thou shalt not seethe (cook) a kid in its mother's milk'. Later commentaries on the Bible enlarged on this concept to forbid the use of milk products and meats in the same meal. As a result, a kosher kitchen becomes two separate domains, one for meat and one for milk, with a whole set of different dishes, pans, cutlery, bowls and other utensils. There is, of course, also a neutral *parev* category of foods, containing neither milk nor meat.

In addition to the specific or implied Biblical prohibitions, many of the early laws – for example, the distinctions between clean and unclean animals, birds and seafood – are traceable to measures for the preservation of health in ancient Palestine (London and Bishov, 1952). But even today, when these health considerations are no longer relevant, the dietary laws retain for the observant Jew meaning and significance in their application.

For Judaism is 'an intricate and committed way of life rather than merely a theologized set of intellectual beliefs and it is only in the fulfilment of the religious law, with both its positive and its negative commandments, that the inner, intuitive life of the Jew is formed' (Stavroulakis, 1986, p. 9).

Responsibility for the full observance of the dietary laws in the home is, of course, the woman's, for it is she who makes a *kosher* home. In this, her role encompasses not only the everyday cooking but especially the preparation of meals for the Shabbat and festivals, each with its specific requirements and traditional foods. In the fulfilment of the dietary laws and in the providing of the daily and the celebratory meals the woman has always been crucial. Little wonder then that the kitchen and the home could become the focus of her activity. Traditionally, this focus has been portrayed as a source of pride and dignity. Inevitably it must also have confined her creativity (Duncan in Heschel, 1983; Cooper, 1991). Being denied the kind of education obligatory for her brothers, the woman's intellectual capabilities were concentrated on a task often considered menial in other communities but of supreme importance in Judaism.

Whilst feminists and psychotherapists warn that the woman is impoverished by an overemphasis on her constantly-giving-to-others role, writers such as Kupferman (1976), Myerhoff (1978), Stavroulakis (1986) and Rose (1989) depict this central role as being also an enriching one. Rose comments that, because food has always played a major role in Jewish home-based ritual, 'Jewish women have had to spend more time in the kitchen, and have therefore concentrated more thought and accumulated more folk knowledge than any other parallel group' (1989, p. 5). Much emphasis was placed on food in the Bible and the Talmud. Subsequently, particularly during the Middle Ages, it was one of the few pleasures available to Jewish families. The ability to cook was traditionally considered as being as important as a good dowry and, 'if both cooking and dowry came together, it was the best *shidduch* [match] of all!' (p. 6)

I spend far more time in the kitchen than I should; it's not demanded of me; it's just conditioning.

(Traditionally observant mid-life woman)

In our own day, how a woman feels about her role in relation to food is a very subjective matter. Many – not only the Orthodox – see their ability to maintain a Jewish home, especially expressed in terms of food, as giving a particular meaning to their lives. Lingering awhile in the kosher shops – the butcher, fishmonger, baker, delicatessen – on a Thursday or a Friday morning or on the days preceding a festival, one becomes very aware that the women as they bustle about buying and chatting have a real sense of their value and dignity. Similarly in their homes, even if the minutiae of the dietary laws are not followed, they convey to their family a feeling of Jewishness which is informal and personal. It is this, even in the absence of Orthodoxy, which becomes the often unconsciously internalized cultural message. But how this message is received and expressed depends also on the individual family dynamics.

One final point needs making about the dietary laws: fully observed they effectively ensure the Jew's separation from the non-Jew. Being prevented from dining together, the likelihood is lessened of other social mingling and, above all, of intermarriage.

Probably in no other religious or ethnic tradition do the requirements relating to food occupy a more important place. For the Jewish people, influenced originally by Biblical prohibitions and mandates, certain dishes and ways of cooking become associated with the Shabbat and with particular festivals. And, of course, the cookery of a people, like all other aspects of its culture, is a reflection of its history.

Food for Shabbat

Come into my kitchen on any Friday afternoon. Shabbat begins at sundown, so in winter you must come early. What will you feel? First of all, a sense of expectation, a home waiting for something special. Then, the aromas; yes, of course, the proverbial chicken soup, and fish, and apples and cinnamon: a medley of fragrances which tell you a little about Jewish cooking and a little about *Shabbat shalom,* a peaceful Shabbat. What else? A white-clothed table, candles, *challot* (the two special Shabbat breads); in the corner, a hot water urn, turned low. An idealized picture, naive? An Orthodox home? No. An ordinary traditional family, mine – with a peaceful Shabbat by no means guaranteed (after all, Howard Cooper has challenged the myth of untroubled Jewish family life) – but a home in which there is an expectation of a family's pausing awhile from all their activities. On Shabbat, I don't cook, we don't drive, we don't work. We have time to sit as a family and talk and eat together.

The amount of variation in observance is considerable. The Orthodox ideally keep everything from the beginning of the Shabbat on Friday until its conclusion one hour after Saturday's sunset. It is a day of rest, set apart from the working week. In terms of domesticity, no cleaning, washing, shopping or cooking may be done, nor may gas or electricity be used unless they are pre-set and then used only for keeping warm already-cooked food. The housewife is therefore involved before the Shabbat in considerable preparation. At the other end of the spectrum, even in non-observant homes the woman may still make a special Friday evening meal in the hope that husband and children will spend this time together.

Whilst the range of observance has been discussed earlier, an idea of Shabbat food depends on an understanding of religious requirements and shared traditions within the context of specific cultural backgrounds. For this understanding, the Orthodox ideal is presented with the realisation of variation from it.

Shabbat is a day so holy that the rabbis have said that the other days of the week were created for its sake, so that we could fully appreciate its joy and rest. Amongst the rules for its observance are those forbidding the kindling of fire and the undertaking of any work. Therefore all shopping and cooking must be completed before it begins, which influences the type of cooking done. On Shabbat, as on all days of great rejoicing, three complete meals must be eaten and the different types of foods created for these usually relates to the Ashkenazi or Sephardi origins of the woman.

Traditional foods will either be those which can be eaten cold – chopped liver or *gefilte* fish, followed by chicken or meat with salads and then, maybe, strudel is a fairly typical Ashkenazi summer meal – or those which can be left in a slow oven from the beginning of Shabbat on Friday until lunch on Saturday. The classic dish, an incidental reminder of poor people's cooking when simple ingredients were made tempting, is *cholent*. Deriving from the cold countries of Eastern Europe, its main ingredients are beans, potatoes, onions, a large dumpling and a little meat. Just as Ashkenazi food may include *borscht* from Russia, *kishkas* from Poland and a dozen ways of cooking carp, Sephardi food equally draws on recipes from many lands – Spanish, Portuguese, Moroccan, Turkish, Iraqui, Iranian. It tends to be sweeter than Ashkenazi food and make more use of spices. In both, though, the characteristic is that it is labour-intensive cooking, deriving from a time when families were relatively poor and the housewife substituted her time and energy for the lack of rich ingredients.

There are cookbooks galore on Shabbat and festival foods, a folklore handed down from mother to daughter in all the lands of the dispersion. They tell of the culinary ingredients. What they cannot know is how much variation from the religious ideal there will always be. Maybe these are the tacit understandings.

Food for Festivals

The celebratory meals contain within them symbolic reference to the religious or historic meaning of the festival. On the major festivals they must, as on Shabbat, fulfill the *halachic* requirements of being prepared in advance. It is the festive meals, above all, which emphasize the family-based aspect of Judaism and the woman's role in maintaining this. Inevitably, therefore, whilst feminism questions the fairness of this time-hallowed responsibility, the day-to-day reality again highlights how disadvantaged in this respect is the woman without a family. The unmarried or childless woman, the separated, divorced or widowed, unless she is part of an aware and caring community, will frequently feel excluded from this most central aspect of any festival. It is a curious paradox; the very demands which so erode a woman's time and energies simultaneously give her an awareness of herself as the pivot of family life and of religious observance.

A description of the special preparations for each different festival is in itself a subject for a book. Of them all, the one which in its requirements always overwhelms the woman – and the more religiously exacting she is, the more overwhelmed she will be – is Passover. But before embarking on this weighty topic – the preparations are so demanding that even a description of them needs pause for breath! – let us savour just a hint of the traditional foods and their festive significance.

The year begins with Rosh Hashana, the New Year, when Jews pray for happiness in the year to come. It is a two-day festival in which the foods symbolize sweetness, welcomed in with blessings over wine and then over apples and honey; the apples are the sweet-sour reality of life, the honey the hoped-for sweetness of the year to come, a theme recurring in all the New Year foods such as honey cake (*lekach*) or carrots cooked with sultanas and brown sugar (*zsimmes*).

Yom Kippur, the Day of Atonement, the holiest day of the Jewish year, comes ten days later. It is a fast day, hence the evening meal after which it begins is one of solemnity; this meal must make fasting possible and has no salty or highly spiced foods. Twenty-five hours later the fast ends with the blessings repeated for a good New Year, again over wine, apples and honey. Of all the festivals, Yom Kippur is the one which, even for the usually non-observant Jew, carries with it the deepest inner meaning. The coming together of a family after a day of prayer in which everyday concerns are somehow transcended imprints a special feeling on the meal with which the fast is ended.

There follows Succoth, its name deriving from the biblical injunction that, during this pilgrim festival, Jews should dwell for eight days in tabernacles, huts with makeshift walls and a roof of branches. Decorating the *succah* with leaves and fruit is a family task and the foods eaten during Succoth convey the harvest symbolism of the festival, strudel especially combining the themes of sweetness and plenty.

At the end of this group of autumn festivals is Simchat Torah, celebrating the completed reading of the Scrolls of Law and its new beginning. The festival's traditional meal pictorially represents the scrolls – holishkes, rolled cabbage leaves, stuffed with meat and rice and simmered in rich, sweet gravy, and its Sephardi equivalent rolled in grape vine leaves.

Throughout the year the festivals have their family meals and symbolic foods. In winter there is Chanukah, with doughnuts or potato pancakes (*latkes*) which, by their cooking, are reminders of the oil which miraculously lasted eight days, when the Jews rededicated the Temple in Jerusalem after its desecration by the Greeks. Spring has Tu B'Shevat, celebrating the blossoming of trees, when all types of fruits are eaten. Later comes Purim, when the downfall of the tyrant, Haman, is remembered in *hamantaschen* (Haman's pockets!), triangular poppy-seed filled pastries. Shavuoth commemorates the giving of the Law to Moses and is also the time of the wheat festival in Israel, a land flowing with milk and honey and, in all the lands of the disperion, Shavuoth has been traditionally celebrated with dairy foods – cheese cake and cheese pancakes (*blintzes*), or the Sephardi delicacies, *bougatsas* or *kassates* – for the Law is likened to milk.

Passover
If men had to make Pesach it would be simplified!

(Observant woman)

Above all others, in terms of the woman's role, is Passover, *Pesach*. It is an eight-day festival infused with symbolism and significance which celebrates the freeing of the Jewish people from slavery in Egypt and their flight through the wilderness. They fled from Egypt in haste and the bread they were baking remained unleavened. Over 2,000 years later Jews the world over still commemorate this flight to freedom. Symbolically, it is remembered by the eating of only unleavened bread (*matzah*) during the whole festival. No foods containing anything which is leaven (i.e. which has risen through fermentation) are permitted.

That, in itself, would be simple. The requirement, however, is that the whole house be cleansed before the festival of anything leavened (*chometz*). In theory, even that should be simple; it sounds, after all, like a good spring clean. But there is more; lest any fragment of *chometz* may adhere to cooking utensils, to crockery and cutlery, it must all be changed. The observant Jewish home is required to have two sets of everything – pots and pans, everything. However poor the household, the Orthodox Jew changes everything except that which may be soaked for a specified period, such as glassware, or which may be burned in a flame after scouring, such as tureens with no separate handle (which might harbour leaven).

Nor is that all. The removal of leaven is seen in symbolic terms. The 'spring clean' is not confined to rooms in which during the year meals have been eaten. It must take place in every room. Every cupboard, shelf and drawer in every room has to be dusted and cleaned and scoured.

There is a hymn, '*dayenu*', that is sung during the *Seder*, the Passover festive meal. It gives thanks for all that God did for the Jews in their redemption from Egypt; *dayenu* means 'that would have sufficed'. It is more than likely that the observant housewife thinks 'this would have sufficed' as she undertakes the massive preparations which must be completed before she can even begin the cooking and baking of the special *Pesach* foods and of the two festive meals, the Seder meals, with which Passover begins. Many observant women begin this 'scouring' of the house a month before Passover; they begin after Purim. Often they become so overwhelmed by the work involved – particularly in the final week when the whole kitchen has to be meticulously cleaned and scrubbed, seals around fridges and cookers scraped, surfaces scalded then covered with foil – that they lose sight of its spiritual feeling:

> I sat at the *Seder* table and I wanted to contribute – a story, some thoughts about *Pesach* – and I realised I hadn't had a moment to sit down before then and reflect.
>
> (Young wife at her own *Seder* table)

On the eve of the festival, the man of the house – he who has not done the cleaning – performs a symbolic final act of cleansing, the 'search for *chometz*'. It is a search by candlelight in which he gathers up with a feather a few crumbs, to be burned early the next morning, and pronounces a blessing.

> One of the strongest memories of my childhood was all the work for *Pesach* and then, *erev Pesach*, in comes my father who looks around, sees that everything is done and makes a blessing! I likened him to the Egyptian taskmaster and we, the women, were the slaves.
>
> (Asphodel Long, feminist writer, 'secular' Jew)

Chaim Bermant, a perceptive chronicler of the Jewish world, wryly observes:

> Their onslaught on the kitchen is particularly merciless ... They savage the cupboards, fall upon tiles and floorboards with a knife, purge sinks with boiling water, disembowel their ovens, and all but immolate themselves .... Then there is the cooking and the baking, the roasting

and the grilling, the steaming and the frying, as they prepare, not for a meal, or even two meals, but for a siege. . . .

When the family sits down to the *Seder* the men, according to tradition, are kings, and the women, in theory at least, queens, but they function as serving maids, so that when the king has to wash his hands his womenfolk bring a jug, basin and towel to the table. They also, of course, bring on the *kneidlech* [dumplings], and ladle out the soup, and when the repast is over they clear up and wash up, and that is the limit of their participation. . . .

According to tradition, we were liberated from slavery by virtue of our women – and we now celebrate the occasion annually by making them slaves.

(*Jewish Chronicle*, 1.4.88, p. 26)

The *Seder* meals require special symbolic foods and, more than at any other festival, the service around the family table has many beautiful and elaborate customs, with variations coming from the different cultures of origin. At the head of the table will be placed three whole *matzos* covered with a napkin. Beside them will be a *Seder* plate on which are placed a roasted egg, a roasted shankbone, a dish of *charoses* (a mixture of nuts, apple and wine), some horseradish and bitter herbs, a bunch of parsley, a bowl of salt water. Each has its meaning: the egg is a symbol of the freewill festival offering brought to the Temple; the shankbone symbolizes the Paschal lamb, sacrificed on Passover eve during the days of the Temple; the *charoses* symbolize the mortar used by Israelite slaves in building the pyramids of ancient Egypt; the horseradish and bitter herbs and the salt water into which the parsley is dipped remind participants of the bitterness of slavery; whilst the parsley itself symbolizes the festive nature of this meal which celebrates the redemption of the Jews.

Why such a detailed description? Partly to convey a little of the complexity of the whole set of expectations which preoccupy the woman, partly to hint at the difficulty of facing this whole historic legacy, rich with symbolism and memory, and deciding to abandon it, or even a part of it.

HANDING ON TRADITION

The cynic – or the objective observer – may comment on the historically often-changing emphasis on woman's roles in Judaism. The centrality of the wife-mother role is constant but whereas the biblical 'woman of worth' combined this with a role in the public sphere, during the talmudic period the Jewish woman was not encouraged to go out to do business but rather to stay at home and supervise her household (Schlesinger, 1987). Then, post-talmudically and in many subsequent periods, her role changed again from passive guardian of her home to that of active financial supporter of her household.

The Jewish woman's changing expectations of what she should do and be – and, of course, the source of these changing definitions – is much commented upon (Rich, 1977; Myerhoff, 1978; Kraemer, 1989; Burman, 1982, 1986, 1990). It is hardly provocative to suggest that, in a male-defined system, the destiny of women permitted little real choice.

'Freed from responsibilities for making a living... the Jewish woman could fully focus her attention on her family and on the needs of the less fortunate within the community': Kraemer (1989) shows how affluence allowed the re-establishment of sharply demarcated gender roles. At the same time, and increasingly concerned by assimilation, communal leaders placed great emphasis on the woman's responsibility as educator: 'As the guardian of the hearth in the period of bourgeois domesticity, the Jewish woman was held responsible for the behaviour of her husband and children' (Hyman, in Kraemer, p. 180).

Many assumptions are made in seeing the woman-as-mother naturally becoming the woman as transmitter of culture. Yet for many women it was – and remains – a valid progression. This was so not only in the Jewish world. Looking at turn-of-the century American society, Westkott (1986) points out that the rapid social and economic changes 'bred a quest for stability and a desire to reaffirm the traditional religious and ethical values that seemed to be eroding. The domesticated world of women became the locus of preservation.' (p. 21).

Whilst women's access to religious study has been earlier discussed (Chapter Three) and the subject of women's wider education is considered in Chapter Nine, it is relevant to note here that the Jewish mother's duty regarding the education of her children is that she must teach her sons until they reach the age of six, but continue always to teach her daughters. She teaches her daughters *chinnuch*, the totality of Jewish morality – and this indicates the disparity between traditional attitudes towards women and men in religious education. 'Women learnt by observing – learning and doing; men learnt by arguing. It was a differentiation that made both parties feel they were masters of the situation. That worked until informal education collapsed as a basis of Jewish learning' (Rabbi Dr. Jonathan Sacks, in The *Guardian*, 25.7.90). Except in Orthodox families, the traditional role of the parents as transmittors of religion was gradually, often unknowingly, relinquished. When this happened – and believing that they could be the ones to stem the risks of assimilation in an increasingly secular word – religious education for women was urged:

> The well-being of the community depends as much – more, perhaps – on the religious education of these future mothers, as it did on the religious education of the future fathers.
>
> (*Jewish Chronicle*, 24.2.1922)

Burman (1982 and 1986) asks how it is that Jewish women have seemingly always acquiesced in the flux in their roles, which were prescribed from a male perspective and then, apparently, internalized. She finds a partial answer in recognising that it is often the social construct rather than the reality which changes – 'few women conformed to the stated ideal'. However, primarily, Burman suggests, it is because the woman recognises herself as mediator between the family and the outside word. Therefore, in the ghettoes of Eastern Europe she was the buffer between the hostile host society and the unworldly male domain of religion; in contrast, in the open society of Britain she became the one who, by keeping up the traditional practices in the home, helped to define the Jewish identity of the household. 'The identity of a community, and consequently the way in which its women's role is defined within it, is shaped in part in response to the society in which it is located' (Burman, 1982, p. 37).

Feminism has offered women, even Jewish women, other options. Understandably, the backlash has stressed the clash between feminism's apparently egoistic push and the needs of Jewish family life. How can a woman pursue educational opportunities and a career, how can she strive for financial equality and a life outside the home and remain firmly rooted within a system which expects her to be primarily there, at home, giving stability and religious direction?

Cooper sees the dilemma expressed in conflict: 'The anger in Jewish women ... is an inevitable consequence of a system of traditional values which seeks to assign a place to them without recognising and valuing their own autonomous desires' (*Jewish Chronicle*, 31.5.91). The dilemma is highlighted by the fact that educated Jewish women expect and receive respect for their knowledge in the wider, non-Jewish society, whereas within 'traditional' Jewish society they are still respected primarily – and often only – in their home roles. It remains a question of who defines the culture and who transmits it.

Interestingly, in this male-defined culture, it is the mother, not the father, who *halachically* (i.e. according to religious law) has the sole right of transmitting Jewish status. The privilege carries with it expectations superimposed on the fact of matrilineal descent; they relate to women's 'crucial position as agents of acculturation in the home', a position which Webber (1983) suggests that, contrary to appearances, has changed hardly at all. And Danzger, studying the *ba'alei t'shuva* (those who return to religious Judaism), makes a similar point; that although the man's religious role is the more visible, the woman's role in the home is the more crucial to Orthodox life.

But, as Hyman (in Heschel, 1983) emphasizes, it is a myth to suggest that the Jewish woman always played the central role in transmitting Judaism to her children. That is an over-simplification. Firstly, 'learning and teaching were traditionally the preserves of men – the father and the *melamed* [teacher]'. Secondly, whilst women make possible the religious celebrations within the home, it is the man who presides over them. Yet the image of women as culture bearers is a tempting one for women to believe: 'it connotes power and a recognition of the value of the mothering role, which certainly includes teaching by example'. Hyman's message is that, whilst the Jewish mother has always strongly influenced her family, 'that should not become an argument for suggesting that the only good Jewish mother is one who stays home and spends her time teaching her children in some indefinable way how to be Jews' (p. 21).

7 Marriage, Childbearing and Sexuality

THE MEANING OF MARRIAGE

The Lord God said, 'It is not good for man to be alone. I will make a fitting helper for him.'

(Genesis 2.18)

Women are not...obliged to marry, whereas a man is obligated to marry...A married woman is entitled to receive from her husband food, clothing and sexual gratification.

(Webber, 1983, pp. 148–9)

Marriage in Judaism is considered essential for the preservation of society and the Jewish religion believes that a person is not fulfilled until he or she is married. Interestingly, marriage has never been regarded as a sacrament (and therefore indissoluble) yet, since earliest times, the contractual aspects of the marriage union have been imbued with holiness. Marriage is looked upon as a contract blessed by God in which the conduct of the partners is closely regulated by divine law.

Unlike the early Christian Church, Judaism has always discouraged celibacy. On the contrary, sex within marriage is regarded as an essential part of a complete life and the denial of sexual relations is seen as a prime ground for divorce.

There are many misconceptions regarding Jewish marriage. For example, as Gubbay and Levy (1985) point out, it is a 'commonly-held fallacy that a Jewish husband "acquires" a wife as he might acquire a chattel' (p. 24). In fact, the *Gemara* (the talmudic commentary on the *Mishnah*, the oral tradition codified in 200 CE) makes it very clear that the bride must consent to her own marriage. Also, although they were first codified at a time when women in other contemporary cultures had few rights, the Jewish marriage laws actually safeguard the wife's rights. The marriage contract (*ketubah*) has two aims: to guarantee her material, social and sexual rights during marriage and, by means of the marriage settlement, to protect her financial position if a divorce should take place or her husband should die. The marriage settlement specified in the *ketubah* is claimable by the wife in case of divorce and becomes the first charge on the husband's estate after death (Gubbay and Levy, p. 28).

147

However, the idea that a wife was 'acquired' originates in the Bible. Bird and Hauptman in Ruether (1974) and Biale (1984) discuss marriage in biblical and post–biblical literature and Biale points out that the religious law relating to marriage relies on *interpretation* (her italics) of the biblical text. 'The cornerstone of this legislation is the legalistic interpretation of the term "taking" which characterizes biblical references to marriage' (p. 45). Hauptman considers the development of biblical law in the Talmud and explains how Jewish marriage traditionally was effected in two stages: betrothal and, a year later, the marriage ceremony. A man could betroth a woman by presenting her with a gift or by 'taking possession' (Hauptman, p. 185). Betrothal was therefore sometimes compared with purchase (i.e. marriage as the purchase of the woman who then becomes her husband's property). But Hauptman points out that there is a difference, because the consent of the woman had to be obtained before betrothal could take place (Kiddushin 2a, 2b, 4la). Biale further emphasizes the clear disapproval in talmudic discussion of betrothal taking place by means of a sum of money or by intercourse (Biale, pp. 53 & 56).

In earlier times, marriage was arranged by the parents. 'This is not surprising when we realize . . . the centrality of marriage in Jewish society.' On it depends 'social status, economic stability, personal fulfilment, sexual satisfaction and control and of course biological continuity'(Biale, p. 61).

Although traditionally – and still amongst the Orthodox – arranged marriages have always been the norm, Judaism also cherishes the idea of a young couple being attracted to each other before the marriage. One of the most beautiful prayers, the Song of Solomon, extols romantic love. It is interpreted allegorically as the courtship between God, the lover, and the children of Israel, his beloved:

> Behold, thou art fair, my love; behold thou are fair;
> Thine eyes are as doves behind they veil; . . .
> Thou has ravished my heart . . .
>
> I am my beloved's and my beloved is mine, . . .
> For love is strong as death, . . .
> Many waters cannot quench love,
> Neither can the floods drown it . . .

Essentially marriage in Judaism is seen as having two purposes. The first purpose is for companionship: 'And whoever lives without a wife lives without well-being, without blessing . . . ' (Even Ha'Ezer, quoted in Biale, p. 62). Procreation is the second purpose of marriage. 'Therefore, a man is required to marry a wife in order to procreate and multiply, . . . for it is written "And you shall be fruitful and multiply", Gen, 9:1' (Even Ha'Ezer, quoted in Biale). Interestingly, these two requirements relate to the man – his need for companionship and his duty to procreate. But Feldman (1972) points out that an important aspect of *halacha* is the principle of enabling others to discharge their obligation (p. 35)

In addition to companionship and procreation, marriage serves another purpose: the control of the sexual impulse. 'The rabbis in all generations saw temptation as an ever-present force in the lives of men' (Biale, p. 64). Therefore, again defined in terms of male needs, marriage should provide a channelling of erotic desires and should also prevent the 'improper emission of seed' (*Shulchan Aruch*, vol. 4, ch. CLI). At the same time, as Goodman (1965, p. 291) stresses, the sexual aspect of marriage is not given just a 'compromised legitimacy by the necessity to propagate the race'. On the contrary, in Judaism it is seen as a desired end in itself.

As in so many aspects of Jewish life, there are contradictory perspectives. For example, considering marriage historically, Biale highlights the essentially passive role which the woman had. In the first place, although in principle she could withhold her consent to a marriage, the choice of a husband was essentially made by the parents, as were the negotiations over dowry and marriage settlement. Secondly, it was (and is) the woman's role to fulfill the man's needs: to be a companion to him, to enable him to fulfill the *mitzvah* (commandment) regarding children and to satisfy his sexual desires within the constraints of the Laws of Family Purity. In marriage the woman's role becomes one of central importance as mother, yet prior to marriage she was 'expected to pass from one protected status, that of daughter, to another, that of wife' (Biale, p. 65). 'Women much more than men, are controlled by others in traditional Jewish society' (Biale, p. 69).

At the same time, the woman has always had an esteemed status within Jewish marriage; it is the woman on whom the responsibility rests for the hallowing of the Jewish home and for the observing of the Laws of Family Purity. In religious law, the wife has always been seen as an equal partner in the marriage relationship. Interestingly, too, her desire for sexual fulfilment is equally respected. Also, as earlier discussed, the marriage contract has always offered her protection. Throughout the religious texts, marriage is seen as a sacred bond in which the man is enjoined to honour his wife: 'for she is responsible for all the blessings found in his household . . . A man must not cause his wife to weep for God counts her tears' (Baba Metzia 59a).

CHOOSING A PARTNER AND THE WEDDING CEREMONY

A gift most precious has that man in life
Who has secured a good and loving wife,

(Yevamot 63b)

Happy is the husband of a beautiful woman;
the number of his days is doubled.

(Yevamot 63b)

That a young man or woman will marry – or will marry within the Jewish fold – is no longer a foregone conclusion, as the statistics amply reveal. Nevertheless, the strength of feeling still surrounding the subject of Jewish marriage suggests powerful unconscious expectations and a deeply-ingrained, archetypal desire for the continuity of the Jewish people. Although many partnerships today are far removed from it, this chapter will attempt to portray what was – and for many still is – the ideal.

Courtship

For the majority of young Jews today, finding a partner is a process of choice and, despite the increasing rate of marrying out or of not marrying at all, it is likely that most still consciously hope for a Jewish partner.

For the Orthodox the *shadkhan* (matchmaker) still exists. He or she arranges an introduction not just of two young people, but of young people of compatible backgrounds, thus bringing about a union of two families, with obvious advantages in terms of shared values and of family support for the match. Many factors are taken into account in the *shidduch* (match) and Orthodox families take great pains to ensure that there should be no blemish to detract from a good *shidduch* for their son or daughter.

The courtship of an Orthodox couple is often short; they may not touch each other or in any way be physically intimate but it is a time in which they discover and confirm an attraction for each other and a sense of harmony. Pre-marital sex is forbidden in Jewish religious law. Sexual relations are sanctified only within marriage. The engagement, as in all traditions, is an occasion of rejoicing at the future coming together of two families. But in Judaism, since medieval times, the actual betrothal, in which the man and woman become legally bound to each other, is the first part of the marriage ceremony.

As in so many of the ceremonies surrounding major life events, there are similarities and differences between Ashkenazi and Sephardi customs relating to the marriage ceremony and even, sometimes, to the finding of a partner. Within these two groups there are also further variations, depending on the culture of origin and the degree of religious observance. Yet central to all Jews is the concept of marriage as much more than a merely contractual union between two people. Its spiritual significance is expressed in the word *kiddushin*, meaning sanctification, which is an integral part of the wedding ceremony. The union is blessed by God.

The prelude to the marriage

On the Shabbat before the wedding, the bridegroom is given the honour in the synagogue of being called to the reading of the Torah (the scroll of law). This ceremony, the *aufruf* (calling up), is the beginning of the celebrations and often the two families will offer hospitality to all the congregants. In some synagogues, this will be wine and sweet biscuits; in others, particularly Sephardi ones, it may be an elaborate spread; a celebration calls for a feast. In Orthodox communities, it is a custom that the bride and groom do not meet from the Shabbat preceding the wedding, so that their reunion under the *chuppah* (wedding canopy) will have new joy and significance. Often, therefore, the bride is not present at this Shabbat ceremony.

The evening before the wedding, the religiously observant bride immerses herself in the *mikvah* (ritual bath). It is then that she first takes responsibility for the Laws of Family Purity (*taharat ha mishpachah*), discussed later in this chapter.

On the day itself, bride and groom fast until after the ceremony, so coming to their *chuppah* in a spirit of solemnity, as on Yom Kippur (the Day of Atonement). Their fast emphasizes the significance of the occasion.

Prior to the start of the actual ceremony, the rabbi asks the bridegroom, in the presence of two witnesses, to accept the obligations written into the *ketubah*. The *ketubah*, written in Aramaic, the spoken language of talmudic times, is signed by the bridegroom and becomes the wife's property. Although usually only of symbolic significance it is a document of great importance in guaranteeing the material, social and sexual rights of the woman during the marriage and after, if it should end by divorce or death.

The marriage ceremony

Blessed art thou, O Lord our God . . . who created joy and gladness . . . Blessed art thou, O Lord, who makest the bridegroom to rejoice with the bride.

Originally the marriage ceremony was in two distinct stages; the betrothal, which established a legal bond between the couple, and then a year later the marriage itself. Only then did the couple live together as man and wife. Since medieval times, however, the betrothal and the marriage have been combined into a single ceremony.

The wedding ceremony therefore consists of these two separate ceremonies – the betrothal (*kiddushin*) and the nuptials (*nissuin*). The marriage is solemnized beneath a *chuppah*. The *chuppah* symbolizes the new home which bride and groom are to build together. It is a simple canopy, held aloft by four poles, usually twined around with flowers and leaves. In good weather, it is often erected in the open air 'that their descendants may be as the stars of the heavens' (*Shulchan Aruch*, vol. 4, ch. CXLVII, 1). There is symbolism, too, in the *chuppah's* being flimsy and portable, suggesting that the couple's future happiness should be independent of material possessions.

The bride and groom are escorted to the canopy, usually by their parents, sometimes carrying lighted candles. It is an emotional and beautiful procession during which psalms of joy are sung. The groom then goes to his bride for the ceremony of *bedecken* (veiling the bride). As he lifts the veil over her face, the congregation say: 'May you be the mother of thousands of myriads' (Genesis 24:60) – the blessing bestowed upon Rebecca by her family when she went to marry Isaac. The bride then encircles her groom, walking around him seven times, following the verse in Jeremiah 'A woman shall go around a man' (31.22), then joins him under the *chuppah* at his right hand: 'At thy right hand doth the queen stand' (45.10), for the bride on her wedding day is as a queen.

The betrothal begins with blessings over wine, praising the sacred covenant of marriage. The couple share the cup of wine.

The essence of the ceremony follows; it is the placing of a ring by the bridegroom on his bride's forefinger as he declares: 'Behold, thou art consecrated to me with this ring, according to the Law of Moses and of Israel.' His declaration affirms his intention to undertake the obligations of married life in accordance with religious law, and it confirms that his bride is sacred to him and forbidden to other men. The bride's willing acceptance of the ring in the presence of witnesses completes the ceremony of betrothal. The ring must be unadorned; it is a symbol, not to to be detracted from by jewels.

There follows the reading aloud of the *ketubah* and its translation into English:

Be thou my wife according to the law of Moses and of Israel, and I will be a true husband unto thee. I will honour and cherish thee; I will work for thee; I will protect and support thee . . . as it beseemeth a Jewish husband to do.

And this bride has consented and become his wife . . . and has taken upon herself all the duties incumbent upon a Jewish wife.

The seven nuptial blessings, praising God for creating love and harmony, are then recited over a second goblet of wine. Bride and groom drink from the goblet and the ceremony ends with the bridegroom's breaking a glass, placed under his foot. It is an act imbued with symbolism; it is a reminder of the destruction of the Temple, the one element of sorrow amidst the celebrations; it is also a warning of the fragility of relationships.

The guests greet bride and groom with '*mazeltov*' (good luck) and the religious ceremony is concluded. Finally, the secular (civil law) wedding ceremony is enacted by the signing of the marriage register. Then bride and groom are escorted joyfully to the *yichud* – a room in which, at last, they are alone together and where in privacy they break their fast.

After the ceremony, there are great festivities and the celebratory meal at which the *sheva berachot* (the seven blessings) are again recited. The religiously observant follow the wedding day with a week of festive meals for the bride and groom and at each the blessings are once more sung.

Thus is the traditional celebration of a Jewish wedding. Since time immemorial it has brought light and joy to a people who have frequently known sorrow. Of course, over history and within different cultures of origin there have been many variations, as there are today relating to particular religious groups. Sometimes now, too, there are innovations reflecting feminist thought – sometimes the bride also gives her husband a ring, with the accompanying declaration. Yet, despite all diversities, the basic laws rooted in the Torah together with a deep belief in the sanctity of marriage remain part of a common heritage.

A detailed discussion of the symbolism of the marriage ceremony appears in Kaplan (1983). Although it is written from a traditional viewpoint, there emerges a clear impression of the ceremony symbolizing the responsibilities of each partner to the other. For example, the bride's encircling her bridegroom before the *chuppah* 'indicates that she is binding him with certain obligations'.

Yet from a feminist perspective there are inevitably aspects of the ceremony which cause disquiet. Schneider (1985) suggests that 'the marriage contract is an act of acquisition by the man' (p. 323), a view discussed in the first part of this chapter. She looks at three main areas of concern: The first is the *ketubah* which is written by the man. He therefore initiates, with the bride remaining in a 'passive and dependent role'. In the *ketubah* he 'spells out what she has brought to the marriage and what will be returned to her if they divorce or if he dies first. He also makes explicit his obligation to support her'. Secondly, it is the man who gives the woman a ring; '*he* is "acquiring" *her* in exchange for the ring'. Finally, one of the interpretations of the bride's covering her eyes with a veil is that it is a symbol of trust in her husband. Schneider observes that there is no place in the ceremony in which the bridegroom symbolically places himself in such a vulnerable position.

Some current proposals aimed at avoiding the status of *agunah*

However, the main focus of concern – and not only of feminists – remains the woman's disadvantaged *halachic* position should a divorce take place. It is in this area that modern Orthodox rabbis acknowledge the greatest difficulty. Britain's Chief Rabbi Sacks (1991) has called for a '*halachic* response that will remove the great disadvantage to women in this situation' (*Jewish Chronicle*, 9.8.91). Rabbi Riskin (1989) painstakingly documents how legal solutions can be *halachically* acceptable, but they have not yet been implemented. He refers, for example, (p. 137) to an important proposal of Rabbi Eliezer Berkovits (1967) that a conditional clause should be written into the *ketubah*. This clause would eliminate the possibility that a wife might become an *agunah* by her husband refusing or being unable to issue a *get*. More recently, Dayan Berel Berkovits (a *Dayan* is a rabbi and a judge) put forward a seemingly acceptable proposal, based on precedents in New York and in Ontario, to overcome the obstacles placed by a recalcitrant husband (*Jewish Chronicle*, 15.6.90, p. 26). His proposal would operate not through a 'conditional' marriage contract but through the civil courts; his suggestion is that they be empowered 'not to grant the petitioner a decree absolute ... where a *get* is being unreasonably withheld'.

A consideration of marriage and the marriage ceremony carries with it the understanding that, however undesirable, some marriages end. The major problem for Jewish women wanting to stay within a *halachic* framework is for a way to be found around the discriminatory aspects of the divorce laws as they are presently interpreted. That is the issue facing Orthodox Judaism today.

THE MARITAL RELATIONSHIP AND THE LAWS OF FAMILY PURITY (*TAHARAT HA MISHPACHAH*)

This is perhaps the area over which observant women and feminism are in greatest discord. The commonly held view is that these laws deem a woman 'impure' during and immediately after menstruation. This section of the chapter discusses the actual *halachic* meaning of these laws and the feminist response.

Biale (1984) observes that 'all Western religious traditions walk a tightrope between legitimation of sexuality and ascetic denial of the libidinal drive' (p. 121). Orthodox Judaism resolves this tension by fully acknowledging the importance of sexual relations within marriage and, through the laws of *niddah* and *onah*, prescribing the times for absention and the times for intercourse. The laws of *niddah* refer to 'one who is excluded', specifically a menstruating woman; the laws of *onah* encompass the sexual rights of a married woman and the marital obligations of her husband. As Webber (1983) writes: 'in contrast with the popular belief that sex is a man's right and a woman's duty, the *halacha* tends rather to view marital relations as the duty of the husband and the privilege of the wife' (pp. 160–1).

'Marital relations are holy, pure and clean, when done in the correct manner, at the correct time' (Nahmanides, quoted in Meiselman, 1978, p. 117). The *halachic* requirement is that, from the time a woman has her period until she immerses in the *mikvah* (ritual bath), she has the status of a *niddah*. During this time, all sexual activity and physical contact with her husband is forbidden (Kaplan, 1982). The origin of these laws is in Leviticus, 15:19: 'And if a woman have an issue and the issue ... be blood, she shall be in her impurity seven days'. The rabbis extended the seven days of impurity to twelve and defined all vaginal bleeding, including that of the bride and that of the mother having given birth, as menstrual (Leviticus 12: 1–8). Curiously, the *niddah* period of the woman who has given birth depends on the baby's gender: after the birth of a son, a woman is impure for forty days; after the birth of a daughter, the period of impurity is eighty days.

Taboos against the menstruating woman are found in primitive societies and in other religions (Douglas, 1966) and the assumption is often made that these *halachic* restrictions are similar. Gubbay and Levy

(1985) also observe that the idea of ritual purification by means of immersion is deep-seated in human consciousness and they compare the Hindu practice of bathing in sacred rivers. Barbara Cohn Schlachet (in Brody, 1984, p. 60) refers, too, to 'the historical relation to woman's body as both worshipped and despised for its fecund and earthly quality'.

In fact, the rabbinic explanations for these laws are complex (see Meiselman, 1978, ch. 19; Biale, 1984, ch. 6). Anyway, as Gubbay and Levy point out, for the observant Jew, all explanations are unnecessary; the laws were given by God and, although discussion within a framework has always been encouraged, ultimately they must be obeyed. *Niddah* falls into this category; it is a decree for which no reason is given.

Adler in Koltun (1976, pp. 63–72) discusses *niddah* in terms of endings and beginnings – 'menstruation is an end which points to a beginning'. She sees the menstrual blood, which carries the potential for new life, as a token of dying when it is shed. But the human life cycle encompasses death and birth; while the woman is *tumah*, 'connected with death', (i.e. the loss of potential life), she must withdraw from those acts which re-affirm life. Then, at the end of this time of dormancy, she must be *tahara*, 'reborn', by immersion in living water.

The woman must count five days from the start of her period and then, if she has no show of blood, a further seven 'clean' days. She then bathes and goes to the *mikvah*, a specially constructed pool with running water, in which she immerses herself and makes a blessing. Immersion is seen as an act of spiritual purification and it is incumbent upon the observant woman to follow the requirements of *niddah* very strictly.

Because the Laws of Family Purity are regarded as fundamental to religious life, observant families rarely live in a town without a *mikvah* although, if necessary, immersion can be in any place of running water.

The emphasis during the period of *niddah* is on the emotional – i.e. non-physical – aspects of the marriage. It is, of course, pertinent that the resuming of sexual intimacy occurs at the very time when ovulation is most likely. But, equally important, observant women often feel that the monthly periods of separation and then reunion give a sense of renewal to their marriage.

Whilst these laws have many critics, much is also written – including discussion by non-orthodox women – on their value. For example, Pirani (in Cooper, 1988, p. 56) writes 'woman's knowledge ... is intuitive knowledge ... of creative life and death cycles and processes ... a woman's body knows the creation of the new and destruction and death of the old'. Kupferman (1979) similarly finds in the time of *niddah* and then in the ritual of *mikvah* a natural rhythm, a space for women to go down into themselves, to be apart and to reflect. From living amongst them (1976) she feels that Orthodox women seem much more content than women without such faith. However, discussing this view, Sophie Laws (1990) suggests that 'the satisfaction these women refer to is that of feeling integrated into their community, their religion, of marking their commitment to their particular forms of marriage'(p. 27).

From within tradition, Frankiel (1990) writes: 'Jewish mysticism tells us that when husband and wife unite at permitted times, and especially on Shabbat or at the end of her period of *niddah* when it is a *mitzvah* (commandment) to do so, their union reflects the union of masculine and feminine in the divine' (p. 82).

The Laws of Family Purity are one of woman's three prime obligations (the other two being *hallah*, which symbolizes her role as homemaker, and the lighting of the Shabbat candles, which symbolizes her bringing religion into the home). By observing them, she brings God's presence into their family life. That is the Orthodox position.

Feminist Approach to *Taharat ha Mishpachah*

In contrast to the Orthodox belief is the feminist interpretation. Koltun sets this out (1976, pp. 63–72) and suggests particularly that these laws represent 'the residue of an ancient taboo based on male fear of woman's creative biological cycle'. She sees a special stigma in the concept of *niddah*, with its implication that menstrual blood has 'powerful contaminating properties which must be guarded against'. The feminist contention is that *niddah* suggests a 'repugnance on the part of men for the uterine lining in which they themselves grew to life'. Finally, Koltun asks, if the concept of life and death is inherent in the laws of *niddah*, why is it that only the wife must immerse herself at the end of this period; surely it is the couple together who embody the potential for new life and should therefore immerse themselves together. She claims that the Laws of Family Purity exemplify the *halachic* method in which woman is viewed 'purely as an object with which the man may do *mitzvot* or commit sins'. In a spirited reply, Adler (in Koltun, pp. 63–72), points out that 'a dominant strain in Talmudic thought stresses woman's . . . different-ness from man'. She suggests that the *mitzvah* of *niddah* is 'an enabling activity through which women safeguard the purity of the family'.

An important consideration arises in the context of these laws for the Orthodox. Although the woman's most fertile period is usually halfway through the menstrual cycle, i.e. when marital relations are just resumed, it is not always so; occasionally ovulation is earlier. The conflict that this causes for an Orthodox couple is movingly described in Gold (1988) p. 99.

> For us, the monthly menstrual period was a sign of death. Once again, that potential child would not be born. . . . On the other hand, the monthly trip to the *mikvah* was a time of hope and rebirth. Perhaps this month a child would be created.

'BE FRUITFUL AND MULTIPLY': LAWS AND ATTITUDES ON CHILDBEARING, CHILDLESSNESS, CONTRACEPTION, ABORTION

> I feel shell-shocked when I think how many children we have had, but each one has been a blessing.
> > (Orthodox woman, university lecturer, mother of eleven)

> You know, I've got no family; my mother came to this country as a child and all her family perished; my father's parents died, too, when he was little and he was separated from his only sister. The most important thing for me to do was to become a mother, a Jewish mother.
> > (Reform woman, psychotherapist, mother of three)

In Judaism, having children is seen as fundamental to family and society. Procreation is also seen as one of the prime purposes of marriage. Yet surprisingly, as mentioned earlier, the commandment regarding procreation is incumbent only upon men; for women it is a matter of choice. Therefore, in theory the use of contraception is a possibility for the woman. At the same time, it is the woman's responsibility to make possible the man's fulfilling of the commandments and the first commandment that God gave to Adam was: 'Be fruitful and multiply' (Genesis 1:28).

Whilst *halacha* takes the view of Rabbi Hillel (first century BCE) that this *mitzvah* is fulfilled after the birth of one male child and one female child (Gubbay and Levy, 1985, p. 33), traditionally the Jewish ideal has always been a house full of children. In fact the rabbis teach that, for a man, the *mitzvah* of procreation never stops; he has a continued duty to produce children.

What is very striking about modern Orthodox women – who theoretically have the option of using contraception – is their *choice* to have as many children as possible. By doing so they enable their husband to fulfill his *mitzvah*. At the same time, they obviously feel a sense of pride and status in their ability to have and care for such large families and in their husband's ability to provide for them. Although average family size amongst the Orthodox is estimated at only 5.6 children (Loewenthal, 1990) that means, of course, that many families are much larger.

But there is something more, too: many Orthodox women feel they share a responsibility to try to compensate for the losses of the Holocaust. It is an emotion spoken of even by non-Orthodox women (who do use contraception), that creating a family is important to Jewish continuity. Indeed, for survivors of the Holocaust, both Orthodox and non-Orthodox, there was a very conscious decision to have children to try to replace their own and other lost families and, for the generations which followed, having a child became 'an almost holy commitment that the Jewish people must continue' (Schiff, in Linzer, 1984, p. 186).

Having children, in Judaism, is more than a blessing; it is a commandment. However, contrary to assumption, procreation was never seen as the sole purpose of marriage. The first purpose of marriage is companionship and Judaism has always regarded sexual intercourse in marriage as desirable in itself, for the love it expresses and the happiness it gives, and as an obligation owed by the husband to the wife; indeed rabbinic law sees it as a husband's duty to please his wife even after her menopause, when she is no longer able to conceive.

Childlessness

And when Rachel saw that she bare Jacob no children, Rachel envied her sister and said unto Jacob, 'Give me children, or else I die.' And Jacob's anger was kindled against Rachel and he said, 'Am I in God's stead, who hath withheld from thee the fruit of the womb?'

(Gen. 30, 1– 2)

Childlessness by choice is seen in Judaism as a transgression; it is a man's transgression, for the rabbis have always assumed that a woman has a natural desire to bear children. Whilst contraception is permitted for the woman, it is only after she has enabled her husband to fulfill the command of procreation.

In contrast, a couple's infertility is regarded as a great misfortune. Iris Singer (1992), a therapist working with the infertile, sees the 'mourning' of infertile Jewish women as being even more than the loss of an unrealized part of self; she sees it as an existential grief at their inability to preserve the continuity of their people.

I was never made to feel in any way lesser. I had the belief that things happen the way they have to happen. But we are required to do everything we can to help ourselves.

> (Orthodox woman in Gateshead who for twelve years remained childless and then, after fertility treatment, gave birth to triplets).

Unable to conceive a child, although it is emphasized in rabbinic texts that husband and wife can still live a life of good deeds, they are encouraged to seek medical intervention. The *halachic* view on artificial insemination permits it as long as the husband's sperm is used. There is, however, much disquiet over issues raised by artificial insemination by donor and by surrogacy (Gold, 1988, pp. 103–30).

Adoption

Adoption is as old as the Bible – after all, Moses was adopted by the daughter of Pharaoh – and it is seen as a great *mitzvah*. Yet there are many difficulties for, as well as the emotional strain on the potential parents, few Jewish children become available for adoption. As a legal procedure, adoption does not exist in Jewish law because *halacha* emphasizes the importance of a child's biological identity. Therefore, if a non-Jewish child is adopted, the child does not automatically become Jewish; he or she must be formally converted. The *halachic* conversion of the child often imposes further stress upon the parents for it requires confirmation that they are fully following a religious way of life (see p. 176).

In a culture which is so family based, to be denied the blessing of children is a deep sorrow. The psalmist understood this when he praised God:

> He sets the childless woman among her household to be a joyful mother of children.
>
> (Psalm 113, 9)

Contraception

Possibly the feminist view would be that the Orthodox woman merely complies with the expectation that she be 'the mother of thousands' (Gen. 24:60). But the reality feels different; many discussions with Orthodox women indicate a feeling of positive well-being which these women have, surrounded by their large families (Loewenthal, 1990; Baker, 1990). It is not that they are particularly affluent (which would buy domestic help); in fact, most of them also work outside the home. It seems that their contentment is to do with feeling needed, useful, constructive and to their being strongly integrated within the community.

Interestingly, there is only one reference to male contraception – which is forbidden – in the Torah; it tells how Onan was punished by God (Gen. 38, 9–10) because he had 'spilled his seed on the ground'. Regarding the woman's use of contraception, there is unequivocal rabbinic support for it in any situation where childbirth could have fatal consequences for the wife (Biale, 1984, pp. 203–18). However, there is complexity of interpretation as to other circumstances in which a women may use a contraceptive device. In the past, strictly Orthodox rabbis ruled that, unless the saving of life is involved, contraception is not permitted. The non-Orthodox position is more lenient, permitting contraception where further pregnancies are deemed undesirable. However, the modern Orthodox position shows sensitivity to a wife's potential inability to cope with too-frequent pregnancies and psychological stress is taken into account, as well as risks to physical health (Wiselberg, 1991). Regarding method of preference, it is for oral measures, particularly the pill. Unlike Catholicism, Judaism has never suggested abstention, for abstinence is regarded as contrary to the very concept of marriage.

However, central to this discussion is the recognition that, amongst the Orthodox, it is the woman herself who is frequently reluctant to relinquish what she perceives as her divinely-given task.

Abortion

The Talmud teaches that the embryo is to be considered as a part of the mother and not as an independent entity. Similarly, the *halachic* position is that a foetus in the womb is not an actual life until born. Abortion is not prohibited in Jewish law and, in fact, the *mishnah* (the oral law, codified in the second century) distinctly states that the life of the mother takes priority over the life of the child whilst still in the womb. Subsequently, Maimonides (a twelfth-century sage and physician) advised that where the life of the mother is threatened, therapeutic abortion should be mandatory, not optional. However, once the child's head has emerged 'he may not be touched for we do not set aside one life for another' (quoted in Biale, 1984, p. 230).

As with the issues regarding contraception, where the mother's life is not threatened there is more difficulty. Biale writes: 'The contemporary debate revolves around the question of whether a woman has the moral and/or legal right to choose to abort the foetus she carries' (Biale, p. 219). At the one extreme, abortion for merely social reasons, even during the first forty days before the foetus is fully formed, is not sanctioned (Gubbay and Levy, 1985, p. 35).

The more complex situations are those in which the mother's mental or physical health is at risk, or pregnancy as a result of rape, or where there is a probability of the birth of a malformed child. In such cases, there is considerable rabbinic discretion. The strict position permits abortion only to save the mother's life, in cases of the mother's extreme mental anguish; or where there is danger to the health of an existing child. Other rabbinic rulings allow 'disgrace' of the woman to be sufficient cause to warrant an abortion. Concern has also focused on circumstances where there is danger to the future child, but not to the mother. Whilst *halacha* does not countenance killing a foetus to prevent its future suffering, the principle has been clarified that the woman's pain comes first; therefore the abortion of a potentially deformed foetus is permitted on the grounds that its birth would cause severe anguish for the mother (Biale, p. 236).

In summary, *halacha* does not recognise a woman's right to abort a child because it is unwanted or to limit the size of her family. It does, however, fully recognize her right to abort the unborn child if this is necessary to protect her own life. The more contentious areas relate to the woman's mental anguish or disgrace. In all situations abortion is seen as a decision of grave concern.

In the context of women's striving to redefine their roles, these considerations raise vital issues. Now that women have choice as never before, traditional Judaism seems to erect strong prohibitions against the exercise of such choice. For the feminist, motherhood may be among her options but it is rarely the all-absorbing source of her fulfilment. Yet a new understanding – as distinct from a rationalization of the old one – is emerging in the writing of Jewish feminists (see, for example, Kaufman, 1987; Frankiel, 1990). There is a plea that the maternal role should not be denigrated, that feminism should not be coercive. Greenberg (1981) asks: 'Is there an archetypal feminist source which still gives a woman fulfilment in nurturing?' (p. 158). Frankiel, looking at the archetypal mothers of the past, believes that they symbolize generativity, 'that dimension of creativity that looks toward the future' (p. 19). In tending and caring for what came forth from them, in using their energies to direct the inner life of their family, they developed their own sense of self-worth in a spiritual context.

Kaufman, listening to *ba'alot t'shuva* (women returning to Orthodoxy), similarly remarks that 'from the imagery of their language and the descriptions of their experiences, a symbolic framework for social existence emerges which transcends the self . . . and embraces, ultimately, the entire community'. She suggests, as Frankiel writes, that from our foremothers 'we have the gift of a deeply feminine reality'.

SEXUAL MORALITY

> . . . and thy desire shall be to thy husband, and he shall rule over thee . . .
>
> (Genesis, 3:16)

Judaism discourages celibacy and elevates sex within marriage to a holy act. The *halachic* ideal requires absolute abstinence from sex before marriage and total fidelity afterwards. In both biblical and post-biblical legislation, the prime concern is with the danger that adultery poses to marriage and to social stability. Considering these laws, Biale (1984) points out that they were conceived 'within a patriarchal marital structure and male terms of reference' (p. 196). In fact, polygamy was still accepted in biblical times and, although subsequently its practice became less frequent, there was no ban on it until the twelfth century, and that was observed only by Ashkenazim until relatively modern times.

Although the *halachic* ideal has always been extolled, it seems that special emphasis is placed on the woman's purity and fidelity, for Orthodox Judaism maintains that a bride's virginity strengthens the marriage and establishes the mutual respect essential for family life. The values implicit in this belief are shown in biblical law, in which it was a capital offence for a woman to pass herself off to her husband as a virgin when she was not, yet the act by which she lost her virginity was not deemed a transgression.

Throughout the discussions on sexual morality, the theme is one of what Biale describes as a 'one-way exclusiveness':

> The married woman is the exclusive sexual partner of her husband, forbidden to all other men. The married man, on the other hand, is not precluded by his marriage from relationships with other women provided those women are single, although such promiscuity is condemned for both sexes.
>
> (p. 197)

Binstock (1991), commenting on this, observes that at its root is the aim to preserve the sanctity of the marriage, particularly in relation to children, for if a married woman were permitted sexual relations outside marriage, the child's paternity would always be in question.

In questions of sexual morality it seems that since earliest times there has always been the ideal expected of the woman, and beside this a different male reality, so that adultery by a married woman was regarded as a capital offence whereas the same offence committed by a married man with an unmarried woman carried much lighter penalties. This did not, of course, amount to permission for the man, but the level of prohibition was not the same for a man as for a woman.

Yet the Torah condemns casual relationships between men and women and, as Bermant (1974) points out, although 'there is no definite, outright condemnation of fornication between unmarried, unrelated men and women in the Bible . . . the sense of disapproval is evident in every page' (p. 55).

Biale further comments that normative sexuality in Jewish law is heterosexual and any sexual relations outside marriage are regarded as deviant (1984, ch. 7). Within this 'deviant' category, there are further distinctions: incest and adultery are considered sexual transgressions, whilst lesbianism or sex between unmarried people, although condemned, are not sexual transgressions. These prohibitions and taboos are specified in Deuteronomy, 22 and 23, and Leviticus, 18 and 19.

Attitudes which view the married woman as ideally asexual are not unique to Judaism. Westkott (1986) writes:

> the idea of the motherly wife creating what Christopher Lasch (1979) calls a 'haven in a heartless world' was entwined with a middle-class ideology of repressed female sexuality . . . Historians note that . . . men and women alike were subject to the strictures that equated respectability with control over sexual impulses . . . However, for the middle-class Victorian woman, self-control was presumed to be physically inherent. This presumption undergirded the ideal of spiritual motherhood . . . [and] also formed the psychological basis for the imperative of maternal selflessness . . . a wife was considered to live only for others – especially husband and children.
>
> (p. 22)

STAYING SINGLE

As a single Jewish woman over the age of thirty, you don't fit into the pattern of things. It's to do with creating your own family. The older you get, the more men's attitudes change; they see you as being past childbearing. You're made aware of being different by women, too – it can be quite innocuous, it's the way they introduce themselves saying they're married with children – but it means somehow you're not complete. And in a way you're not complete because the festivals are oriented to families with children, so if you're not a family, you're out. And in most of the synagogues I've been to, I feel invisible as a single woman.

(Ina Randall)

The married woman, especially the mother, is the paradigm idealized in Judaism. Hers is seen – even by single women – as the 'normative experience'. 'Normative' and 'deviant' are recurring words in discussion of woman's marital status and the woman who does not marry, whether out of choice or not, often feels that she is perceived as deviant.

In fact, according to the written law, a woman has the right not to marry and not to bear children (Yevamot 65b; Biale, 1984, p. 16). But alongside the written law there is the oral law in which there is the clear expectation that the woman will do both; after all, every man is obligated to take a wife so that he may fulfill the commandment incumbent on him to procreate.

Halachically, the single woman is disapproved of if she has a sexual relationship and casual sex is construed as *zenut* (prostitution). But there is much complexity to the situation for, if a married man has sex with an unattached woman, he is not regarded as committing adultery. If a single woman has sex with an unmarried man whom she could legally marry, that relationship is construed as a 'common-law marriage' and *halachically* she is not then able to change her partner without a religious divorce (Biale, p. 190).

There are no statistics estimating the numbers of unmarried Jewish women, although in the States there is ample evidence of Jewish women's choosing to marry – if at all – much later than they did a generation ago. Yet women who marry late and, even more so, women who remain unmarried (whether or not out of choice) are alienated by a still-existing assumption that 'normal' Jewish life is lived in a traditional nuclear family.

The contemporary dilemma for all but the most Orthodox rabbis is in recognising that remaining single is now an option for Jewish women. To exclude single women from communal life is usually to lose them. The choice facing the communal leaders is either to legitimize non-normative Jewish lifestyles or, alternatively, to deny or 'pathologize' them. But for the unmarried woman no such dilemma exists; the still predominantly male rabbis can hardly define her reality. They can even less presume to evaluate it in terms of establishment norms.

LESBIANISM

I learned early about being an invisible member of a minority.
(Adrienne J. Smith in *Seen But Not Heard: Jewish Women in Therapy*
(1991))
The assumptions within Jewish society, of what is normative and what is
seen as deviant, come from men. In terms of definitions, it is significant
that sexual acts between women are not considered a violation of the law
because no act of intercourse takes place – in other words, it is the male
experience which defines what is a sexual act.

Biale (1984, pp. 192–7), looking at the early texts, points out that lesbianism is not mentioned in the Bible at all and there is only scant reference to it in the Talmud. It was obviously considered rare and no parallels
were drawn with male homosexuality which is deemed 'an abhorrence'
and is forbidden (Leviticus 18:22). Later rabbinic discussion seems to
regard lesbian relationships as improper and as falling within the category
of sexual deviance but not as a legal violation of sexual prohibitions.

Considering the minimal comment on lesbianism in the early sources,
Biale raises an important point which, of course, is relevant to the lives of
women generally: she asks if lesbians were written out of history. *Halacha*
was defined by men, inevitably remote from women's most intimate experiences. Pronouncements on 'sexual deviance' came from 'within a patriarchal marital structure and male terms of reference'.

As in so many other areas of life, our understandings and judgements
come not from the reality but from male definitions of reality. 'Normative
sexuality in Jewish law is heterosexual, initiated by the male, and confined
within marriage' (Biale, p. 197).

Rabbi Elizabeth Sarah is an English Reform rabbi and a lesbian. Her
being a lesbian has been acknowledged and accepted right from the start
by the community which chose her as their religious leader. Her partner
participates in religious communal celebrations as would the wife of a heterosexual rabbi. For Rabbi Sarah, her lesbian relationship and her communal role are not mutually exclusive.

Exploring my Jewishness and understanding that society is male-
dominated, I wanted to focus not on the negative aspects – i.e. that
women have been marginalized – but to assume that change is possible.

She explains Jewish attitudes to lesbianism in that 'procreation is a commandment incumbent upon men, not women, therefore lesbianism can be
tolerated. As long as the majority are heterosexual, then lesbianism is not a
threat'. She sees no conflict between being lesbian and her duty as a rabbi:

'the teaching, the parochial role are what matter. Just as Reform have accepted women as rabbis, there is no reason why they shouldn't accept lesbian women as rabbis. It depends on the movement towards tolerance within society at large'.

Yet the Reform rabbi Charles Emanuel reacts differently, expressing disquiet about lesbian rabbis: 'It feels very wrong that a role model, which is what a rabbi is, should represent in her way of life something deviant from the Jewish norm.'

The prevalance of lesbianism in the Jewish community is not known, but it is reasonable to assume that it is similar to that in the wider society. Rogow (1990) points out that 'as long as "coming out" places women in danger, statistics on lesbians will be impossible to obtain' (p. 72) but she quotes studies by Kinsey and Masters and Johnson (1979) and Bell and Weinberg (1978) which suggest that at least 10 per cent of the general population is gay or lesbian.

Whilst Jewish lesbian visibility is a recent phenomenon, Jewish lesbians are not. There is evidence of woman-identified culture in ancient Near Eastern goddess traditions (Litman, 1983, in Rogow). In our own times, many Jewish lesbians have been and are active in both radical politics and radical feminism; in being Jewish and lesbian they have a personal understanding of the meaning and consequences of oppression. However, lesbianism remained outside 'normative' definitions of Jewish women's experience until the publication of Beck's lesbian anthology in 1982. In claiming that lesbians were 'Nice Jewish Girls', too, it 'exploded restrictive stereotypes that limited Jewish women to marriage and subservience' (Rogow, p. 71).

Inevitably, Orthodox and traditionally observant Judaism (in Britain, the United Synagogue; in America, the Conservative movement) make no provision for groups which acknowledge the existence of lesbians in their communities. In fact in England, the setting up of a Jewish Lesbian and Gay helpline in 1990 was strongly criticised in the 'establishment' media.

As might be expected, both in the States and in Britain, initiatives to meet gay needs have all come from the more progressive synagogue groups – Reconstructionist, Reform and Liberal – sometimes led by lesbian rabbis, sometimes forming *Havurah* groups of gay men and women, many of whom had opted out of Judaism until finding a form of service to meet their spiritual needs.

Rogow (1990) documents the struggles which Jewish lesbians in the States went through to combat homophobia. Public discussion of Jewish lesbians first took place in 1969 with the so-called Stonewall 'riot' which sparked the gay rights movement. The first gay synagogues were founded in the early 1970s in Los Angeles and New York City and others followed, yet they were often dominated by men and the language of prayer often remained male-defined. At the same time, not all lesbians who lived Jewishly wanted to affiliate with Jewish communal institutions, and many Jewish feminist lesbian groups became support networks unrelated to synagogues.

Within the Jewish community there are different contradictions in relation to lesbianism. The 1980s and 1990s have seen an increasing number of publications and books (Beck, 1982; Balka and Rose, 1989) by and for Jewish lesbians, yet non-lesbian Jewish feminists often react with ambivalence. Similarly, despite the acceptance of lesbian rabbis in the Reconstructionist and Reform movements in the States and in the Reform and Liberal synagogues in Britain, homophobia remains a common reaction. For example, as Rogow (1990, p. 74) points out,

> though the Reform movement has passed supportive resolutions and accepted gay synagogues, Hebrew Union College still does not support the ordination of openly lesbian rabbinical candidates. And though the Reconstructionist Rabbinical College currently ordains lesbians, several women have discovered that gaining entrance to the school does not guarantee a welcoming atmosphere.

Lesbians still feel marginalized, not only by the Orthodox but by the 'normative' Jewish community which condemns them as deviant. 'By their very presence...lesbians challenge the patriarchal model of authority which has, for so long, served to keep women from defining Judaism' (Rogow, 1990, p. 76).

Little wonder then that a request to a lesbian couple to meet and listen to their particular experiences within the Jewish community was met with the defensive response: 'Why? Do you want to anthropologize or pathologize us?' It was a valid question.

Interview with one partner of a lesbian couple, 26.9.91.

We began with my asking four questions (very unlike the Seder four questions!) which I hoped might guide our discussion:

(1) As you recognised your lesbian self, was this a transition in self-image?

(2) What do you feel about your seeming abandonment of the 'ready-made me' – ie. the whole complex of expectations coming from 'normative' society and from 'normative' Judaism?

(3) Have you personally felt – or been made to feel – that being a lesbian is 'deviant' from the Jewish experience? In fact, is our talking in a way 'anthropologizing' or 'pathologizing' this part of your life?
(4) Do you experience your religious involvement differently now?

The transition in self-image from my being heterosexual to my being lesbian went hand-in-hand with a transition from my being able-bodied to my being 'physically challenged'. In fact, it was the diagnosis of my having multiple sclerosis which was the turning point, the watershed. It was that which gave me permission to become comfortable with myself and with my body. Before that, I thought I might be bisexual. It was a tremendous effort for me even to use the word 'lesbian' in therapy for the first time.

My breaking up with my husband was not precipitated by my lesbian affair. It was much more that when I knew I had MS, I knew I wanted physical intimacy and spiritual intimacy which I had never had in marriage. It sounds clichéd, but I found God when I became ill. I remember that M. and I sat on the floor, on Shabbat, wearing *tallithim* [prayer shawls worn by men], and I suddenly understood a phrase in the *siddur* which had puzzled me – 'Give me the courage to accept God's chastening hand':

I realised it was about asking for courage to deal with my diagnosis. It freed me to make changes in my thinking and way of being.

Honesty was an enormous relief and yet there is also a lot of loneliness. For example, if I am in a group of 'dykes' – as they label themselves – I am as out of place as if I were with a group of Orthodox women. When I hear the word 'dyke', if feels quite pejorative; it's masculine and butch and that description of a lesbian doesn't fit me; I still feel feminine. There is no contradiction; I can be lesbian and feminine, too.

The loneliness is the other side of the 'high'. It is a wistfulness; if we've had an argument, I sometimes think 'I just want to go home'. 'Home' then feels where my marriage was, where my daughters are. Just sometimes I think I'd like to go back to the old ways. Then I remember how withered and dead I was becoming inside. I'm living life feeling very passionately involved in it now. It's as if all experience now is in technicolour whereas before it was grey. *My soul was withering away.*

On a superficial level, society is changing; the boundaries and acceptances are greater now and attitudes are changing in society generally. But Jewish society is very judgmental. I feel there is little acknowledgment of gay men and women in Orthodox or traditional Jewish society. That had to come from Reform and Liberal or from much more 'alternative' communities like Rabbi Sheila Shulman's.

I haven't felt any desire to flaunt my lesbianism but the people with whom I have shared this have not been thrown – only my mother. My daughters are very aware of how much it has opened me up emotionally. They are very supportive. I think it will become easier to talk about it as it becomes more a part of me, but I don't need to flaunt it; it's my private affair. Yet some lesbians take a political stance; it becomes a challenging statement.

I share aspects of myself with people for whom they are relevant. Like lesbianism, my MS is not instantly visible and I don't need to bring that into everyday conversation either. I don't see either as a 'pathology'. I realise that my generation and my parents' generation had to suppress their feelings about being gay; they married.

The Jewish straitjacket is the conforming: the wedding with all the trappings, the extravagant house; being impressed and trying to impress. Keeping-up the whole time was such an effort. Yet the early years were good; in my naivety I thought I was happy, should be happy; after all, I had all the material wants I could wish for. I *chose* to overlook a feeling within myself for years until a feminist friend opened my eyes *and then I couldn't un-know what I knew*: this relationship was not making me happy.

Acceptance and understanding come slowly to my mother's generation. There's a lot of guilt – 'Where did we go wrong?', etc. She won't invite me home with my partner. My mother had indoctrinated me since childhood to marry and marry well – which I did – and yet virtually throughout my marriage I felt dead, lacking in self-confidence. I was untouched emotionally and physically then and yet my mother says, 'How could you? He was such a gem!' And suddenly living as a lesbian is a much more equal sexual experience than in a heterosexual relationship in which one is the penetrator and the other is the one who is penetrated. In his way my husband was sad and oppressed; the son of a very, very powerful father.

At first I felt a lot of guilt – but do I give up *my* life to help him feel better? Yet I don't know if I would have given up my marriage if I had not been approached by M. It was her awakening of me. Otherwise I might have stayed repressed. The friends who support G. don't articulate what they feel about me. But they want him to go on having a 'normal' Friday night, etc.

I wouldn't mind if my daughters were to become lesbian; I don't have a problem about that. If they want children, there are even gay men who will co-parent with a lesbian. With my daughters I am much more alive and real. I cry freely these days; they are happy in the warmth of our physical touching. They see us as two *people* deeply in love, not solely as two women in love – and this gives them strength.

It is important to me that M. is Jewish. Our very deep bonding on a spiritual level came first: we were very close Jewish friends. But my involvement with the synagogue has undoubtedly changed. I was very, very involved. I used to go every single Shabbat morning. I belonged to a study group there, a women's group there. G. was chairman of the synagogue till I got ill and then he resigned. When I became ill, the community supported me; they thought I was a wonderful brave invalid. But when I picked up my bed and walked, some didn't want to know me; I'd reneged on the idealised image they'd created of me.

When I became lesbian, I moved away from the synagogue: it was too rigid and patriarchal; there is no place in the service for me. It doesn't any longer feel right. Religion is not to do with ritual now; it is much more to do with spirituality. We read not specifically Jewish readings, but spiritual readings. *Havura* groups are developing to meet the religious needs of women and men who had opted out of mainstream Judaism until they found something which met their spiritual needs. What are my feelings? Well, for example, the High Holydays; the girls had always gone with G. and me to *shul*, sat in their lovely new clothes. But now, this year, my elder daughter felt unable to go and my younger daughter felt that what happens formally in synagogue – sitting, repeating, repeating – no longer has any relevance to her. They are discovering their Jewishness more intimately – almost as if they are doing in tandem what I'm doing.

Yet community is very important for me: it's not in isolation that I can find these things. I need language in a prayer book that recognises the female aspect of God and therefore validates the God within me.

(S.L.)

8 Areas of Difficulty

INTERMARRIAGE

> As long as a limb is attached to the body there is hope of a cure. But when it is severed it cannot be restored, and every Jew is a limb of the Shekinah (the presence of God).
>
> (Ba'al Shem Tov)

> Intermarriage, as soon as it appears on a large scale, marks the end of Judaism.
>
> (Arthur Ruppin, writing in the 1940s)

Intermarriage is feared as both an index of and a route to assimilation. Ruppin warned that it occurs when Jews abandon Orthodoxy and live for a few generations amongst Gentiles who are kind and cultured. In America, particularly, his doom-laden prophecy is being realised. Whereas the 1930s saw an intermarriage rate of no more than 3 per cent, the rate for the years 1985–90 was estimated at slightly over 50 per cent (National Jewish Population Survey, 1991). Similarly in Britain: one is three marriages, it is estimated, is now of mixed faith.

Inevitably, as young Jews mix freely with non-Jews in all spheres of life, they intermarry. Only the strictly Orthodox can be sure that their grandchildren will be Jewish; for them, the possibility of marrying a non-Jew is not even an option in their thinking; for the non-Orthodox, it is often a reality in their lives. Nor is intermarriage only a phenomenon amongst non-Orthodox or secular Jews: it happens increasingly in traditionally observant families, too.

Whether intermarriage involves the conversion of the non-Jewish partner or not, it remains an issue of intense concern. The concern is to do with Jewish communal survival, for high rates of marrying out lead to great losses: the children of mixed marriages – particularly where the non-Jewish partner does not convert – usually have little involvement with Judaism. In fact, if the mother is the non-Jewish partner, the children are not *halachically* Jewish, although they are now welcomed into Reform and Liberal congregations.

Conversion – and the extreme difficulty of being converted *halachically* – is discussed in the next section. This section of this chapter begins with a consideration of the different religious responses to intermarriage, an occurrence which is seen by each group as undesirable, and then looks at the communal debate about its implications.

The overriding need today is to find effective deterrents to contain this plague which has already reached disaster proportions ... the continued erosion of Jewish life, now threatened by intermarriage more than by any other single factor.

(Lord Jakobovits, *L'Eylah*, September 1986, vol. 22, pp.22–3.)

Orthodox rabbis in both America and Britain will not under any circumstances officiate at marriage ceremonies involving a non-Jewish partner. The only marriage recognised as a *halachically* Jewish marriage between a couple, one of whom was non-Jewish, is where the formerly non-Jewish partner has undergone a strictly Orthodox conversion, and this is rare. An equally strong stand – with the same restrictions–is also taken in Britain by the United Synagogue, which is the majority group.

Theoretically, similar *halachic* considerations govern Conservative rabbis in the States but, in practice, their application of the laws is often more liberal. Whilst they will not officiate over a mixed marriage, they facilitate conversion – an approach similar to that of the small Masorti/Conservative movement in Britain. However, moving to the left, the American Reconstructionist movement permits its rabbis to participate in *civil* marriage ceremonies between a Jew and a non-Jew.

The issue of mixed-faith marriages highlights an important distinction between Reform in America and Britain. In Britain, neither Reform nor Liberal rabbis will perform a religious ceremony where the non-Jewish partner has not converted. As a result, virtually all such marriages are *civil* marriages and, although some Liberal rabbis may be persuaded to give a blessing, even the most progressive will not permit a synagogue wedding.

In America, too, Reform is still in principle against intermarriage and tries to persuade the non-Jewish partner to convert before marriage. But an increasing number of its rabbis are willing to officiate at a *religious* ceremony between a Jew and a non-Jew, although they make every effort to persuade the non-Jewish partner to convert after marriage.

Intermarriage is a complex and emotive issue, and one of the forces impelling American Reform rabbis to officiate even where there is no conversion – and sometimes even in partnership with a Christian priest – is the deeply-ingrained feeling within society which still regards it as important for a marriage to be religiously blessed. And, within Jewish society, there is the notion that the participation of a rabbi gives legitimacy to something of which lingering Jewish loyalty disapproves.

So it can be seen that religious reactions to intermarriage range from that of the Orthodox, by whom it is deplored, to that of the Reform and

Progressives who, whilst not being in favour of mixed marriages, are increasingly having to accommodate to them, particularly if the non-Jewish partner converts.

Traditionally, those who married outside the faith knew that they were cutting themselves off from the Jewish community. Their families often sat *shiva* and mourned them as dead. In contemporary society, except for the Orthodox, such extreme reactions are rare yet, not long ago, a British politician, Edwina Currie, described how, from the time of her marriage to a non-Jew, her father never spoke to her again, not even when she had children.

William Frankel, a former editor of the *Jewish Chronicle*, suggests the fear of intermarriage is 'a primeval desire to perpetuate the tribe'. Lord Jakobovits views it in terms of duty, declaring that the primary task of the Jew is to perpetuate his Jewishness (both in Brook, 1989). But even non-religious Jews express concern at any act that further depletes the strength of the Jewish population. Richard Hirsch – interestingly, a Progressive – urges 'we must zealously differentiate between making the best of a bad situation *ex post facto* and *ib initio* forsaking the legitimate and vital expectation of Jewish parents and the Jewish community that Jews should marry Jews' (1986, p. 77).

In the face of high intermarriage rates, particularly in America, where, by 1990, it was estimated that there were between 400,000–600,000 Jewish-Christian marriages (Seltzer, pp. 10–11, *Congress Monthly*, May/June 1990, vol. 57(4)) there are conflicting reactions. The Orthodox inevitably view it in terms of an assimilation/disappearance scenario: to be avoided at all costs. At the other end of the spectrum are those who claim that 'intermarriage is likely to be a quantitative and qualitative gain for the American Jewish community' (Goldscheider 1986, p. 16). But, when evaluating this claim, we must note those who emphasize that 'since conversions to Judaism take place in only about one-quarter of intermarriages, the net effect is a loss to the Jewish people, both in terms of numbers and quality of Jewish life' (Himmelfarb, 1986, p. 69).

The reality is that marriage to a Jew results in about one in every six of the non-Jewish partners – mostly the women – immediately converting. Usually they become committed to a Jewish way of life, observing some of the home rituals, becoming part of a network of Jewish family and friends and involved in synagogue or in communal activities. The difficulties arise for the children: although the children of mixed marriages in which the non-Jewish partner has converted (albeit non-*halachically*) often do see themselves as Jewish, this is usually not so in families where the non-Jewish parent has not converted. Ironically, where the mother is

Jewish, her children are *halachically* Jewish, even if their father has not converted – yet, even if they are brought up with Jewish family rituals, these children are usually lost to Judaism. It is partly to stem this loss that the Reform movement in both countries is increasingly willing to educate and convert the children of mixed marriages.

There is a tension even for the more progressive leadership. It is between admitting the reality of mixed-faith marriages and condoning them. Reform and Liberal synagogues are opening their doors to couples who have intermarried and their discussion groups reveal many sensitive areas: that the Jewish partner would have married a Jew had the opportunity arisen; that the intermarried do not necessarily wish to opt out of being Jewish; that family opposition was felt less in religious terms than in socio-cultural 'tribal' terms – 'she is not one of us'. Ironically, many mixed-faith couples express a desire to bring up their children as Jews – a desire which has eventually prompted the Liberal synagogue group in Britain and the Reconstructionists and Reform in America to set aside *halacha* and accept patrilineal descent.

The decision to marry 'out' is always a painful one. In the past, it tended to be one taken primarily by the man – sometimes as both a real and a symbolic separation from a style of family life and a set of cultural expectations seen as too all-pervasive. But, increasingly, Jewish women are also intermarrying. They are no longer held back by a socialization process conveying traditional gender roles, internalized as they matured. In times gone by, the daughter was less expected to succeed professionally and more expected to fulfill her parents' wishes by marrying an educated Jewish man. The parental message was 'don't fly too high; marry well; stay close'. 'Intermarriage would therefore not only be a 'failure' for the Jewish daughter but would also cut her off from warm ties with her family' (Schneider, 1985, pp. 336–7). However, feminism has challenged these sex role differentiations, and a major repercussion of women's wider career opportunities has validated Schneider's predictions: daughters have become 'less dependent on parental validation of their identity and . . . thus less susceptible to their push toward suitable marriage'.

CONVERSION

> Neither shalt thou make marriages with them; thy daughter thou shalt not give unto his son, nor his daughter shalt thou take unto thy son.
>
> (Deut. 7:3)

As I have often said, we should concentrate on converting should-be

Jews, rather than would-be Jews.

(Lord Jakobovits, *L'Eylah*, September 1986, p. 23)

It is extraordinary when one thinks of the requirements involved in being an observant Jew that anyone should want to convert to Judaism. To convert to Orthodox Judaism – and therefore to become a *halachically* accepted Jew – is an exceedingly difficult process. In contrast, the Reform synagogue is more welcoming but their converts are not *halachically* accepted. This section of the chapter will look at both processes.

There are two main situations in which conversion becomes relevant: the first, when a non-Jewish child has been adopted; the second, when an adult wants to become Jewish.

The conversion to Judaism of a non-Jewish adopted child is considered essential by the Orthodox and desirable by most adopting parents. For an Orthodox couple who satisfy the *dayanim* (religious judges) that they observe all the commandments there is little difficulty: the *Beth Din* (Court of religious law) issues a certificate accepting the child as a *halachic* Jew. The procedure is considerably more problematic for a non-observant couple wanting an Orthodox conversion for their child: they have to become fully observant themselves first and to convince the *dayanim* of their intention to remain so. In contrast, Reform and Liberal rabbis are willing to convert a non-Jewish child if they are assured that the child will be brought up in a Jewish way, but such conversions, not being *halachic*, would exclude that child in the future from the possibility of marrying in an Orthodox synagogue.

The much more contentious area is adult conversion. Judaism is not a proselytizing religion. Those who want to convert often do so because they are hoping to marry a Jew who does not want to distress his or her parents by 'marrying out'. However, in the eyes of the Orthodox *Beth Din*, this is not a satisfactory reason to proceed with conversion. Jewish law requires that the would-be Jew sincerely wants to embrace Judaism for its own sake; seeking conversion because of marriage is regarded as an ulterior motive.

Since biblical times there have, of course, always been converts; Ruth, the Moabite, daughter-in-law of Naomi, was the most famous. But, historically, the main reason why Jews resisted accepting converts wanting to marry a Jew was to do with self-preservation. Bermant (1974) observes that 'the more Jews were accepted in the outside world, the more ... the zealots pulled back into their own' (p. 225). Intermarriage has always been feared and never more so than at present, with estimates of one in three in Britain and over 50 per cent in America.

Why should it matter? There is, firstly, parental pressure; (and this applies to non-Orthodox parents, too. The Liberal Jewish woman commenting: 'I was more sad than I thought I would be when my son married a non-Jewish girl...I was surprised that it upset me so much' was expressing a still-common reaction). But, secondly, there is the crucial question of the religious status of the couple's yet-to-be-born children. Whilst the child of a Jewish mother is *halachically* Jewish, even if the father is not, the child of a non-Jewish mother is not *halachically* Jewish unless the mother converts according to the rigorous requirements of the Orthodox *Beth Din*. A Reform conversion is not regarded as valid by the Orthodox. It is difficult to obtain accurate current figures but, historically, more men than women 'marry out'. The non-Jewish woman's potential conversion therefore has special significance.

There are many obstacles to a *halachically*-acceptable conversion, particularly if the reason is for marriage. In these cases, when the would-be convert approaches the *Beth Din*, their first response will be negative, for *halacha* requires the applicant to be without 'ulterior motive'. Even a second application on the same grounds will be rejected. But if the applicant shows persistence and is able to convey that his or her wish is to become Jewish for its own sake, then stringent requirements must be fulfilled. For the woman, this involves going to live with an Orthodox Jewish family and undergoing a prolonged course of instruction in the Jewish religion and in Hebrew. It often takes up to two years. During this time, the *Beth Din* involves itself with her Jewish partner who must convince them that – even if he had not formerly been observant – he will now take upon himself all the obligations incumbent upon an observant Jew. If he is unwilling to do so, the woman's conversion cannot proceed. If, however, he does convince the *Beth Din* of his intention to behave in a strictly religious way, then his partner's conversion may take place. She will be examined on her religious learning and, if this meets the high requirements, she must then undergo a ritual immersion in the *mikvah*. She emerges a *Ger* (a convert), a fully-accepted Jew before God.

Only about 25 per cent of the applications received each year by the Orthodox *Beth Din* will be converted. Why conversion is made so difficult is explained in terms of the need for both partners to be willing to take on the full yoke of obligations in order to live and bring up their children as observant Jews. Ironically, the convert often becomes more Orthodox than many born Jewish!

Non-Orthodox Judaism (i.e. Conservative, Reconstructionist and Reform in America, Masorti, Reform and Liberal in Britain) takes a different stance; it claims that its more hospitable attitude towards conversion lessens the effect of marrying out. It also argues that, if the non-Jewish partner is not converted, the family will be lost to Judaism. Non-Orthodox conversions also demand a serious programme of study and practice, but their requirements are far less rigorous and the major difference lies in the would-be convert's not being initially rejected, even if marriage is the reason. They believe that marriage may be a starting point, but it is not an end point. Regarding ritual immersion, although observing the laws of *niddah* is not an expectation within non-Orthodox Judaism, prior to conversion the would-be convert is required to undergo the *mikvah* ceremony.

Where the non-Jewish partner has not converted before marriage, Reform rabbis make every effort to persuade him or her to convert after marriage and to encourage their involvement in synagogue and communal life. But if, despite these efforts, the non-Jewish partner does not convert, Reform is willing to educate the children of mixed marriages as Jews and, if requested, to convert them. In the States, there are estimated to be between 10,000–15,000 non-Jewish partners annually choosing to convert. Whatever their *halachic* status, the children of such marriages are more inclined to identify as Jewish.

Where the non-Jewish partner does not convert, it is far less likely that the children will identify as Jewish. In sombre illustration of this fact Elazar (1992, p. 19) gives figures from the North American 1990 National Jewish Population Survey: he states that 700,000 children under the age of eighteen of mixed faith marriages are being raised as Christians – that is between 35 and 40 per cent of all Jewish-parentage children in that age group.

In terms of the need for conversion, the religious status of yet-to-be-born children no longer becomes a consideration if a child born of either a Jewish mother or a Jewish father *and brought up as a Jew* is entitled to Jewish status. So here conversion is sought primarily to please the Jewish partner and his or her family. Even non-Orthodox conversions require a study of Hebrew and of the Jewish religion, but the more progressive the group, the less daunting the procedure. However, none of the non-Orthodox conversions are *halachically* accepted.

Conversion, of course, has its emotional consequences. Schneider (1985) asks 'what do women feel who, like Ruth in the Bible, leave their own people and take on another religious identification?' The most difficult aspect 'may well be in forging the synthesis of two different family backgrounds' (pp. 346–7). These problems are particularly pronounced with the Orthodox. One woman who became *Lubavitch* (a strictly-Orthodox *chassidic* sect) talked about her sorrow when her parents died at being unable to sit *shiva* (the seven days of ritual mourning) for them. Another described her difficulty in explaining to her young children why they took sandwiches when they went to eat at her parents' home.

Susan Rose, denied conversion by the Orthodox *Beth Din* and then, after extensive learning, granted it by the Masorti synagogue, discussed her thoughts:

> Becoming Jewish – and more Jewish – was a gradual process for both of us. Conversion, which the rabbis see as a loss to the Jewish community, is in fact a gain. They believe that unless it is made an exceedingly difficult task, the families will use it just as a convenience for marriage and will then drift away. An Orthodox conversion can come about only if the couple are prepared to become extremely Orthodox ... But what results is a way of life in which the emphasis is so heavily on the performance of *mitzvot* [commandments] that every day is like a kind of obstacle race. They see religion as a seamless garment in which you can't do one thing without another. I don't think a convert should be expected to do more than most Jews do. The sincerity of a conversion is to be proved over a lifetime.

FAMILY BREAKDOWN AND DOMESTIC VIOLENCE

In the past, there has been a disinclination in the Jewish community to admit that all is not well in family life; it is reassuring to retain an idealized picture. But the communal social work agencies have increasingly revealed a different reality: that the Jewish community mirrors the wider society. This is particularly relevant in terms of single parent families, with the prime carer mostly being the mother.

This part of the chapter attempts to look at two areas of family breakdown which particularly concern the woman: domestic violence and being a lone parent. It also considers women as carers in a wider context, in relation to family members who are handicapped or elderly. In all of these, accurate statistics are difficult to obtain and, certainly with domestic violence, much, inevitably, remains unreported.

Domestic violence: Wife beating

In this, above all, there is much shame and secrecy. In Jewish family life, emotional or physical violence remain taboo subjects and within Jewish society, myths are perpetuated powerfully enough to make a woman blame herself if violence erupts. Mimi Scarf (in Heschel, 1983) makes this point:

Jewish women who are beaten by their husbands are almost always convinced that it is their fault. *Jewish men do not beat their wives* [her italics] ... Thus a situation has been created in which a very strong image contradicts reality; this in turn leads to a cognitive dissonance, for those involved deny what is happening to them by clinging to what they believe ought to be the reality.

(pp. 51–2)

Biale (1984) suggests that wife-beating must certainly have taken place in traditional societies. Considering the sources, she finds differing attitudes towards it amongst *halachic* authorities. Some regarded it as completely unacceptable and ruled that a violent husband should be forced to grant his wife a divorce if she wished it; others (such as Maimonides) were more lenient towards the husband and permitted 'beating a bad wife as a form of discipline' (quoted in Biale, p. 95); yet others distinguished between wife-beating by an aggressive husband and that caused by a provocative wife.

That it occurs in modern Jewish society is not in doubt. Wiselberg (1991), working with poor Oriental Sephardi families in London, sees marital conflict leading to violence and, in that particular community, attributes it to the women's internalizing different expectations from their often more unwordly husbands. However, Grazin (1991), who set up the first helpline for Jewish women in Britain, suggests wife-beating takes place in all sectors of the community, a similar finding to that of Finkelhor et al. (1983) in the States.

In terms of specifically Jewish resources, one of the most important initiatives is the Family Violence Project, started in 1983 in Los Angeles. Its findings highlight the fact that violence may happen in both religious and non-religious groups and at all socioeconomic levels, it occurs with both Ashkenazim and Sephardim and amidst both immigrant and non-immigrant groups. Yet information about the incidence and the at-risk groups is still inadequate and, frequently, the fact of marital violence is discovered not via the telephone helplines or the women's refuges but by social workers who are already involved with a family because of anxiety over a child.

Giller, in *Jewish Women in Therapy* (1991, pp. 101–9), offers two very specific explanations of this conspiracy of silence. There is, firstly, the discrepancy between the Jewish value system and what actually occurs within the Jewish family. Violation of the internalized ideal of *shalom bayit* (peace in the home) 'has such stigma attached to it that reaching out for help to treat problems such as family violence is rarely even considered within the Jewish community' (p. 102). And, secondly, there is the tension between how Jews want non-Jews to view them – the myth of Jewish family harmony – and the reality, which may, indeed, be dysfunctional.

Much of the literature suggests that Jews, like non-Jews, transmit family violence from one generation to the next. But Giller makes a further point: that the direct experience of persecution may contribute: 'the experience of survivors of the Holocaust and their families serve to generate rage and model violent means of interaction which find expression within the family' (p. 105).

Domestic Violence: Child abuse

Experience and research show that child abuse transcends all cultural, economic, ethnic and religious boundaries
(Jim Harding, Director of Children's Services, NSPCC,
Jewish Chronicle, 16.8.91)

Child abuse is a problem profoundly affecting women as mothers. Norwood Child Care, which covers the areas of most dense Jewish population in London, reports annually increasing referrals of child abuse. In 1989, from a caseload of 600 families, there were a total of 181 children seen who were suffering from or at risk of physical, sexual or emotional abuse. The increase, of course, partly represents increased awareness by the public and professionals. At the same time, these are only reported figures and only for certain areas of London. Norwood's 1990 Annual Report expresses the fear that many in the community 'prefer to look away, to pretend that the old certainties still exist'.

The report emphasizes that with a divorce rate of one in three marriages, family breakdown is high, often accompanied by domestic violence. Women are always at the epicentre of the struggle and very often struggling, too, with poverty. Sam Brier, Norwood's director, points out that child abuse takes place right along the religious/non-religious continuum, even in the Orthodox community, and Norwood is seen at crisis point as being the 'umbilical cord' even for the totally non-affiliated. But Brier suggests that child abuse in the Jewish community is of a less sadistic long-term nature and, secondly, abuse is less drink-related.

It is reasonable to assume that, as in all communities, much child abuse remains hidden even from Jewish social workers in the community. But in the summer of 1991, the Orthodox community of Stamford Hill was torn apart by a mother's seeking help from an agency outside the community, alleging that her daughter had been sexually abused by a young Orthodox man. The horror was not only to do with the allegation but with the mother's seeming betrayal of 'her own'. Amongst the volume of comment was an article by a Liberal Rabbi, Sidney Brichto (*Jewish Chronicle*, 16.8.91), suggesting that 'the desire to create a sub-state by ethnic minorities is not uncommon. It did not work in Stamford Hill because the community could not cope with the repressed sexuality implicit in the allegations'. A similar understanding came from Jim Harding of the NSPCC:

> Child sexual abuse, perhaps more than any other form of abuse, arouses such a degree of feeling that wherever it occurs, secrecy and taboo have served to keep it well hidden ... In communities which strive to maintain a separate religious and cultural identity, revelations of child abuse raise additional issues such as the need to protect the community from uncomprehending and possibly hostile outsiders.
>
> (letter quoted above, 16.8.91)

It is important to acknowledge that child abuse is not restricted just to poor families or to insular, close-knit Orthodox communities. Many of the factors which ignite violence in the wider society are relevant within the whole spectrum of the Jewish community, too.

There is, of course, social work support for families in crisis and, in situations where it is deemed unwise for a child to remain at home or when the child's own family has broken down, there are foster families and group homes – but, as so often with children received into care, they are often found too late to repair the emotional harm that has been done. David Amias, a family therapist in a group home, discusses the extra dimension of caring for Jewish children from families which cannot cope:

> It's difficult to know whether these are extreme situations resulting from family breakdown, from pathological families with no boundaries, or whether we are dealing with the untouchable end of a spectrum – the 'untalkable-about'. I suspect there are elements of pathology in many so-called normal families. For example, we see eating disorders – bulimia and anorexia – in families with too high expectations of their children; they seem to be symptoms of the 'never-good-enough' child. Similarly, you could regard anorexia as a Jewish symptom of the rejection of love.
>
> In terms of the continued Jewish identity of a child who has had to come into care, I am pessimistic. A child who has been abused is often so hurt by what has happened to them that it is too late for us to atone, as if we were not just rescuers but substitute parents making it alright again. In a way it is as if we are atoning for the transgressions of the

abusing parents – as if we are taking on a sort of collective guilt and responsibility. Yet the children in many cases try to throw off the Jewish yoke, as if they resent not only their parents but us as representatives of the community who did not come to their rescue until after the damage had been done.

Children who come into care appear to represent Jewish mothers who have failed adequately to care. Inexplicably, we always have many more girls in care than boys. Why does the breakdown between mother and daughter seem to matter so crucially? Is it that boys' 'acting-out' behaviour is somehow more 'normal'? Or is it that a Jewish girl child has to go along a particular path which will prepare her also to be a mother and, if she has lacked adequate mothering, her consequent deviance from the expected norm is seen as pathological?

There is massive denial in the community that things go wrong in Jewish family life. Behind this is the fear about 'what will the others think?' – i.e. non-Jews. It's as if we daren't acknowledge that we have a problem. One of the myths is that 'it doesn't happen to us'.

(Amias, 11.10.91.)

SINGLE PARENT FAMILIES

Single mothers are the new Jewish poor.

(Schneider, 1985)

Commenting on the situation in the States, Schneider notes that single-parent families, almost all headed by women, make up half the total of Jews living in poverty. It is paralleled in Britain: 'There remains a commonly held view that all Jewish families are affluent. The evidence of Norwood Child Care suggests otherwise.' Its Annual Report states that single-parent families represent over half of its ever-increasing caseload (a caseload of 600 families in the London area in 1990). As an indicator of these lone mothers' financial problems, Norwood points out that over 75 per cent of the families with whom they work are reliant on state benefits, especially single-parent families and even more so where there are children with special needs.

With a Jewish divorce rate of one in three marriages, it is divorced women who are the largest group of lone parents, followed by widows. They suffer not only from the emotional trauma of loss – family break-up or bereavement – and the usually accompanying poverty: also, even today, single parents still suffer from their deviant status in the community. The sense of exclusion comes from being part of – and not being part of – a community which is normatively so family-based. The projected values, the way of life, appear to invalidate the lone mother – her son has no father to sit with in synagogue; she cannot celebrate a *Pesach seder* (the ritual Passover meal) with her children alone. And, despite belated communal acknowledgment of her needs, in Britain the lone mother continues to feel excluded. In contrast, in the States single women and single mothers with their children are increasingly coming together to celebrate the festivals in different ways, their ceremonies and rituals reflecting new insights and understandings.

But the realities of daily life for the single mother remain difficult: state child support provision is inadequate, maintenance payments from ex-husbands are almost impossible to enforce and the need to find work which is flexible enough to fit around child care necessitates their taking 'any old job'. Often, too, the woman who has been out of the workplace during the early years of mothering lacks confidence and has no readily marketable skill. So, she is faced with a financial crisis and a crisis of self-definition simultaneously. The discussion which follows highlights many of these issues. It took place amongst a group of Jewish single mothers in a Gingerbread group in Stoke Newington, North London.

A discussion with Jewish women, 2.10.91

Sandra, Carole, Diane, Michelle, Pauline, Irene.
D: The Jewish community is *not* a very caring community. There's no support for single parents.
S: I went to Norwood and I had this social worker who said: 'I know how you feel' – and I said to her: 'You don't know at all how I feel; you have a nice home, enough money, a car, holidays. How can you know how I feel?' I managed better with the non-Jewish social worker; she was more on my wavelength.
C: The hardest part is having full responsibility – care and control – and then having the father interfere; no financial support, just interference. For me the difficulty is, after being fairly affluent, in being very poor. Now I think twice before buying anything at all. Maybe it's a good thing but my son said to me: 'Some children, when they ask their mothers for something, the mothers say "No, you can't have it." But when I ask you, you say "I'm sorry I can't afford it."'
M: Three of us here haven't been married. You're even worse off financially if you're a single parent never having been married. Single parents have to fight to be able to claim maintenance, whereas a

divorced woman has an automatic right to maintenance. The system is a lot easier for divorced women. Even if I got maintenance the courts would deduct it from my benefits.

D: As for the myth of the warm Jewish community, I don't find the Jewish community supportive. Whereas non-Jewish people can go and talk to their priest, we can't: the rabbis are unapproachable and they make judgements.

D: You crack up: there's no safety net: not Norwood, not Child Guidance, no-one.

C: It's the full responsibility of being with a child twenty-four hours a day during the weekends and holidays and when they're ill that gets you. Mine follows me around the flat. It got so bad during the summer that I took him to my mother for a week.

S: Child Guidance talked to me as if I have the problem: I'm the one with the problem.

D: But when it boils down to it, we are the problem.

C: It's the full responsibility for everything, and for the discipline, that's difficult.

S: You know in your mind that you've got to be consistent with a child and yet you reach the end of your tether and there's no-one you can turn to, so you give in.

P: I'm disabled and a widow. Until my husband died I was well off. I miss having someone to talk to. I don't like having to make decisions. I don't like being Atlas – having to hold everything up.

S: You have to do it. You have no choice except to crak up.

I: My mother lives with me. She has Alzheimer's. Jewish Care give me virtually no help. All they can offer her is the day centre twice a week. I've just come out of hospital; no one from Jewish Care has come to see me. They don't care for the carers.

S: There's no worthwhile help in the Jewish community. There's no financial help. There's no safety net.

C: Where I'm lucky is that I work for myself, but only very part-time. But I still need income support because I'm below subsistence level.

M: We're all on income support.

S: It was important for me that my child went to a Jewish school. Yet, if your child is at a Jewish school, you have even more difficulty in finding work because you're stuck with the Jewish festivals and the State holidays.

C: We all have our children at Jewish schools. It's not that I'm so religious, but I want my son to know he's Jewish.

S: I feel Jewish but not in any way religious. I don't do anything that I should be doing, but my son tells me the things to do which he's learned at school.

I: My daughter has taught me to light candles. She knows her heritage in a way that I don't.

D: Yet there's no sense of belonging here to a community.

I: The girls I work with have such a wrong idea: they say: 'You Jewish people are so close to each other.'

M: The Orthodox community looks down on us because we're single parents. It's a terrible disgrace. I feel completely dismissed by them. They used to spit at us and call us names. As far as they are concerned, we are not Jewish. They don't respect you. There's more feeling of acceptance in the non-Jewish community as a single parent. In the Jewish community it's still hidden, like in my family. Even now my parents don't admit to anyone that I'm an unmarried mother. I met an old friend of theirs the other day and she asked me how my husband is. She couldn't believe that I hadn't been married. It would have been better to have been divorced.

S: I've learned how to fight. You're not only fighting for yourself; you're fighting for your child.

WOMEN AS CARERS

In Britain of the 5,000 clients annually looked after by Jewish Care, 1,000 are in residential homes – Jews who are elderly, physically disabled or mentally ill – and a further 2,000 attend day centres. One in three of the mental health referrals are Holocaust refugees. By far the majority of those who are elderly are women. A comparable situation exists in the States.

Schneider (1985), discussing elderly American women, comments on the many areas from which they feel excluded, especially the synagogue world. A similar view was expressed by a woman living in a home for Jewish elderly people in London: the visiting rabbi pronounced himself unable to conduct the Shabbat service as there were not ten men (a *minyan*) present! Yet, at the same time, Schneider and, particularly, Myerhoff (1978) describe the greater resilience of elderly women and their early-learned resourcefulness.

Inevitably it is the (usually middle-aged) woman who takes on the prime concern for elderly parents. It is a predictable enough dilemma – the work versus family conflict – and comparable to that which she probably had earlier with young children. Like that earlier one, and particularly if this time round the daughter decides to pursue her career, it is a conflict in which guilt is ever-present.

The woman who primarily devotes herself either to the needs of elderly parents or of a child who has a handicap faces different tensions. In fact, the unspoken problem for Jewish women in these circumstances is that the burden of primary care nearly always falls on them. Partly it is unspoken because it is an expectation. Although the welfare agencies act as a safety net with residential care when families cannot cope, a major focus of their work is often supportive services for the carers. Yet the carers may themselves be single parents or widows or elderly, at constant risk of 'burn out', and they themselves not infrequently become the clients.

There is a contradiction: the communal conscience is a strong one in terms of fund-raising and vast sums are raised annually for the welfare organizations. At the same time, as Melanie Kaye/Kantrowitz (1991) writes, 'poor Jews, especially women and the elderly, are invisible, disguised by assumptions of Jewish wealth' (p. 8). Those with a handicap, particularly a mental handicap, could be added to these invisible groups, for they are not included in the idealized depictions of Jewish family life. And, inevitably, so could their mothers. The woman as continued carer is a theme throughout, but particularly so in families where a mentally-handicapped adult child still lives at home, for there her working opportunities are severely limited by the hours offered by the day-care training centres. This is when the realization dawns that her adult-child will always need her at home and that the freedom that other mothers gain as their children become independent will never be hers.

The problems of the woman as carer are far from being a uniquely Jewish phenomenon. But there are specific Jewish cultural assumptions: of communal awareness and of an extended family life, sensitive to the needs of all its members. Not all of these assumptions are valid.

Part IV
Areas of Change

9 Changing Perspectives

SECULAR EDUCATION

> These data indicate that, in general, Jewish men are more highly
> qualified than men in the population at large. However, the opposite is
> true for Jewish women. The situation was changing in the younger age-
> groups.
>
> (Waterman, 1989, p. 43)

The observation is a surprising one, even with its acknowledgment of
change in the younger age-groups, yet the Jewish population which he
describes is very representative of modern Anglo-Jewry. In fact, what has
occurred is a marked generational change, with women now at mid-life
having had different expectations for themselves from those they convey
to their daughters. The mothers had often matured viewing educational
goals and careers as less important than marriage and motherhood (Baker,
1990). But there is much evidence of younger women following the
American pattern: becoming well-educated, with vocational or professional qualifications, and continuing with their careers even after children
are born.

Surveying the North American scene, Fishman (1989) shows how feminism focused the educational goals of Jewish women. Unlike the liberal
arts studying of the 1950s and 1960s, the educational achievements of
younger women are strongly oriented towards occupational and career
objectives. As a result, the high-earning woman with a challenging career
tends to marry late, she has children when she is older, and continues
working during the early years of family life.

In terms of secular education, there is obviously a striking difference
between the attitudes of Orthodox and non-Orthodox families to what is
deemed suitable for their daughters. However, what is more surprising is
the divergence between ultra-Orthodox and so-called 'modern Orthodox'.
These expectations are discussed below, as are the still-existing ambiva-
lences of non-Orthodox Jewish women.

University education is rarely even now an option deemed appropriate
for the daughters of the strictly Orthodox, and this is so even if their own
mothers may have been university-educated (Loewenthal, 1990). The
overt reasons given always refer to the perceived risks – promiscuity,
drugs, etc., – but behind these may be more profound concerns about the
potential cognitive dissonance between the freedoms of the secular world

191

and the requirements of the religious world (Cohen-Nusbacher, 1987). Yet historically, and particularly in Europe, Orthodox girls and young women, excluded from intensive study of the religious sources, were frequently given a liberal education and became more widely accomplished than their male counterparts (Webber, 1983, p. 156). In fact, as 'agents of acculturation', they were often the mediators between the family and the outside world.

Cohen (1988) discusses three levels of education: (a) that which could be described as basic acculturation; (b) that which provides practical skills for working; (c) that which equips the student for leadership. She notes that, traditionally, Orthodox girls were provided with only the first two: great care was always given to their learning the basic laws of Judaism which would enable them to run a religious home; they were also taught the skills needed for them to take their place as useful members of society. Indeed, Kraemer (1989) points out that 'the expectation that the woman should play an active role in supporting the family was taken into account during the prenuptial bargaining, and it also dictated the character of the education considered suitable for one's daughters' (p. 167).

However, the role of leadership in male-defined Judaism has not been viewed as relevant to women. For example, Judaic law, except in certain exceptional circumstances, prohibits women from being witnesses or judges. Despite the exceptional women from biblical times onwards (always quoted by apologists) who were judges and scholars, it was taken for granted until relatively recently that women could not attain even limited positions of community leadership; and the assumption was also made that they did not aspire to such roles.

Yet increasingly, 'modern Orthodox' women have realised that, without education and real knowledge, their roles will remain the caring, 'expressive' family and communal ones and they will continue to be excluded from the 'instrumental' roles which they see more liberated women exercising in the wider society. Partly to meet – or quieten – their demands, modern Orthodoxy in the States and in Britain has begun to make academic provision for women in Jewish studies to a level which their more secular counterparts would reach at university. In Britain, the inauguration of Rabbi Sacks as Chief Rabbi in 1992 witnessed the setting up (on his initiative) of a working party of women, with the express purpose of ascertaining areas where change is needed. Whilst, for the secular woman, the opportunity to discuss innovation within *halachic* parameters seems a merely cosmetic exercise, for the modern Orthodox woman, it is much more; it is acknowledgment of the possibility that knowledge may, indeed, be power.

Very different considerations concern non-Orthodox women – women of a generation who now expect fully to develop their professional potential, who recognise their mothers' tremendously underdeveloped abilities and who determine not to repeat that pattern in their own lives. Yet, ironically – and in this women in Britain may lag far behind women in the States – they often contend with mixed messages:

> My friend, a very bright woman, was told by her mother:, 'Don't be too clever; the men won't like it.' The norm among my friends – even when they are educated – is still, even today, that they stay at home as a mother and housewife. But I don't know if this is a specifically Jewish thing; it's important to recognise that even in non-Jewish society, girls' educational and career aspirations have always been set lower then boys'. And even if you are determined to continue working, as I am, your career – as distinct from your job – is shot to pieces as soon as you take maternity leave.
>
> (Judy Wolfson, 30-year-old teacher, mother of two)

Therefore, even in the context of equal educational opportunities and even with the understandings coming from feminist research and teachings, it seems that in Britain, at least, ambivalence remains. Inevitably two factors still strongly influence the younger woman as she embarks on her career: her mother's own educational/professional achievements and, where relevant, her parents' differential expectations about sons' and daughters' educational goals. Naomi Cohen, a recent graduate, discusses this ambivalence in the context of a traditional Jewish upbringing:

> Having attended an all-girls school, womanhood was not an issue for me. I knew it would all end in matrimony and motherhood. My expectations of the life ahead had been set long before – a product of an education by, and the example of, others . . . You knew what the mother did – she fed and tended. If she did go out to work . . . she was always sure that it never interfered with her domestic responsibilities.
>
> Yet I had never accepted the argument that women couldn't achieve in whatever career or other endeavour they chose to pursue, or that education was a male prerogative . . . Nevertheless this was not consistent with the prescribed formula.
>
> It was not until I went away from home to university that I found a label for these contradictions – feminism. In the years since, I have gone through a process of almost complete re-education – politically, culturally and religiously. I have come of age. My entry into the student community shook up my ideas, expectations and norms radically.

But my education in feminism was by non-Jews in an entirely secular context and before very long seemed to pose an enormous threat to the very essence of my Jewish self. If I was a feminist, which I was, then how could I ascribe to a way of life as inherently sexist as that in which I had been raised? But if I was an observant Jew, which I was, then how could I possibly claim to hold to an ideology – feminism – that so blatantly challenged all I had been brought up to believe? I am still learning that the Judaism of my childhood was as much that of social convention as of religious rule and that I do not have to become ostracised from Judaism simply because I want something different for myself and my daughters than my mother and her mother had.

VOLUNTARY WORK

Once the primacy of the Jewish home and education is safeguarded, by all means we should mobilize for community service the enormous resources of our women.

(Lord Jakobovits, *L'Eylah*, 23 Pesach/Spring 1987)

The entire glory '*Kol Kevudah*' of the King's daughter is within.

(Psalms 45: 14)

Since biblical times, women in Judaism have been persuaded of the primacy of their roles within the home. David Feldman (1972) suggests that this ideal of '*Kol Kevudah*' was never a norm, in that women were never barred from seeking gainful employment outside the home. Yet throughout this consideration there is a paradox: the woman's home roles bring the rewards of family and societal approval and yet within that lies the tension which questions whether – except in economic necessity – her outside roles are valued and valid. How this paradox was traditionally reconciled is explained by Kraemer (1989): her 'aspirations for meaningful work were channelled into the realm of philanthropy' (p. 181).

Voluntary work – welfare work within the community – is an expectation equally incumbent upon men and women. There are many laws enjoining acts of kindness, *gemilut chasadim* and *chesed*, which make it a duty to concern oneself with the needs of the sick, the widowed, the orphan and of all who are needy. However, in terms of the enactment of these expectations, as distinct from the giving of charity, this has primarily become the woman' sphere. Whilst the 'Woman of Worth' of Proverbs 31 fulfilled her obligations to the poor, she was also depicted as a business woman. As earlier noticed, in our own times it was affluence which led to women's concentrating their surplus energies into charitable work. It was a vocation not unique to Jewish women and, in fact, the lives of Jewish women have frequently resembled those of other contemporary women of similar economic, cultural and educational backgrounds (Schlesinger, 1987, p. 35).

But several factors have combined to make women question this traditional role: the economic recession and, at the same time, the climate of opinion which sees money as a metaphor for worth. And, as well as the realities within society, there is an emotional truth in Virginia Woolf's memorable phrase in *A Room of One's Own* (1929) – 'money dignifies' – which resonates even today! Also, for many women there is often the disturbing feeling that voluntary work may indeed be a 'compassion trap' (Adams, 1971).

> In my terms, worthwhile also has be paid.
>
> (Librarian)

> Payment makes a difference to the way you feel about work. In the eyes of other people, the payment aspect earns respect . . . Then, too, in voluntary work you frequently have to defer to someone whom you would rather be and you are constantly aware of not using your talents.
>
> (Teacher)

Historically, it is interesting to note the important role which Jewish women played in both the States and Britain in the establishment of communal institutions and their day-to-day running. Yet now the situation has changed and increased educational and career opportunities have resulted in the long-established welfare committees reporting a serious depletion of volunteers as younger women turn to paid employment.

Fishman (1989) described the way in which, in the States, communal voluntary work has strikingly been affected by feminism. She notes the high percentage of Jewish women substantially involved in it a generation ago – for voluntary welfare work had always earned family and communal approval. However, by the 1960s and 1970s it came under the scrutiny of the Jewish feminist movement, with writers like Doris Gold and Aviva Cantor calling it 'pseudo-work', 'a placebo' and 'a distorted form of occupational therapy', inevitably making the volunteers themselves question not its worth but their own needs in doing it. Similar changes came about in Britain, although slightly later, resulting in the voluntary roles being retained primarily by older women.

However, while younger women rejected the expectation that they would find a sense of purpose in everyday welfare tasks, they did not totally reject an allegiance to communal work. They turned, instead, to the traditionally male areas of politics and power and began to seek and gain leadership positions. They also began to take on professional paid roles within the communal organisations. These became the most significant changes in women's voluntary involvement.

JOBS AND CAREERS

Women should acquiesce in their role, just as men do . . . Women's freedom is too new: they've not learned to use it appropriately yet. Feminism has probably brought as much unhappiness as the earlier situation when women knew they needed to stay at home while the children were small . . . Now they have careers and they strive for the same level of achievement as men. So the women lose out if they compromise and their children lose out if they don't. There is a price to be paid for freedom.

(Lucien Gubbay, in interview)

One felt – one was made to feel by other women – quite ambivalent about mothering . . . You wanted the best for your children, but that shouldn't involve staying at home with them. As for the creation and provision of food for a family – that was considered negligible stuff. The woman who stayed at home was ridiculed. In contrast, women who had real careers were enormously respected by other women – 'ah, but hers is a real career, it can't be set aside!' – and enormously envied.

(Norma Black, Glasgow woman, former television producer,
mother of three)

The subject of women and work is an enormously emotive subject as well as a factual one and here it will be considered from several different perspectives. Firstly, it will be looked at historically and then in terms of its specifically Jewish aspects. These considerations are followed by a description of the current situation in the States and Britain. The chapter ends with possibly the most sensitive area – peer group pressure and personal needs.

Historical

Employment outside the home for women with children inevitably raises complex problems. Yet before industrialization the practical difficulty was not as great, for there was no separation of work and home; the woman could work and earn and not be away from her mothering role. In contrast, with the separation of home and workplace, the woman needing to contribute to the family's income or even to be the bread-winner had to make alternative arrangements for the care of her children.

Oakley, in *Subject Women* (1981), discusses this point: she refers to a study on the nation's health by Frederick Maurice in 1903 in which, reviewing Whitechapel in the East End of London, he found that 'Jews were healthier and lived longer because Jewish mothers, unlike their Christian counterparts, did not go out to work' (quoted in Oakley, p. 211). They worked, of course, often in sweated workshops, but his otherwise puzzling observation pinpoints the crux of the dilemma, which is to do with child care.

In the absence of economic necessity – and definitions of this are often culturally relative – many other factors become relevant to a woman's work expectations: currently held theories about child care exert powerful influence – for example, Bowlby's writings of the 1950s on attachment and maternal separation held sway over at least a decade of mothers. Also enormously important are generational attitudes and male insecurities about the 'rightness' of married women's working. But the revolution in women's thinking emanating from the writing and speaking of feminists, from Gavron and Friedan in the early 1960s onwards, reached all women, exhorting them to question their rigidly defined roles.

Specifically Jewish considerations

Jewish women have worked throughout history and have always had roles additional to that of motherhood. There are over 200 occupations listed in the Bible and Schlesinger (1987) points out that many of these – agriculture, the buying and selling of land (as in Proverbs 31), business, textiles and weaving – were also performed by women. Post-biblically, we read (in the *Mishnah Ketaboth*) that even if a woman has servants she should at least spin her own wool because 'leisure leads to idiocy'.

The 'Woman of Worth' of Proverbs 31, whose praises are sung every Shabbat, worked as both homemaker and breadwinner to enable her other-worldly husband and sons to become religious scholars. The scholars, of course, were few but since earliest times it was acceptable, if there was economic need, for a wife to work and earn. Often she worked alongside her husband in manufacture or trade but Schlesinger also shows over different periods of history the change in attitudes towards the acceptability or otherwise of the wife's having an economic role outside the home. Similarly, Hyman (in Heschel, 1983) sketches the work roles of Ashkenazi women in Central and Eastern Europe and the fact that 'the *halachic* tradition ... accommodated itself to the expanding economic role of women'. But she also notes how 'the economic aspect of the Jewish mother's role has tended to be omitted from the popular image' (p. 23).

Notions of there being 'appropriate' and therefore rigidly demarcated gender roles have, historically, always been set aside because of economic necessity (Rich, 1977; Myerhoff, 1978; Burman, 1990). Ironically, it was affluence which resulted in women's role becoming more confined – affluence in the context of the increasing secularisation of society. As men fully took over the economic role, it became a sign of their success that they no longer needed their wives to earn. The woman was therefore left with little option but to withdraw into the full-time mother-housewife role and, as Kraemer (1989, p. 181), quoted earlier, writes, 'her aspirations for meaningful work were channelled into the realm of philanthropy'.

The phenomenon of the woman's withdrawing into the home is discussed in different contexts by Kaplan (in Cohen and Hyman, 1986) and Westkott (1986). Both see it in terms of a quest for stability in a time of rapid social and economic change. 'The domesticated world of women became the locus of preservation' (Westkott, p. 21). As a result, women came to be defined through the family. 'A value system which defined women as domestic, modest, dependent, protective, self-denying, religious and virtuous, gained ... attraction in a period in which these same qualities were viewed as encumbrances by men under pressure to succeed in the world outside' (Kaplan, p. 65).

In our own time, Jewish women are struggling, often unconsciously, to reconcile many different pressures and contradictory expectations, and even the Orthodox, with their seemingly impregnable boundaries, are trying to integrate new possibilities within their way of life. In the context of work, the Orthodox woman is different from more affluent and less strictly religious women. She draws on a tradition of working outside the home, although her work may be confined to a primarily Jewish world. But, however protected, many Orthodox women now work in the non-Jewish world and inevitably there are tensions, possibly even questions about the role of women in religious Judaism. Cohen-Nusbacher (1987), looking at the Orthodox in New York, discusses how women cope with these conflicting influences; she asks whether they deny the cognitive dissonance, or accommodate, or compartmentalize. She observes the strength of the Orthodox reference group and the individual's 'fear of being labelled deviant by the community' (p. 165) if she were to initiate change. Drawing on reference group theory, she explains how the woman, through the family, internalizes the community's norms and perceives, thinks, forms judgements and acts according to the group's frame of reference.

However, the influences confronting the Orthodox woman working in the secular world do not only concern women's wider options; sometimes they involve social mores. Eytah Simons, working in a London housing department, explains:

> All day long, I hear *prosta* [uncouth] language. They joke and speak lewdly without meaning anything by it. But it upsets me; it's difficult to maintain a feeling of spirituality working in that world, yet I want to work in it because I can achieve things for our own community.

Whilst work has always been the norm for the Orthodox woman, it has traditionally been work fitted around family commitments. The imperative is that home and children must come first and work has always been seen as being to help support the family and enable the husband to pursue religious study. However, whilst there are no formal contra-indications, communal pressure as well as family responsibilities make the possibility of a woman's developing a career – as distinct from undertaking a job or running a business – comparatively rare; indeed the concept of 'self-development' is an alien one in Orthodox Judaism which emphasises not autonomy but reciprocity of roles.

Shakdiel (1990), discussing Orthodox women and work, sees throughout history the separation of realms and roles between men and women; whilst women were very much revered in the roles they could fulfil, 'it would be fair to say that men had avenues to develop personal ambitions' and women did not. In effect, the notion of a *career* for an Orthodox woman is a very new one.

For the non-Orthodox, there have been different constraints. Burman (1982, 1986 and 1990), depicts the generations of immigrant women – robust, enterprising, industrious, independent – and their daughters, liberated from such economic need, who 'moved towards a situation of greater economic dependency and a more exclusively domestic orientation' (1982, p. 33). She describes how they gradually took on similar values to those of the long-established Anglicised Jews who 'tended to see breadwinning as a male prerogative and responsibility' and thought that 'a woman's involvement in paid work would have cast a dark shadow on her husband's integrity and social standing' (1986, p. 238).

For the economically favoured generations which followed, it took a revolution in thought for roles to change again and for Jewish women to reach for the wider options that increasingly their non-Jewish counterparts were following. Many factors made it a difficult transition; partly the still-strong pull of old ways of thinking (their own and their menfolk's); but, especially for the religiously observing, there were, and are, all the extra dimensions. They are more than merely practical demands – the cleaning and shopping and cooking and preparing for the Shabbat (particularly in winter when it begins early) and for the festivals throughout the year, with all their special requirements – they are a way of life.

Yet, despite the difficulties, women who married and became mothers in the sixties and early seventies were the first to respond to the realisation that they had choices: they could expand their roles or remain confined within them.

And this time Jewish women struggled not with economic need but with psychological and socio-cultural conflicts (Baker, 1990). And, eventually, they found new 'steady states' which often, for the sake of marital harmony, involved tacit agreements reconciling their awareness of their own potential with their perception of other people's expectations.

Schlesinger (1984 and 1991), also considering married Jewish women's return into the paid workforce, makes similar observations about the adjustments between desire to work and a family context of patriarchal assumptions. She notes how women learn to juggle roles and cope with guilt, 'because they were not fulfilling their original marriage contract as they understood it in traditional Jewish terms'. However, 'they slowly came to realize that their roles within the family did not have to depend on how well they cooked, but on who they were' (p. 85).

The Contemporary Situation

So, after all this discussion, what is the reality? Writing on the North American experience, Fishman (1989) sees later marriage and childbirth and smaller families as being the now-established pattern for Jewish women. It is a pattern within the context of Jewish women's high levels both of education and of professional training and their consequent career expectations and occupational achievements. Alongside these trends, she notes inevitable changes in the types of work which Jewish women are choosing: the numbers opting for teaching careers have dramatically dropped and, especially in the younger age groups, there is a striking advance into careers in medicine, law, engineering and science and into executive positions in business.

How these careers have been reflected in terms of child-care decisions is shown by the fact that in 1957, only 12 per cent of Jewish women with children aged under six worked outside the home. By the 1980s, the majority of Jewish mothers continued to work, at least part-time, even when their children are quite young. Fishman points out that, whilst perceived economic need is still probably the single most important factor affecting the proportion of Jewish mothers who work outside the home, there is also strong peer group pressure to do so.

In contrast to this quite specific picture, what Jewish women in Britain, do if they remain in or return to the workforce is still inadequately documented. However, Waterman's (1989) study of female employment amongst Jews observed no significant difference between Jewish and non-Jewish women living within the same districts. Anecdotal evidence also suggest that the work experience of Jewish women is similar to that of non-Jewish women of similar backgrounds.

Commenting on women's work experience in the population at large, the 1991 report of the Equal Opportunities Commission observes: 'we see so graphically that women's experience and skills are still under-utilised and under-valued. Women continue to get less and a lower level of training, less pay and fewer senior jobs than men and, as compared to other women in the European Community, they fare badly on maternity rights and access to child care.' Of all the statistics, maybe the most telling is the fact that, in 1989, only 28 per cent of employed women were in managerial and professional work (*Social Trends*, 21, 1991).

Peer group pressure and personal needs

Social pressure affects not only behaviour but, even more powerfully, the internalized attitudes which influence behaviour (Ajzen and Fishbein, 1980). In terms of women's roles, peer group pressure to transcend previously-held options, to strive and achieve outside the home, creates change. It also often creates emotional conflict for the homemaker who becomes polarized into the defensive position of defending that which matters to her. It is a conflict frequently voiced by younger women who enjoy being mothers and homemakers but who feel guilty at doing so, as if this should not be, as if they are somehow letting themselves down. And, of course, it is a sad paradox that the struggles and achievements of feminism have so deeply entered women's collective psyche that for women to continue doing what feels most natural – to nurture – becomes a way of life needing to be defended.

This time round, the gradual evolution in women's roles came about because of a painful awakening in each woman's awareness that maybe she could do more. It was an awakening which was acknowledged: her seemingly individual frustration was not hers alone (Friedan, 1963) and nor was it a sign of pathology (Scarf, 1980; Showalter, 1987).

But both the awakening and the acknowledgment did not in themselves change the roles; the change for each woman came about as a result of her own struggle, made in the context of her early parental influence, her own mother's example, her marriage, her peers; and it was never an easy one. Each eventually found her individual way and collectively they became the role models for women born in the sixties and seventies. The daughters represent a historically significant new generation, theoretically the beneficiaries of their mothers' struggles. The options they have inherited are no longer specifically Jewish options, but neither are the conflicts. For, inevitably, for younger women who choose motherhood as one of their roles, the juggling act remains. Rabinovitch describes it:

> Today's Jewish mother is pushed this way and that: by the ancient culture within her which tells her to stay with her baby, and by the much more forceful culture without, which tells her to cherish her own sanity first. Remarkably, among more and more of the young women whom I meet, the ancient call is prevailing.
>
> (*Jewish Chronicle*, 28.12.90)

The conflict is not a new one and the seeming 'regression' is much chronicled, on which particularly see Rossiter (1988). She describes the inner conflict between what seems natural – to mother her children and to respond lovingly to their need of her – and her intellectual realisation of the consequences: 'I stayed home with the kids; consequently, I lived isolation, financial dependency, deprivation of work and depletion of my energy from constant caretaking. But I *chose* to stay home' (p. 12). Friday (1977, p. 25) discusses it also in terms of the double messages which women give to their daughters:

> Little girls are raised to live by a hidden agenda. On the surface we say, 'Yes, you have as much right as a boy to have a career, to be a doctor, a lawyer', but there is a hidden message: 'first, you are going to be a mother too.' So the girl says, 'Yes, I'm going to be a lawyer, but I'm also going to have a family.' No recognition is given to the fact that in our society it is structurally very difficult to be a mother and a lawyer, too.

Looked at historically, it seems that women's decisions about work are never reached in a vacuum. Ironically, for many the cycle has gone full circle as economic necessity once more overrules traditionally demarcated gender roles. Even where that is not a prime consideration, as they pursue their careers and delay marriage and motherhood, other younger women ask: 'have we learned too well the message that our mothers conveyed?' And somewhere in the middle, new-old contradictory expectations still tug. Young mothers speak of having to balance their very primitive desire

primarily to be mothers with their own conflicting need – as well as peer
group and ideological pressure – to prove themselves in the world of
work.

The tugs are there in a letter from my daughter to me, as she prepared to
return to work:

> It seems so strange and impossible to imagine my leaving him for
> someone else to look after for a whole big chunk of day. I know he's
> grown and developed incredibly since being such a little helpless lamb
> at birth; but he's still so tiny and helpless, so in need of constant holding
> and loving and being near my breast the whole time. And yet I also
> know that if I am to leave him, it's probably better to begin now, when
> he is happy to be cared for by anyone who is gentle and loving and
> sensitive, rather than in two or three months' time when he'll be much
> more specifically attached to me and much more painfully aware of
> being left with a stranger. The woman whom I've found is very caring. I
> hope all will be well.
>
> But what will I do without him? I'll burst with milk and with missing
> him.
>
> (Caroline Hacohen, 6.8.91)

10 Feminism

> The bias of Jewish culture . . . is toward the collectivity. Not that the individual should be sacrificed to the community, but that the individual is profoundly connected to the community, so profoundly that separation is not truly possible without extreme loss. But even feminist therapists . . . who know better than to idealize individuation and demean connectedness . . . sometimes miss the point about Jewishness and see it only as an archaic construct to shed.
>
> (Melanie Kaye/Kantrowitz, 1991, p. 13)

> There is nothing more beautiful for a wife than sitting in the corner of her house.
>
> (Maimonides (1135–1204), quoted in *L'Eylah*, September 1991, p. 45)

> Yet the truth is, Jewish women *have* disrupted the family. We have challenged patriarchal authority. . . . We have created a Jewish women's peace movement in support of Israeli and Palestinian women working for peace. We have argued unequivocally for reproductive choice. We have been among the leaders of the feminist movement, challenging the traditional nuclear family.
>
> (Melanie Kaye/Kantrowitz 1991, p. 16)

Jewish feminism enquires how women achieve self-respect within a religion and within a culture which have been male-defined. All the literature analyzes the way in which existing roles incorporate in their structure male-dominated attitudes and values; (Priesand, 1975; Koltun, 1976; Greenberg, 1981; Heschel, 1983; Schneider, 1984; Adelman, 1987; Neuberger, 1983 and 1991). Whilst Greenberg in particular maintains a strong commitment to Jewish tradition, other writers discuss the ways in which changes have to be made in the traditions and, above all, in women's legal position, stressing that much in Jewish law sets women apart, not only as separate but also as disadvantaged.

Feminism in its widest sense and Jewish feminism with its specific issues have touched Jewish women right along the religious/non-religious continuum. Yet for different women there are different issues: for some, feminism is about roles within the family; others focus on roles within religion; many demand change of woman's status within *halacha*, particularly in relation to divorce and *agunah*; yet others see feminism ideologically *vis-a-vis* Israel and her policies.

WITHIN THE FAMILY

Greenberg (1981) writes that, in previous generations, the Jewish woman was completely fulfilled as wife and mother: 'No one ever told us that we should expect something more for and from ourselves'. For many British Jewish women, even in the 1990s, their home, sometimes together with voluntary work, has remained their prime sphere of fulfilment (Baker, 1990). But for others – and much earlier for American Jewish women – the ripples emanating from the women's movement led to their questioning seemingly predestined roles and redefining their expectations for themselves. And, in their turn, the daughters of these women have even begun to question marriage and motherhood.

This, of course, is not a uniquely Jewish phenomenon, Swirsky (1989) suggests that 'the generation into which a woman is born has a critical effect on the way in which her identity is constructed'. Whilst women in the context of economic necessity have always worked outside the home, the radical change has been for women who do not economically need to work, in their choosing to work for its intrinsic satisfaction. Their changing perceptions of what they can do were contingent on the understandings of feminist writers and psychotherapists from Friedan (1963) to Orbach (1986), who enabled women to think about their own potential as well as their time-honoured role as enablers of others.

But there is an extra dimension for Jewish women and it is partly to do with assumptions: that taking on work roles might threaten traditional Jewish family life (Schlesinger, 1984). Historically – and still in the unconscious of many women – there is the feeling that 'self-development' is contrary to a religious-cultural ethos which emphasises not autonomy but reciprocity of roles. How this delicate balance between awareness of one's own potential and awareness of the needs of others is maintained is often through 'tacit agreements', eloquently expressed by one (traditionally observant) woman: 'I'm aware of how I and many, many other intelligent, able women maintain an unnecessarily low profile career' (Baker, 1991). A culture which has always accommodated women in the breadwinning role – when that accorded with necessity – had to evolve through a more confining view of a woman's 'rightful realm' to a new equilibrium in which outside roles once more became valued and valid.

WITHIN RELIGION

It is this area within Orthodox and traditional Judaism which has been the most complex, where feminist pressure for change has met both powerful male opposition and seemingly incomprehensible female ambivalence. Whilst in Progressive Judaism women fully participate in all aspects of religious and communal life, the conflict within Orthodoxy is epitomised by Greenberg's cautioning against too radical change, stressing the rewards built into existing roles (1981).

Acknowledging the extent to which woman is idealized in her 'proper' sphere, Jewish feminists emphasize how *halacha* constrains women in the other central areas of religious life – Torah study, synagogue ritual and communal leadership. But Hyman (in Koltun, 1976) sees the most formidable barrier to change as lying 'in the psychological rather than the *halachic* realm'. Her view (that Orthodox women do not want involvement in synagogue ritual and that traditionally observant women are equivocal about it) is borne out by the reaction expressed by Orthodox women that 'These questions are from outside; they're not relevant to our lives'. Yet Pnina Peli suggests that 'worried about losing everything to an open society, prevailing conditions are frequently "enshrined" and painful problems are swept under the carpet in the name of some undefined piety' (*Jewish Chronicle*, 31. 10. 86.) Meiselman (1978) – very much from within Orthodoxy – suggests that women are uniquely private beings, endowed with humility and therefore with no need of the public arena for the expression of their innermost spiritual thoughts (pp. 12–15). Commenting from outside this system of thought, Julia Neuberger writes:

> A better justification for the exclusion of women from the requirements of public worship it would be hard to find, and a more clearly apologetic explanation of how it is that women are excluded from the congregation of ten [men] required to conduct a full service in orthodox Judaism it would be hard to create.
>
> (1991, p. 154)

Yet within modern Orthodoxy the debate has gathered momentum and there are strong and knowledgeable women well able to argue both perspectives. Some uphold the rightness of separate spheres and maintain that within these there is an intrinsic dignity (Loewenthal, *Jewish Chronicle*, 23.3.84, p. 10). But Loewenthal also points out that 'the idea that a woman shouldn't learn, shouldn't pray, should spend her whole time cooking and cleaning and looking after the children – there is nothing in *halacha* that says she has to live this way'. Other women within

Orthodoxy focus on public prayer and argue that evolution is both desirable and, in fact, *halachically* feasible. Greenberg (1981) and Rosen (1984) both challenge accepted wisdom and affirm that there is nothing to prevent women from making up a *minyan*, their own *minyan*, separate from men. Rosen also suggests that there are other areas, too, which are *halachically* permitted to women – to recite *kaddish*, to dance with the scrolls on *Simchat Torah*, to approach the Ark in the synagogue (*Jewish Chronicle*, 23.3.84, p.10).

Significantly, a seminal issue of *L'Eylah*, the journal of modern Orthodoxy, gave central place to a symposium on Judaism and Feminism (September 1991). In it Gila Rosen looked at radical feminism which exposes 'hierarchical patterns between men and women and social injustices perpetuated by men', but stressed that it did so 'away from their extenuating social contexts' (p. 9). Inevitably, therefore, it is alien to Orthodox Judaism, for it 'rejects Jewish law as a "man" made system, rather than a Divine system with different roles for men and women'. Rosen finds the liberal feminist view 'with its emphasis on women's equivalent potential... more amenable to synthesis with the tradition'; it is a potential stimulus 'to evaluate the *halachic* possibilities of increased participation of women in various religious experiences'. Similarly, Erica Brown draws on feminist ideas: she cautions that 'female spirituality is so often woven into the care for others that women have not learned to grow up spiritually on their own', and urges women to increase their commitment to study and prayer (1991, p. 8).

But what remains within modern Orthodoxy – despite the eloquence – is often a sense of disinclination for fundamental change: 'What I think is necessary is to be aware of *halachic* definitions and their deeper psychological roots, whilst at the same time attempting to maximise one's individual potential' (Dansky, 1991, p. 12). Despite Greenberg's often-quoted rallying call – 'Where there is a rabbinic will there is a *halachic* way' (1981) – what modern Orthodoxy seems to want is circumspect evolution within the parameters of what is permitted by *halacha*.

WOMAN'S LEGAL STATUS IN RELATION TO DIVORCE AND *AGUNAH*

Chapter Three discussed the divorce laws and the tragic position of the *agunah*. The feminist case for change is an eloquent one, for it is in this area above all that religiously committed women are potentially affected by *halachic* inequalities. As Tager writes, 'Women who desire to practice their religion remain victims of a patriarchal system which considers them as unable to take full responsibility for their destiny' (1991, p. 5). But the implications of these laws are even more far-reaching: even women remote from traditional Judaism are not immune for they risk conferring onto the children of their subsequent partnerships a status of religious limbo. The *halachically* 'tied woman' must remain loveless or her future descendants become non-*halachic* Jews.

The demands for change come from many who are well-informed in terms of religious-legal possibilities – Greenberg (1981), Judge Aron Owen (1988), Judge Myrella Cohen (1989), Rabbi Riskin (1989), Dayan Berkovits (1990), and many others – but they are confronted by learned *halachists* who insist that the laws cannot be changed. Nor it seems, is there much hope of their being re-interpreted (Ruth Winston-Fox, personal communication). Focusing specifically on one aspect, Owen examines legal options to prevent a recalcitrant spouse from withholding consent consent to the giving or acceptance of the get. He concludes 'we should not have to look to non-Jewish legislation for ways to remedy problems relating to . . . Jewish religious problems. These should, can and must be solved *by our own religious leaders*' (his italics, *Jewish Chronicle*, 17.6.88. p. 29).

To the feminist striving to combat injustice, the status of *agunah*, whether resulting from a husband's non-granting of a *get* or consequent on a husband's disappearance, symbolizes woman's powerlessness within religion. The irony is that strictly Orthodox women remain seemingly accepting of their disadvantaged position. Asked about a desire for possible *halachic* re-interpretations, they reply 'these questions are from outside our frame of reference'. But it is, after all a reply understandable within its historical context and within a belief system so resistant to change, a resistance eloquently expressed by Lord Jakobovits:

> Above all it should be more widely realised that for every instance of personal hardship caused by applying the laws of marriage and divorce there are thousands of Jewish homes sanctified by the strict adherence to these very laws over the ages. It lies in the nature of every civilised system of law that individuals occasionally suffer for preserving the interests of society at large, just as there are inevitable causalties in any army defending the nation's survival and freedom.
>
> (*L'Eylah*, 1986, no. 22, p. 22)

In contemporary terms, little has changed since Greenberg wrote that for rabbis 'to say that their hands are tied, or to say they can resolve an individual problem but not find a global solution, is to deny their collective responsibility' (1981, p. 142).

Feminism and *halacha* – ideologically poles apart – yet, as Greenberg (p. 143) points out, underlying Judaism is the principle of *tikkun olam* – improvement of the social order. 'And if there is one woman in each generation who suffers unnecessarily as a result of the law, then the law is biased against all women.' So is there, then, a point of contact between feminist ideals, which challenge injustice, and this mystical Kabbalistic doctrine, *tikkun olam*, which emphasises human responsibility for the perfecting of our world? Believing that there must be, a new generation of women are informing themselves of the facts about women 'trapped' as *agunot*, are acquainting themselves with the methods of reasoning and, no longer as supplicants, are petitioning for change. There is a Chassidic saying: 'Whether it be an individual or a people, whoever shuts out the realization of their flaws is shutting out redemption.' It applies most of all here.

FEMINISM AND ZIONISM

> I was a universalist. I believed that as a woman I have no country. Being Jewish was what I was born into; it is my tribe, my heritage. I was never *not* Jewish. But during the major part of my life this tribal affinity was not important. It became important because of anti-Semitism associated with Israel: I was driven back into my Jewishness by my sisters in the Women's Movement. The pro-Palestinian propaganda was an acceptable cover for anti-Semitism.
>
> (Asphodel Long, in interview)

> The *Spare Rib* affair faced Jewish feminists with a classic choice: to speak out against other feminists and be accused of betraying their sisters, or to continue to struggle within the women's movement and be accused of betraying their community.
>
> (Julia Bard, 1991, p. 93)

In Britain and America, many Jewish feminists severed themselves from the wider feminist movement in the late 1970s and early 1980s. The initial cause of disquiet was the proposal at the United Nations Decade on Women's first conference in Mexico City in 1975 that 'Zionism equals Racism'. The proposal (which was passed as a resolution of the UN General Assembly and only eventually rescinded in 1991) was the first indication of anti-Semitism within the women's movement.

However, the need for Jewish women in the feminist movement to define their ideological position became very apparent with Israel's 1982 invasion of Lebanon and her indirect responsibility for the subsequent massacre by Maronite Christians of women and children in the Sabra and Shatila refugee camps. This tragic war starkly highlighted the responsibility of Jewish women to speak out against oppression – and yet how could they do so in the context of an increasingly vocal anti-Semitism amongst their non-Jewish feminist sisters? The issue of anti-Semitism in the women's movement was confronted in the States by Letty Pogrebin in *Ms* magazine (June 1982). In Britain, the conflict was brought to a head by an article in *Spare Rib* magazine entitled 'Women Speak Out Against Zionism' (Boyd et al., August 1982); protesting letters from Jewish feminists were refused publication.

It had become a very painful 'double-bind' situation in which Jewish feminists felt unable to remain within the women's movement and yet unable to identify with the 'normative' Jewish community which was seen to silence any public criticism of Israel by Jews. (Ironically, these inherent contradictions were later intensified by Israel's own sharply divided response to the *intifada*.)

Yet no specifically Jewish feminist stance emerged. There were too many issues, no unifying agenda. Mostly, as Rogow points out, Jewish feminists 'defended Israel against anti-Semitic criticism while they condemned Israel's treatment of Palestinians and searched for ways to shrink the chasm between Palestinian and Jewish women' (1990, p. 70).

At the same time, sharp divisions developed – and remain unbridgeable – between Jewish feminists: there are those who believe that Israel should return the territories occupied in 1967 whilst supporting her right to exist within secure borders (the position of the women's peace groups in the States and Britain); there are those who will not countenance any defence of what they see as Israel's imperialist stance; and there are those from the 'normative' Jewish establishment who consider any criticism of Israel as traitorous (Solomon, 1990, p. 45).

There is a further issue: it is to do with the centrality of Israel in Jewish thought. Since the Holocaust it has, for the majority of Jews, been hard to imagine Jewish survival without the existence of Israel. Yet, at the same time, identification with the oppressed should be an ethical foundation of Jewish identity. In this lies the conflict: Jewish women doubly identify with oppression, as women and as Jews, and cannot reconcile Israel's policies towards the Palestinians with their own ideological understandings.

The alienation which Jewish women felt within the wider feminist movement was mirrored for the more radical of these women by what they felt about the Jewish religious and communal establishment. 'Normative' Judaism sees Israel as the heart of the Jewish world. Jews who do not hold this view perceive themselves as not being regarded as *bona fide* members of the community. Julia Bard (1988) writes: 'The central assumption is that Jewish identity rests on a Middle Eastern foundation; that it is always seen through the prism of the Israel/Palestinian conflict' (p. 3). The community, according to this perception, claims that to break with Zionism means to shatter one's Jewish identity.

The chasm, therefore, became not just about the freedom to define right and wrong for, in fact, even within 'establishment' Judaism there is not one view about Israel. It concerned something more contentious: the possibility of making other alliances, specifically of seeing validity in Palestinian claims. 'Zionism is the acid test, the one issue on which all Jews, whatever their other differences, are supposed to agree. If they don't, then there is no place for them in the community; they are no longer entitled to ... make political statements *as Jews*' (Bard, 1988, p. 4, her italics). It is a position which urges responsibility, not opting out, but which suggests that one's identity as a Jew can and should exist distinct from either religion or Zionism.

The rift became an issue about Zionism and also about something wider, for it concerned 'marginality'. Cesarani (1985/6) writes:

> To most people in the Jewish community, this ... [concern about intermarriage] along with ... Zionism and a paranoia about anti-Semitism, constitutes the sum total of Jewish awareness ... The Jewish community defines itself according to religious and racial characteristics; it is deemed to be united by a common religion, including Zionism, and a common enemy – anyone who isn't Jewish (p. 51). Those defining their Jewish identity differently are united by a sense of exclusion.

Yet, within what Cesarani calls the 'Alternative Community', he notes contradictory trends; 'for Jews who were leftist and non-affiliated in any Jewish sense, anti-zionism forced them to re-evaluate their sense of self, often leading them to explore the Jewish community' (p. 52) – a position expressed above by Asphodel Long. At the same time, 'the problems within Israel and Zionist ideology' led many to move away from this form of Jewish identification and from the early 1980s to find a common ground in the groups supporting the Israeli Peace Movement.

AMBIVALENCE AND CHANGE

Is there, then, a unifying factor for Jewish feminists? Shulman (1987), from a radical feminist perspective, suggests there is: 'even when I have been most estranged, my sense of myself as a Jew has affected everything in my life...my ideals...my intellectual life, my politics...the way I think and feel, celebrate or mourn... some kinds of shared understanding that I share with no other people' (p. 12).

Yet within Judaism she also finds dissonances, 'attitudes untenable for any woman in her right mind'. Her unease is one echoed by many feminists, it is to do with being defined by others: 'A patriarchal outlook begins by making men's experiences normative... Not only are women excluded from the process of shaping the outlook, but women's experiences are projected as something..."other" to that norm' (Heschel, 1983, p. xxi). Shulman and Heschel quote de Beauvoir: 'Thus humanity is male and man defines woman not in herself but as relative to him; she is not regarded as an autonomous being...He is the Subject,...she is the Other' (de Beauvoir, 1953, p. 16). Yet this text, so often used to depict women's experience within patriarchal religions, does not, in fact, accurately reflect woman's situation within Judaism. Where de Beauvoir writes 'she is the incidental, the inessential as opposed to the essential' (p. 16), women in Judaism have always had a totally different reality: 'they knew they were as essential in the cosmological scheme of things as men' (Kupferman, 1979, p. 111).

The theory and ferment of ideas are one thing; what is equally relevant is the extent to which they influence Jewish women outside the feminist movement for, without doubt, feminism has reached right along the spectrum. Within the Orthodox community, it is defused defensively in terms of both 'sophisticated' dialectic (Rapoport-Albert, 1988, p. 525) and attempts to resolve cognitive dissonance (Cohen-Nusbacher, 1987). But, in practical terms, its repercussions are felt as measured by the increased incidence of divorce and, within the 'modern Orthodox' world, the heightened demand for in-depth study of *halachic* sources and rabbinic debate on them. 'Knowledge is power' is a recurrent phrase.

Similarly, in the non-Orthodox world, its impact is expressed in terms of questioning, not only of roles but also of fundamental attitudes:

> There are feminist strands, spiritual ones and, not surprisingly, parental ones... repression and confrontation coincided with every ritual observance and family celebration... They are central to my rejection

of a rigid orthodox framework.

(Masorti woman)

Yet, in trying to evaluate the influence of feminist thought on Jewish women's lives, two factors have to be taken into consideration. The first is the meaning of change in individual terms for, of course, there is an enormous diversity of attitudes and values even within the so-called 'normative' community. Challenging stereotyped assumptions, Swirsky (1989) points out that 'Jewish women's identities are constructed and developed within and against historical and life events' (p. 8). For each woman, the external political and cultural influences are internalized through the dynamics of her family of origin, and it is this which partly determines the way in which she receives, filters and interprets new ideas.

A second factor also operates: it is a feeling within women of ambivalence towards change – a simultaneous desire for and fear of it. In this ambivalence there are surprising similarities between the response of Jewish and of non-Jewish women. In other words, hesitation about fundamental change may well come from historically-grounded conditioning about women's roles and expectations in society in general.

Considering Jewish women in a different context, Ardener (1978) comments on the failure of the kibbutz movement to implement the avowed ideology of sexual equality – a failure partly due to women's *choosing* to revert to traditional gender roles – 'one can query the capacity of three generations of self-conscious innovation to obliterate the influence of a historical Semitic culture to whose value-structure sexual polarisation is particularly central' (p. 214). At the same time, there is ample discussion in all the feminist literature of a comparable difficulty in the lives of all women to be whole-hearted about change: Orbach and Eichenbaum (1987), for example, suggest that 'women have an investment in retaining the status quo'. Similarly, Oakley (1986) writes:

> Certain factors act to mould the cultural product of woman . . . difficult daughterhood, ambivalent motherhood, permanent guilt . . . a trivial self confidence, the wish to retreat and deny rather than the will to advance and confront . . . [woman is] the proud possessor of an impossible socialization.

(p. 76)

In the reality of women's lives, change often occurs less as a product of new ideas and more as a gradual evolution – through an internal process of expanding old expectations to take in newer options. In the context of the Jewish culture, both Heschel (1983) and Schneider (1984) observe the negative stereotypes which 'keep women in line' and note how men's experiences are the normative ones. Heschel emphasizes that only by addressing these 'unspoken hidden images ... and the theological positions which legitimate them' can wider possibilities be envisaged. They focus on the heart of the matter: the internal dialogue, the hidden images. Two centuries ago, Mary Wollstonecraft (1792) wrote 'I do not wish women to have power over men, but over themselves'. Since then, increasing volumes of feminist writing, research and rhetoric have told us of both the external and the internal obstacles, the multiplicity of social and psychological factors at force within cultural and historical contexts.

Within the male-defined culture of Judaism, the factors influencing what women do – and choose to do – are enormously complex. Lerner (1986) recognizes in herself a very familiar theme: 'I represented in my own person all the internalized obstacles' (p. viii). She quotes Rosaldo (1980), highlighting the need for theories 'that attend to the ways that actors shape their worlds, to interactions in which significance is conferred, and to the cultural and symbolic forms in terms of which expectations are organized, desires articulated, prizes conferred, and outcomes given meaning' (Lerner, p. 250).

There is often an eventual harmony between the development of ideas and the realities of our lives. Whilst psychologists and sociologists in the 1960s and 1970s (Rossi, 1964; Bem, 1972; Bernard, 1972) urged a redefinition of men's roles and expectations – only through this, they realised, could a healthier equilibrium be achieved – the writers and thinkers who followed (Friedan, 1981; Gilligan, 1982; Giele, 1982; Miller, 1986) put forward a new plea, the plea of 'second wave' feminism, for a revaluing of the caring roles by both women and men.

Jewish women, like women in every other culture, are influenced by the belief system of their world and the values deriving from it. Even for women far from the source of those beliefs, there is often a deep unconscious thread tying them to it and continuing to define aspects of their self-perception and their expectations. Jewish men, like men in every other culture, learn and reinforce a complementary world-view in which gender roles are separate spheres. But there is a difference; the reciprocity which is an integral part of these separate spheres has never within Judaism polarized men into a 'macho' maleness. And the exclusion of women – historically from the ritual and scholarly worlds and traditionally from the material and public worlds – has never inhibited their developing a significant and meaningful counterpart culture, a culture within a culture. Jewish culture, as Heschel writes, has always 'permitted' men to be gentle and emotionally expressive and women to be strong and capable and proud.

Where we go from here, how Jewish women can use and learn from and become part of the struggles and doubts and achievements of feminist women who in every culture show us the way, will depend on our individual definitions – and on our courage.

* * *

Hasidic saying:
We are afraid of things that cannot harm us, and we know it. And we long for things which cannot help us, and we know it. But actually it is something within us that we are afraid of, and it is something within ourselves that we long for.

Martin Buber, *Ten Rings: Hasidic sayings*
(New York: Schocken Books, 1947, 1962) p. 73

Bibliography

Abbreviation: A. J. Y. B.=American Jewish Year Book (Philadelphia, PA: The Jewish Publication Society of America).

Margaret Adams, 'The Compassion Trap': ch. 24, pp. 555–75 in Vivian Gornick and Barbara K. Moran (eds), *Woman in Sexist Society* (New York: Basic Books, 1971).

Pnina Adelman, *Miriam's Well* (Fresh Meadow, NY: Biblio Press, 1987).

Rachel Adler, *'Tum'ah* and *Taharah*: Ends and Beginnings': pp. 63–71 in Koltun, 1976.

Rachel Adler, 'The Jew Who Wasn't There: Halacha and the Jewish Woman' pp. 12–18 in Heschel, 1983.

I. Ajzen and M. Fishbein, *A Theory of Reasoned Action* (NY: Prentice Hall, 1980).

Shirley Ardener (ed.), *Perceiving Women* (London: Dent, 1975).

Shirley Ardener (ed.), *Defining Females: the nature of women in society* (London: Croom Helm, 1978).

Janet Aviad, *Return to Judaism: Religious renewal in Israel* (University of Chicago Press: 1983).

Adrienne Baker, 'Role Expectations of Anglo-Jewish Wives at Mid-Life', unpublished PhD. thesis, Department of Theology, King's College, London University, 1990.

Christie Balka and Andy Rose (eds), *Twice Blessed: On Being Lesbian or Gay and Jewish* (Boston: Beacon Press, 1989).

Julia Bard, 'Face to Face with the Community', pp. 3–7 in *A Word in Edgeways* (London, J. F. Publications, 1988).

Julia Bard, 'Backwards to Basics', *Jewish Socialist* no. 21, Autumn 1990, pp. 20–2.

Julia Bard, Review Essay on *Generations of Memories* (see below under Swirsky), *Feminist Review*, no. 37, Spring 1991, pp. 85–94.

Julia Bard, 'An Abuse of Power', *Jewish Socialist*, no. 24, Oct–Dec. 1991, pp. 18–19.

Pauline Bart, 'Portnoy's Mother: Depression in Middle-Aged Women' in Koltun, 1976.

Charlotte Baum, Paula Hyman and Sonya Michel, *The Jewish Woman in America* (NY: New American Library, 1975)

Evelyn Torton Beck, *Nice Jewish Girls: A lesbian anthology* (Watertown, MA.: Persephone Pr, 1982; Beacon Pr, 1989).

Martin S. Bergmann and Milton Jucovy (eds), *Generations of the Holocaust* (NY: Basic Books, 1982).

Berel Berkovits, 'Breaking the bond', *Jewish Chronicle*, 15.6.90, pp. 26–7. Also see 'New proposals for *get* process': *Jewish Chronicle*, 23.8.91. and 'Divorce and *Gittin* in the 1990s', *L'Eylah*, Spring 1992, pp. 22–4.

Saul Berman, 'The Status of Women in Halachic Judaism' *Tradition*, 14, no. 2, Fall 1973 pp. 5–28. Reprinted abridged, pp. 114–28 in Koltun, 1976.

Chaim Bermant, *The Walled Garden: The Saga of Jewish Family Life and Tradition* (London: Weidenfeld and Nicolson, 1974).

Bruno Bettelheim, 'Portnoy Psychoanoalyzed' in *Midstream*, June/July 1969, cited p. 89 in Priesand 1975.

Rachel Biale, *Women and Jewish Law* (NY: Schocken, 1984).

Phyllis Bird, 'Images of Women in the Old Testament' in Ruether, 1974.

David Bleich, 'Halachah as an Absolute', *Judaism*, 29, 1980, pp. 30–7.

Barbara Borts et al., *Women and Tallit* (London: Reform Synagogues of Great Britain, 1987).

Roisin Boyd et al., 'Women Speak Out Against Zionism', *Spare Rib*, Aug. 1982.

M. Brayer, *The Jewish Woman*: Vol. 1: *A Psycho-Social Perspective*: Vol. 2: *A Psycho-Historical Perspective*: (NY: Ktav, 1986).

Stephen Brook, *The Club: The Jews of Modern Britain* (London: Constable, 1989).

Sarah Silver Bunim, 'Religious and Secular Factors of Role Strain in Orthodox Jewish Mothers', doctoral dissertation, Wurzweiler School of Social Work, Yeshiva University, NY, 1986

Sarah Silver Bunim, *The World of the Orthodox Jewish Mother* (NY: Ktav, 1990).

Rikki Burman, 'The Jewish Woman as Breadwinner: the changing value of women's work in a Manchester immigrant community', *Journal of the Oral History Society*, vol. 10, no. 2, 1982, pp. 27–39.

Rikki Burman, 'She Looeth Well to the Ways of Her Household: the changing role of Jewish women in religious life, c. 1880–1930', ch. 10 in G. Malmgreen, (ed.): *Religion in the Lives of English Women, 1760–1930* (Beckenham: Croom Helm, 1986).

Rikki Burman, 'Jewish Women and the Household Economy in Manchester, c. 1890–1920' in David Cesarani (ed.), *The Making of Modern Anglo-Jewry* (London: Blackwell, 1990).

David Cesarani, 'The Alternative Jewish Community', *European Judaism*, 1985/6, pp. 50–4.

Nancy Chodorow, *The Reproduction of Mothering: Psychoanalysis and the Sociology of Gender* (Berkeley: University of California Press, 1978).

Naomi Cohen, 'Women and the Study of Talmud', *Tradition*, vol. 24, no. 1, Fall 1988, pp. 28–37.

Steven M. Cohen and Paula E. Hyman, *The Jewish Family: Myths and Reality* (NY: Holmes and Meier, 1986).

Ailene Cohen-Nusbacher, 'Responses to Secular Influences Among Orthodox Jewish Women', unpublished PhD 1987, Department of Sociology, NY University.

Barbara Cohn Schlachet, 'Female Role Socialization', ch. 5 in C. M. Brody (ed.): *Women Therapists Working With Women* (New York: Springer, 1984).

Cassie Cooper, 'The Jewish Mother? An overview of Melanie Klein', pp. 6–19 in Cooper 1988.

Howard Cooper (ed.), *Soul Searching: Studies in Judaism and Psychotherapy* (London: SCM Press, 1988).

Howard Cooper and Paul Morrison, *A Sense of Belonging: Dilemmas of British Jewish Identity* (London: Weidenfeld and Nicolson, 1991).

Naomi Dale, 'Jews, Ethnicity and Mental Health' pp. 68–80 in Cooper, 1988.

Ann Dally, *Inventing Motherhood: The Consequences of an Ideal* (London: Burnett Books, 1982).

Miriam Dansky, 'The Literature of Return', *L'Eylah*, Sept. 1991, pp. 39–41.

M. H. Danzger, *Return to Tradition: The contemporary revival of Orthodox Judaism* (New Haven, Conn.: Yale University Press, 1989).

Simone de Beauvoir, *The Second Sex* (first published 1953) (Harmondsworth, Penguin, 1972/1987).

Mary Douglas, *Purity and Danger* (London: Routledge and Kegan Paul, 1966).

Erica Duncan, 'The Hungry Jewish Mother', pp. 27–40 in Heschel, 1983.

Luise Eichenbaum and Susie Orbach, *Understanding Women* (Harmondsworth: Penguin, 1983/1986).

Daniel J. Elazar, *The Other Half: The Sephardim Today* (NY: Basic Books, 1989).

Daniel J. Elazar, 'Is Momentum Enough? The State of American Jewry', *Congress Monthly*, vol. 59, no. 2, Feb. 1992, pp. 18–2.

Patricia Erens, *The Jew in American Cinema* (Bloomington: Indiana University Press, 1984).

Eric H. Erikson, 'The Problem of Ego Identity' in M. R. Stein et al., eds., *Identity and Anxiety* (Glencoe, Ill.: 1960).

David Feldman, 'Woman's Role and Jewish Law', *Conservative Judaism*, vol. 26, no. 4, Summer 1972, pp. 29–39.

Eva Figes, *Patriarchal Attitudes* (London: Virago, 1978).

Sylvia Barack Fishman, 'The Impact of Feminism on American Jewish Life', *American Jewish Year Book*, 1989, pp. 3–63.

Tamar Frankiel, *The Voice of Sarah: Feminine Spirituality and Traditional Judaism* (San Francisco: Harper, 1990).

Nancy Friday, *My Mother, My Self* (London: Fontana, 1977/1979).

Betty Friedan, *The Feminine Mystique* (Harmondsworth: Penguin, 1963).

Eric Fromm, *Escape from Freedom* (1941) republished (1942) entitled *The Fear of Freedom* (London: Routledge and Kegan Paul, 1960/1984).

Hannah Gavron, *The Captive Wife: Conflicts of Housebound Mothers* (London: Routledge and Kegan Paul, 1966/1983).

H. E. Ghatan, *The Invaluable Pearl: The unique status of women in Judaism* (NY: Bloch, 1986).

Janet Giele, *Women in the Middle Years* (NY: Wiley, 1982).

Betsy Giller, 'All in the Family: Violence in the Jewish Home', pp. 101–9 *in* Siegel and Cole, 1991.

Carol Gilligan, *In A Different Voice: Psychological Theory and Women's Development* (Cambridge, Mass.: Harvard University Press, 1982).

Nathan Glazer, 'New Perspectives in American Jewish Sociology' pp. 3–19 in *A. J. Y. B.*, 1987.

Michael Gold, *and Hannah wept: Infertility, Adoption and the Jewish Couple* (Philadelphia: The Jewish Publication Society of America, 1988).

Calvin Goldscheider, *The American Jewish Community: Social Science Research and Policy Implications* (Providence, RI: Brown University, 1986).

Sidney Goldstein and Calvin Goldscheider, *Jewish Americans: Three Generations in a Jewish Community* (Lanham, MD: University Press of America, 1985).

Philip and Hanna Goodman, *The Jewish Marriage Anthology* (Philadelphia: The Jewish Publication Society of America, 1965).

Blu Greenberg, *On Women and Judaism: A View from Tradition* (Philadelphia: Jewish Publication Society of America, 1981).

Germaine Greer, *The Female Eunuch* (London: MacGibbon and Kee, 1970).

Lucien Gubbay and Abraham Levy, *Ages of Man* (London: Darton, Longman and Todd, 1985).

Yossi Klein Halevi, *Jerusalem Report*, 8.10.92.

Lis Harris, *Holy Days: The world of a Hasidic family* (NY: Macmillan, 1985).

Judith Hauptman, 'Images of Woman in the Talmud', pp. 184–212 in Ruether, 1974.

S. N. Herman, *Jewish Identity: A Socio-Psychological Perspective* (London: Sage, 1977).

Susannah Heschel (ed.), *On Being A Jewish Feminist: A Reader* (NY: Schocken, 1983).

Harold S. Himmelfarb (1986) pp. 64–74 in Goldscheider, 1986.

Richard G. Hirsch (1986) pp. 75–82 in Goldscheider, 1986.

Steven Huberman, 'Repairing the Broken Vase: Reaching our Jewish Grandchildren and our Jewish Grandparents', *Judaism*, Fall, 1991, pp. 498–505.

Paula Hyman, 'The Other Half: Women in the Jewish Tradition', pp. 105–13 in Koltun, 1976.

Paula Hyman, 'The Jewish Family: Looking for a Usable Past', pp. 19–26 in Heschel, 1983.

Paula Hyman, 'The Modern Jewish Family: Image and Reality': ch. 10 in Kraemer, 1989.

Louis Jacobs, *We Have Reason To Believe* (London: Valentine Mitchell, 1957).

Elizabeth Janeway, *Man's World, Woman's Place: A Study in Social Mythology* (London: Michael Joseph, 1972).

Lord Jakobovits, *L'Eylah*, no. 22, September 1986, pp. 22–3.

Paul Johnson, *A History of the Jews* (London: Weidenfeld and Nicolson, 1987).

Aryeh Kaplan, *Waters of Eden* (NY: Union of Orthodox Jewish Congregations of America, 1982).

Aryeh Kaplan, *Made in Heaven* (NY: Maznaim, 1983).

Marion A. Kaplan, 'Priestess and Hausfrau: Women and Tradition in the German-Jewish Family', pp. 62–82 in Cohen and Hyman, 1986.

Debra Kaufman, 'Coming Home to Jewish Orthodoxy: Reactionary or Radical Women?', *Tikkun*, vol. 2, no. 3, July/Aug. 1987, pp. 60–3.

Melanie Kaye/Kantrowitz, 'The Issue is Power: Some Notes on Jewish woman and Therapy', pp. 7–18 in Siegel and Cole, 1991.

Franz Kobler (ed.), *Her Children Call Her Blessed: A Portrait of the Jewish Mother* (NY: Stephen Daye, 1953).

Elizabeth Koltun (ed.), *The Jewish Woman: New Perspectives* (NY: Schocken, 1976).

Barry Kosmin (1987) in *A. J. Y. B.* (1989) quoting figures from North American Jewish Data Bank (1987).

Barry Kosmin and Caren Levy, *The Work and Employment of Suburban Jews* (London: Research Unit, Board of Deputies of British Jews, 1981).

Barry Kosmin and Caren Levy, *Jewish Identity in an Anglo-Jewish Community* (London: Research Unit Board of Deputies of British Jews, 1983)

David Kraemer, *The Jewish Family: Metaphor and Memory* (London: Oxford University Press, 1989).

Jeanette Kupferman, 'The Lubavitch Chassidim of Stamford Hill', unpublished M Phil dissertation, London University, 1976.

Jeanette Kupferman, *The Mstaken Body* (London: Robson, 1979).

Sophie Laws, *Issues of Blood: The Politics of Menstruation* (London: Macmillan, 1990).

Antony Lerman (ed.), *Jewish Communities of the World: A Contemporary Guide* (London: Macmillan, 1989).

Gerda Lerner, *The Creation of Patriarchy* (NY: Oxford University Press, 1986).

C. Levi-Strauss, *The Savage Mind* (University of Chicago Press, 1970).

N. Linzer, *The Jewish Family* (NY: Human Science Press, 1984).

Kate Loewenthal, 'Patterns of Religious Development and Experience in Habad-Hasidic Women', *Journal of Psychology and Judaism*, vol. 12, no. 1, Spring 1988.

Kate Loewenthal, 'Pilot Study of Wellbeing and Distress in Jewish Women', Department of Psychology, Royal Holloway and Bedford New College, London University, 1989/90.

Naftali Loewenthal, *Communicating the Infinite: The Emergence of The Habad School* (University of Chicago Press, 1991)

A. London and B. K. Bishov, *The Complete Jewish Cookbook* (1952) (London: W. H. Allen, 1983).

Bernice Martin, *A Sociology of Contemporary Cultural Change* (Oxford: Blackwell, 1981).

Julia Mazow, *The Woman Who Lost Her Names. Selected Writings of American Jewish Women* (NY: Harper, 1980).

Margaret Mead, *Male and Female: A Study of the Sexes in a Changing World* (Harmondsworth: Penguin, 1949/1962/1976).

Moshe Meiselman, *Jewish Woman in Jewish Law* (New York: Ktav, 1978).

Jean Baker Miller, *Towards A New Psychology of Women* (Harmondsworth: Penguin, 1976/1986).

Kate Millett, *Sexual Politics* (London: Hart-Davis, 1971).

Barbara Myerhoff, 'Bobbes and Zeydes: Old and New Roles for Elderly Jews' in J. Hock-Smith and A. Spring (eds), *Woman in Ritual and Symbolic Roles* (New York: Plenum, 1978).

Julia Neuberger, 'Woman in Judaism: The Fact and the Fiction' in Pat Holden (ed.), *Women's Religious Experience*, ch. 8, pp. 132–42 (Beckenham: Croom Helm, 1983).

Julia Neuberger, *Whatever's Happening to Women?* (London: Kyle, 1991).

Ann Oakley, *Subject Women* (Oxford: Martin Robertson, 1981).

Ann Oakley, *Taking It Like A Woman* (London: Cape, 1984/5/6).

Tillie Olsen, *Tell Me A Riddle* (1956) (London, Virago, 1980).

Susie Orbach and Luise Eichenbaum, *Bittersweet* (London: Century Hutchinson, 1987).

Cynthia Ozick, 'Note toward Finding the Right Question' pp. 120–51 in Heschel, 1983.

Alix Pirani, 'Psychotherapy, Women and the Feminine in Judaism' pp. 50–62 in Cooper, 1988.

Alix Pirani (ed.), *The Absent Mother: Restoring the Goddess to Judaism and Christianity* (London: Mandala, 1991).

Judith Plaskow, 'Standing Again at Sinai: Jewish Memory from a Feminist Perspective', *Tikkun*, vol. 2, no. 1, Jan/Feb. 1987, pp. 28–34.

Letty Cottin Pogrebin, 'Anti-Semitism in the Women's Movement', *MS.*, 12, June, 1982, pp. 45–9, 62–75.

Sally Priesand, *Judaism and the New Woman* (NY: Behrman House, 1975).

Harry M. Rabinowicz, *Hasidim: The Movement and its Masters* (New Jersey: Jason Aronson, 1988).

Ada Rapoport-Albert, 'On Women in Hasidism', pp. 495–525 in Ada Rapoport-Albert and Steven Zipperstein (eds), *Jewish History: Essays in Hounour of Chimen Abramsky* (London: Peter Halban, 1988).

Sara Reguer: 'Kaddish from the "Wrong" Side of the *Mechitzah*", pp. 177–81 in Heschel, 1983.

Theodore Reik: *Jewish Wit* (NY: Gamut Press, 1962).

Bernard Reisman, pp. 99–107 *in* C. Goldscheider: *The American Jewish Community: Social Science Research and Policy Implications* (Providence, RI: Brown University, 1986).

Adrienne Rich, *Of Woman Born: Motherhood as Experience and Institution* (London: Virago, 1977).

Shlomo Riskin, *Women and Jewish Divorce* (Hoboken, NJ: Ktav, 1989).

Faith Rogow, 'The Rise of Jewish Lesbianism Feminism', *Bridges,* vol. 1, no. 1, Spring 1990, pp. 67–79.

Anne Roiphe, 'The Jewish Family: A Feminist Perspective', *Tikkun*, vol. 1, no. 2, 1986, pp. 70–5.

Estelle Roith, *The Riddle of Freud: Jewish Influences on his Theory of Female Sexuality* (London: Tavistock, 1988).

Evelyn Rose, 'What is Jewish Food?', unpublished talk from the first Oxford Symposium on Jewish Food, 18 June 1989.

Amy Rossiter, *From Private to Public: A Feminist Exploration of Early Mothering* (London: The Women's Press, 1988).

Gladys Rothbell, The Jewish Mother: Social Construction of a Popular Image' ch. 9, pp. 118–28 in Cohen and Hyman, 1986.

Lillian B. Rubin, *Women of a Certain Age: The Mid-Life Search for Self* (NY: Harper and Row, 1979).

Rosemary Ruether (ed.), *Religion and Sexism: Images of Women in the Jewish and Christian Traditions* (NY: Simon and Schuster, 1974).

Arthur Ruppin (1943) *The Jews in the Modern World* (NY: Arno, 1973).

Jonathan Sacks, *The Persistence of Faith: Religion, Morality and Society in a Secular Age* (The Reith Lectures 1990) (London: Weidenfeld and Nicolson, 1991).

Maggie Scarf, *Unfinished Business: Pressure Points in the Lives of Women* (NY: Doubleday, 1980).

Mimi Scarf, 'Marriages Made in Heaven? Battered Jewish Wives', pp. 51–64 in Heschel, 1983.

Rachel Aber Schlesinger, 'Jewish Women's Return into the Paid Workforce', *Conciliation Courts Review*, vol. 22, no. 2, York University, Toronto, Dec. 1984, pp. 83–9.

Rachel Aber Schlesinger, 'Jewish Women in Transition' pp. 227–42 in R. Palomba and L. Schamgar-Handelmann (eds), *Alternative Patterns of Family Life in Modern Societies* (Rome: IRP, 1987).

Rachel Aber Schlesinger, 'Midlife Transitions Among Jewish Women: Counselling Issues', pp. 91–100 in Siegel and Cole, 1991.

Marlena Schmool, *British Synagogue Membership in 1990* (London: Community Research Unit, Board of Deputies of British Jews, 1991).

Susan Weidman Schneider, *Jewish and Female: Choices and Changes in our Lives Today* (NY: Simon and Schuster, 1984).

William Shaffir, 'Persistence and Change in the Hasidic Family', pp. 187–99 in Cohen and Hyman, 1986.

Leah Shakdiel, 'The Jewish Career Woman: A Halachic Perspective', unpublished lecture at Traditional Alternatives conference, *Women and the Jewish Future* (London, 1990).

Moshe Shokeid, *Children of Circumstances: Israeli Emigrants in New York* (Ithaca, NY: Cornell University Press, 1988).

Elaine Showalter, *The Female Malady: Women, Madness and English Culture 1830–1980* (London: Virago, 1987).

Sheila Shulman, 'A Radical Feminist Perspective on Judaism', *European Judaism*, 1987, pp. 10–18.

Rachel Josefowitz Siegel and Ellen Cole (eds); *Seen But Not Heard: Jewish Women in Therapy* (NY: Haworth, 1991).

Iris Singer, report in *The Psychologist* vol. 5, no. 2, Feb. 1992, p. 54, of unpublished talk given to Psychology of Women conference, London, Dec. 1991.

Marshall Sklare, *America's Jews* (NY: Random House, 1971) quoted in *A. J. Y .B.* 1989 (pp. 86–7).

Adrienne J. Smith, 'Reflections of a Jewish Lesbian-Feminist Activist-Therapist; Or, First of All I Am Jewish, the Rest Is Commentary', pp. 57–64 in Siegel and Cole, 1991.

Alisa Solomon, 'Building A Movement: Jewish Feminists Speak Out On Israel', *Bridges*, vol. 1, no.1, Spring 1990, pp. 41–56.

Nicholas Stavroulakis, *Cookbook of the Jews of Greece* (Athens: Lycabettus Press, 1986).

Marc D. Stern, *Congress Monthly*, vol. 58, no. 7, Nov.-Dec. 1991.

Ruth Swirsky et al. (eds), *Generations of Memories: Voices of Jewish Women* (Jewish Women in London Group) (London: The Women's Press, 1989).

Arthur I. Waskow, 'Feminist Judaism: Restoration of the Moon', pp. 261–72 in Heschel, 1983.

Stanley Waterman and Barry Kosmin, *British Jewry in the Eighties: A Statistical and Geographical Study* (London: Board of Deputies of British Jews, 1986).

Stanley Waterman, 'Jews in an Outer London Borough, Barnet', Research Paper no. 1, Department of Geography, Queen Mary College, London, Jan. 1989.

Jonathan Webber, 'Between Law and Custom: Woman's Experience of Judaism' ch. 9, pp. 143–62 in Pat Holden (ed.): *Women's Religious Experience*, (Beckenham: Croom Helm, 1983).

Deborah Weissman, 'Education of Jewish Women' in *Encyclopedia Judaica Yearbook* p. 186–7 (Jerusalem: Keter) pp.29–36.

Jack Wertheimer, 'Recent Trends in American Judaism' pp. 63–162 in *A. J. Y. B.* 1989.

Marcia Westkott, *The Feminist Legacy of Karen Horney* (New Haven, Conn.: Yale University, 1986).

Janet Wolf, '"Baruch Ha Shem, Not So Good": Some Concerns of Jewish Women', *Jewish Life*, Spring/Summer 1982.

Ann G. Wolfe, 'The Invisible Jewish Poor' (1971), reprinted *Journal of Jewish Communal Service*, Spring 1972, pp. 259–65.

Mary Wollstonecraft, *A Vindication of Women's Rights* (1972) (Penguin, 1982).

Virginia Woolf, *A Room of One's Own* (London: Hogarth Press, 1929; NY: Harcourt Brace, 1963).

Name Index

Adams, Margaret, 195
Adelman, Pnina, 204
Adler, Rachel, 35, 37, 156, 157
Adler, Valerie, 38
Ajzen, I., 201
Alexander II, Tsar, 20
American Jewish Year Book (*A.J.Y.B.*), 12, 24
Amias, David, 182–3
Amiel, Barbara, 49
Archives Israelites, 53
Ardener, Shirley, 37, 104, 213
Arendt, Hannah, 125
Aviad, Janet, 68, 103, 115

Ba'al Shem Tov, the, 109, 172
Baker, Adrienne
  on roles and expectations, 123, 127–8, 190, 200, 205
Balka, Christie, 168
Bard, Julia 93, 94, 111–13, 209, 211
Bart, Pauline, 132, 135
Bateson, Gregory, 129
Baum, Charlotte, 22, 127
Beck, Evelyn Torton, 167, 168
Bell, Alan P., 167
Bem, Sandra, 214
Ben Azzai, 51
Bergmann, Martin S., 20
Berkovits, Berel, 154, 208
Berkovits, Eliezer, 154
Berman, Saul, 38, 49, 51, 64
Bermant, Chaim, 51, 142, 164, 176
Bernard, Jessie, 214
Bettelheim, Bruno, 134
Biale, Rachel
  on betrothal and marriage, 148–9
  on childbearing, 165
  on contraception and abortion, 161, 162
  on exclusion of women from ritual and study, 35, 36, 49, 51, 77
  on inequalities in divorce law, 54–5, 57–60, 80
  on sexual morality, 163
  on lesbianism, 166
  on religious law, 46, 47, 61, 156, 163–5
  on sexuality and religion, 155, 156, 163–5
  on subservient role of women, 43

on wife-beating, 180
Binstock, Ivan, 163
Bird, Phyllis, 44, 148
Bishov, B.K., 136
Black, Norma, 196
Bleich, David, 64
Blendis, Judy, 83
Boronitz, Eugene B., 21
Borts, Barbara, 81, 90–1
Bowlby, John, 197
Boyd, Roisin, 209
Brayer, M., 127
Brecht, Bertolt, 27
Brichto, Sidney, 182
Brier, Sam, 181
Brody, C.M., 156
Brook, Stephen, 82, 85, 106, 110, 174
Brown, Erica, 207
Bunim, Sarah Silver, 26, 107
Burman, Rikki
  on changing roles, 22, 36, 144–5, 198, 199
  on cultural differences, 11, 127, 199
  on position of women, 2

Cantor, Aviva, 195
Cesarani, David, 28, 29, 92–3, 211
Chodorow, Nancy, 126
Chofetz, Chaim, 53
Cohen, Myrella, 63, 208
Cohen, Naomi, 192, 193
Cohen, Steven M., 110, 134, 198
Cohen-Nusbacher, Ailene, 26, 113, 127, 192, 198, 212
Cohn Schlachet, Barbara, 156
Cole, Rosalind, 97
Community Research Unit, 28
Conway, Joy, 76
Cooper, Cassie, 130–1
Cooper, Howard
  on demography, 31
  on expectations for children, 21, 128–9
  on family life, 138
  on family roles, 128
  on Holocaust, 94
  on male emphasis, 76–7
  on role of food, 135, 137
Cromwell, Oliver, 9
Currie, Edwina, 174

224

Subject Index

abortion, 5, 161–2
Aden, Sephardi emigrants from, 11, 17
adoption, 160, 176
adultery, 163–4, 165
agunah, 55–6, 58–61, 154–5, 207–9
Aliens Act (1905), 10, 20
anti-Semitism
  emigration from, 10, 108
  Israeli issues, 6, 209–11
  Jewish identity, 93–4
  mediaeval, 9
  memories of, 99, 125
  responses to, 97
  threat of, 2
  ultra-Orthodox seclusion, 106
anti-Zionism, 94, 209–11
Arab countries, 10–11, 16
Arab-Israel wars, 10–11, 111
arranged marriage, 48
artificial insemination, 160
Ashkenazim, 16–17, 19–23
  food specialities of, 139
  immigrants to Britain, 9–11, 14, 27
  immigrants to USA, 12, 14
  women, 22–3
assimilation
  fear of, 2, 23, 68
  increased, 27, 93
  integration, 14, 21–2
  'marrying-out', 30
Austria
  Jewish emigrants from, 10, 12, 20
  Nazism in, 10, 12

ba'al t'shuva, 115–19
  appeal of Orthodox stability, 68
  appeal to women, 119, 146
  background, 4, 118, 119
  example, 104
  Lubavitch outreach, 68, 110
  studies of, 68, 103, 115–16, 119, 146, 162
baby-naming ceremony, 85
Balkans, Jewish emigrants from, 17, 67
Baltimore, 24, 103
barmitzvah, 50, 99
bat chayil ceremony, 49, 76, 83
bat-mitzvah, 70, 73, 76, 83, 99
Beth Din
  conversion, 80, 86, 177, 179

divorce, 55–7, 83
betrothal, 147
Bible
  portrayal of women, 42
  status of women, 51
Birmingham, Jewish population in, 28
birth control, *see* contraception
birth rate, 23, 25, 31, 128
Boro Park, ultra-Orthodox
  community in, 103
Boston, Jewish population in, 24
Bournemouth, Jewish population in, 28
Brighton, Jewish population in, 28
Britain, Jews in
  births and deaths, 31
  class and occupations, 30
  denominations, 74–86
  divorce, 31
  emigration, 31–2
  immigration, 9–11, 27
  marriage, 30
  population, 27, 28
  religious composition, 28–9
  synagogue observance, 3–4
  ultra-Orthodox communities, 103

candles, Shabbat, 86–8, 90, 98, 157
cantor, woman, 73
careers, *see* work
carers, women as, 186–7
celibacy, 147, 163
chalitzah, 60
Chanukah, 141
Chassidim, 4, 108–14
Chicago, Jewish population in, 24
child abuse, 181–3
childbearing, 42, 108, 158–9, 200
childlessness, 5, 19, 159–60
children
  adoption of, 160, 176
  care of, 200–1
  expectations of, 21, 128–9
  handicapped, 5, 106, 187
  illegitimate, 57, *see also mamzerim*
  in care, 182–3
  of convert, 177
  of mixed-faith marriage, 71, 73, 93, 172, 174–5, 178
  of working mothers, 200–1

228